The Future of Intelligence

This volume discusses the challenges the future holds for different aspects of the intelligence process and for organisations working in the field.

The main focus of Western intelligence services is no longer on the intentions and capabilities of the Soviet Union and its allies. Instead, at present, there is a plethora of threats and problems that deserve attention. Some of these problems are short-term and potentially acute, such as terrorism. Others, such as the exhaustion of natural resources, are longer-term and by nature often more difficult to foresee in their implications.

This book analyses the different activities that make up the intelligence process, or the 'intelligence cycle', with a focus on changes brought about by external developments in the international arena, such as technology and security threats. Drawing together a range of key thinkers in the field, *The Future of Intelligence* examines possible scenarios for future developments, including estimations about their plausibility, and the possible consequences for the functioning of intelligence and security services.

This book will be of much interest to students of intelligence studies, strategic studies, foreign policy, security studies and IR in general.

Isabelle Duyvesteyn is associate professor at the Department of History of International Relations, Utrecht University in the Netherlands, and author/editor of several books, including the *Handbook of Insurgency and Counterinsurgency* (Routledge 2012).

Ben de Jong is retired lecturer in the Department of East European History at the University of Amsterdam, the Netherlands.

Joop van Reijn is former Chairman of the Netherlands Intelligence Studies Association (NISA), and a subject matter expert at The Hague Centre for Strategic Studies (HCSS) and a consultant for the Geneva Centre for the Democratic Control of the Armed Forces.

Studies in Intelligence Series
General Editors: Richard J. Aldrich and Christopher Andrew

The Future of Intelligence

Challenges in the 21st century

**Edited by Isabelle Duyvesteyn,
Ben de Jong and Joop van Reijn**

Routledge
Taylor & Francis Group

LONDON AND NEW YORK

First published 2014
by Routledge
2 Park Square, Milton Park, Abingdon, Oxfordshire OX14 4RN

and by Routledge
711 Third Avenue, New York, NY 10017

First issued in paperback 2015

Routledge is an imprint of the Taylor & Francis Group, an informa business

British Library Cataloguing in Publication Data
A catalogue record for this book is available from the British Library

Library of Congress Cataloging-in-Publication Data
The future of intelligence : challenges in the 21st century / edited by Ben de Jong, Isabelle Duyvesteyn, Joop van Reijn.
  pages cm. – (Studies in intelligence)
  Includes bibliographical references and index.
  1. Intelligence service. I. Jong, Ben de, 1947– editor of compilation.
  II. Duyvesteyn, Isabelle, 1972– editor of compilation. III. Reijn,
  Joop van, editor of compilation.
  UB250.F87 2014
  327.1201'12–dc23   2013039413

ISBN 13: 978-1-138-95195-2 (pbk)
ISBN 13: 978-0-415-66328-1 (hbk)

Typeset in Times New Roman
by Wearset Ltd, Boldon, Tyne and Wear

Contents

About the contributors

Wilhelm Agrell became Professor in Intelligence Analysis at Lund University, Sweden in 2006. His main areas of research are intelligence history and the study of analytic methods in intelligence assessments, with a broad interest in the Second World War, Cold War military history and security studies. His recent publications include *National Intelligence Systems: Current Research and Future Prospects* (2009), edited with Greg Treverton.

Bob de Graaff is Professor of Intelligence and Security Studies at both the University of Utrecht and the Netherlands Defense Academy in Breda. His most recent book is *Op weg naar Armageddon: De evolutie van fanatisme*, an analysis of the development of apocalyptic narratives that have played a role in the use of violence from the Middle Ages up until the present day.

Ben de Jong is a retired lecturer from the University of Amsterdam. He was one of the founding members of the Netherlands Intelligence Studies Association (NISA) in 1991. He was co-editor of two previous volumes of NISA conference proceedings: *Peacekeeping Intelligence* (2003) and *Battleground Western Europe* (2007).

Monica den Boer holds a position at the Police Academy of the Netherlands and is a member of the Advisory Council International Affairs/Committee on European Integration in The Hague. In 2009, she was a member of the Iraq Investigation Committee in the Netherlands. She has published widely on European internal security cooperation.

George Dimitriu is a Research Fellow at the Netherlands Defence Academy in Breda. He is the author of several scholarly articles on counter-insurgency, strategic communication, intelligence and special forces in journals such as *Small Wars and Insurgencies*, *Public Relations Review*, *Intelligence and National Security*, and other Dutch journals. He currently co-edits a volume on strategic narratives, public opinion and the war in Afghanistan.

Isabelle Duyvesteyn is a senior lecturer and researcher at the Department of History of International Relations, University of Utrecht, and Special Chair in Strategic Studies at the Leiden University in the Netherlands. Her work has been published in several journals, including *Civil Wars*, *Security Studies* and *Studies in Conflict and Terrorism*. Her most recent publications include (together with Paul Rich) *The Routledge Handbook of Insurgency and Counterinsurgency* (2012). She was also guest editor of a special issue of the *Journal of Strategic Studies* on 'Escalation and De-escalation of Irregular War' (2012).

Björn Fägersten is a Research Fellow at the Swedish Institute of International Affairs where he conducts research on intelligence, European integration, security policy and international institutions. Since 2008 he has also been an elected fellow of the European Foreign and Security Policy Studies Program of the Volkswagen Stiftung, the Compagnia di San Paolo and the Riksbankens Jubileumsfond.

Arthur S. Hulnick is Associate Professor of International Relations at Boston University and a veteran of more than thirty-five years in American intelligence. He has written numerous articles on intelligence matters and is the author of two books, *Fixing the Spy Machine* (2000) and *Keeping Us Safe: Secret Intelligence and Homeland Security* (2004), both published by Praeger. He is a member of the editorial boards of *The International Journal of Intelligence and Counterintelligence* and *Intelligence and National Security*.

Mark M. Lowenthal has served as the Assistant Director of Central Intelligence for Analysis and Production, and is President and CEO of the Intelligence and Security Academy. He has written extensively on intelligence and national security issues, including five books and over ninety articles and studies. His most recent book, *Intelligence: From Secrets to Policy* (4th edn, 2009), has become the standard college and graduate school textbook on the subject.

Sir David Omand was the first UK Security and Intelligence Coordinator, responsible to the Prime Minister for the professional health of the intelligence community, national counterterrorism strategy and 'homeland security'. He has been a visiting professor in the Department of War Studies since 2005/2006. His recent publications include *Securing the State* (2010).

Jennifer Sims is currently Senior Fellow with the Chicago Council on Global Affairs. Together with Burton Gerber she co-edited *Transforming U.S. Intelligence* (2005) and *Vaults, Mirrors and Masks: Rediscovering US Counterintelligence* (2009). Her publications on defence technology and arms control include *Icarus Restrained: An Intellectual History of Nuclear Arms Control in the United States from 1945 to 1960* (1985), and 'The American Approach to Nuclear Arms Control: A Retrospective', *Daedalus* (1991).

Gregory F. Treverton is Director of the Center for Global Risk and Security at the RAND Corporation. His recent work has focused on terrorism, intelligence and law enforcement, with a special emphasis on forms of public–private partnership. His latest books are *Intelligence for an Era of Terror* (2009); and (with others) *Film Piracy, Organized Crime and Terrorism* (2009), and *Reorganizing U.S. Domestic Intelligence: Assessing the Options* (2008).

Jelle van Buuren is currently a Ph.D. student at the Centre for Terrorism and Counterterrorism at Campus The Hague, Leiden University. His research deals with historical relationships and correlations to explain the rise in the number of threats directed against state officials in the Netherlands, looking specifically at the rising number of threats by lone wolves, the general level of trust in the government, and political legitimacy in the Netherlands.

Joop van Reijn is a former director of the Netherlands Defence Intelligence and Security Service (NL-DISS). His recent publications include 'Intelligence and the International Security Assistance Force', in *Secret Intelligence: A Reader* (2009), 'Sicherheit und Bürgerfreiheit in den Niederlanden', in *Fehlbare Staatsgewalt* (2009), and, as co-editor, *Inlichtingen- en veiligheidsdiensten* (2010).

Foreword

Michael Kowalski

In recent years there has been a steady stream of publications and debate about new security threats and necessary intelligence reforms. The terrorist threat as it manifested itself during the infamous attacks of 9/11 caused a major upheaval in the international intelligence community. Some eight years later, however, insiders maintain that intelligence services are still burdened by the heritage of the Cold War in their mode of operation, being ill-prepared for proper forecasting in a changed security environment. This is a rather embarrassing observation for organizations that claim to possess early warning facilities as a trademark. There seems to be a pervasive feeling that the twenty-first century may hold more surprises than a mere revival of terrorism, with other major issues (increased nuclear proliferation, cyber warfare) looming on the horizon.

This edited volume is based on an international conference on the future of intelligence organized in 2011 to mark the twentieth anniversary of the Netherlands Intelligence Studies Association (NISA). Its contents address several important questions: What are new security threats and do they also provide new opportunities? Does the development of technology help or hinder the intelligence services? Is it possible to speak of a new intelligence revolution? To what extent do new developments require intelligence sharing, not only nationally but also internationally? And, last but not least: Do these developments pose new judicial and ethical challenges?

NISA is a non-partisan, voluntary association established in 1991. The Association's principal purposes are threefold: (1) to provide informed debate in the Netherlands on intelligence and security issues in the widest possible sense; (2) to support historical research in the field; and (3) to promote and contribute to higher education. NISA members cover a broad range of expertise on the work of intelligence, security and police services: their history, development, organization and structure, the trajectory of intelligence research, debates on methodology, and the significance of new technologies. It comprises an extensive network of national and international contacts, both academic and professional. Through its members, NISA is connected with Dutch and foreign research institutes, study groups and professionals, and works closely with them in a variety of cooperative ventures.

Acknowledgements

NISA is grateful to Routledge Publishers for the opportunity offered to share the outcome of its 2011 conference with a larger audience. NISA is also grateful to the Taylor & Francis Group for the permission granted to include Wilhelm Agrell's article 'The Next 100 Years: Reflections on the Future of Intelligence' in this volume. The manuscript has been completed in the early spring of 2013.

A special word of thanks goes to a number of long-term members of NISA: Isabelle Duyvesteyn (Leiden University) for her support in shaping the volume and for very effectively and smoothly communicating with the authors; Giles Scott-Smith (Roosevelt Study Center and Leiden University) for his editorial work on the draft manuscript; Bob de Graaff (Utrecht University and Netherlands Defence Academy) and George Dimitriu (Ministry of Defence, The Hague) for their introduction and conclusion to the volume respectively; and the editors, Ben de Jong (Amsterdam University) and Joop van Reijn (Maj. Gen., ret.) for a job well done. Last, but certainly not least, NISA would like to express its profound thanks to the authors of this volume for their fine contributions to the project.

Michael Kowalski
Chairman, Netherlands Intelligence Studies Association

Acknowledgements

1 By way of introduction

A systemic way of looking at the future of intelligence

Bob de Graaff

Introduction

It is possible to think of an intelligence organization or an intelligence community as part of an open societal system in transition (De Haan and Rotmans 2011: 90–102; De Graaff 1997: 25–32). In this line of thought the intelligence organization operates in an environment that may be defined in terms of both tasks and values. The task environment consists of all the actors that may have an influence upon the intelligence organization and/or may be influenced by its acts and products. The value environment is the cultural and ideological climate in which the organization has to operate. The larger systems (of security, politics or the military), of which the intelligence organization or community forms a subsystem, set out the wider environment in which this takes place. The interaction between the organization and its environment(s) may be interpreted in terms of input and output.

Input may be divided into support and demand (from the perspective of an intelligence organization these may also be interpreted in terms of threats and opportunities). Support may be defined in terms of money or other material means, but also recruited or contracted employees, or information that has to be processed into intelligence. Demand may be defined as the intelligence consumers' requirements or public expectations. Demands may come from politics or the public at large regarding the organization's performance, products, and legal or ethical restrictions. They may also take the form of information that the organization is forced to act upon in order to maintain itself in its specific environment.

The output of an intelligence organization comprises finished intelligence, but may also include covert actions or active measures. The processes within the intelligence organization that convert support and demand into output could be called 'throughput' or 'withinput'. This throughput covers parts of the so-called intelligence cycle, such as processing the information (decrypting, translation, photo-interpretation and so on), assessment, evaluation and analysis. These are the processes that transform raw intelligence into finished intelligence. Throughputs may also include the decision-making process within the intelligence organization that leads up to certain actions.

It is against this backdrop of a systemic approach that I would like to introduce the various contributions on the future of intelligence which make up this volume.

Future threats

When one addresses possible futures of intelligence one would ideally hope to be able to sketch a picture that would address all parts of this open system: changes in task and value environments, shifts in support and demand functions, modifications in working processes, and alterations in production and output. However, much of the thinking on the future of intelligence merely emphasizes changes in the threat environment.

It is of course difficult enough to foresee the future. Who could have foretold in 1928 the coming economic collapse of 1929, Hitler's rise to power in 1933, the alliance between Nazi Germany and the Soviet Union in 1939, the alliance between the Soviet Union and the Western democracies in 1941, and the division of Europe into a democratic, capitalist Western part and a totalitarian communist Eastern part in the aftermath of the Second World War, all in a mere seventeen years? Some of these occurrences could theoretically have been on the radar screen of the intelligence and security services of that period. A similar case could be made for 1988. Which agency could have foreseen the end of Soviet communism, the reunification of Germany, the Al-Qaeda attacks on New York and Washington DC, the start of a global war on terror, the possibility of an electronic Pearl Harbor, the introduction of the euro and the debate over its possible demise?

Foreseeing the future is of course an intractable problem. Still, intelligence and security agencies have a more than average need to try to predict future probabilities. First, one of their core functions is to provide early warning for both threats and opportunities. If any government organization needs to have foreknowledge of events it should be intelligence agencies. Second, intelligence-gathering capacities often require heavy investment of time and money. Satellite programs, for instance, are very expensive and need to be developed over a long period of time. Human agents generally tend to cost much less, but they need time to be trained and cultivated before they can be activated. A military intelligence service should not only be able to gather the necessary information to protect the armed forces in the present, but should also be considering how forces may be deployed and what adversaries they may face in the future. Assessments of future military opponents and the types of conflict that may be fought have important implications for military investments. Third, as Mark Lowenthal notes in his contribution to this volume, intelligence analysts should have the opportunity to build up deep knowledge about a possible future threat before a crisis develops, instead of rushing from one crisis to the other. Fourth, intelligence agencies are created and used to reduce (or, for Gregory Treverton, assess and manage) the uncertainties of decision-makers and politicians. Few things are as uncertain as the future. The more ominous threats become (the suspicion that a terrorist organization may obtain weapons of mass destruction), the greater the need for 'pre-emptive intelligence' to support 'pre-emptive action' against possible risks and threats, as David Omand phrases it in his chapter.

This tension between mandate and ability regarding the future makes one curious about what students and (former) practitioners of intelligence have to say about the future of their own field. It is understandable that many of the contributors here devote attention to current trends and their extrapolation, rather than to possible futures that cannot yet be discerned in the present. When one looks at the threats that are mentioned, the authors agree on most of them: non-state actors, terrorists, proliferators, organized crime, cyber threats, food shortages, pandemics, migration patterns, and (perhaps the worst of all) information overload (see also Bamford 2004: 111; Shultz 2005; Turner 2006: 57; Treverton 2009: 15; Agrell 2009: 111; Lahneman 2010: 214; Meeuws 2010; Aid 2012: 213, 215).

However, it may not be the threats which these experts agree upon that are the most dangerous, but exactly the ones they do not even mention. The fact that there is so much agreement among them could rather be a cause for concern. Where is the out-of-the-box thinking, where is the imagination that takes us into a dark world of unknowns? Or is the future already dark enough as it is? Above all, is it complex because the threats have become blurred? (Blair 2010: 45–46; Thomas 2008: 146).

I think everyone will indeed agree that the task environments of intelligence agencies have become more complex. Not only state actors, but an increasing number of non-state actors may become opponents. The clustering of possible opponents along the lines of the Cold War dichotomy has been superseded by an ever-increasing multitude of state and (especially) non-state actors that may enter into all kinds of temporary relationships hidden from preying eyes and listening ears. Furthermore, intelligence has become a phenomenon that seems to have penetrated every aspect of social life. Not only is intelligence more and more appreciated in the armed forces and law enforcement circles, as the chapters by Monica den Boer and Jelle van Buuren illustrate, but today almost every individual who uses the internet behaves like an intelligence officer or agent: using passwords, encrypting messages, employing cover names, creating networks, and using satellite pictures to look, for instance, at one's neighbour's estate (Wheaton 2012; Warner 2012: 148). After the Second World War the heads of some Western intelligence agencies were championing a government monopoly on intelligence gathering similar to the government's monopoly on violence, a position that is now unthinkable (De Graaff and Wiebes 1992; Krieger 2009: 100). These days, private intelligence companies and contractors flourish, and no longer only in the United States (Bean 2011: 9, 14). As Wilhelm Agrell argues, the more complicated the tasks of intelligence agencies become and the more technologically advanced the techniques that are required, the more these same agencies will depend on private initiatives.

It seems to be only a question of time before a group of friends will establish an intelligence agency not for a living but for a noble cause or even just for fun.

Treverton mentions the Grey Balloons initiative where people were asked to volunteer working a few hours a week, unpaid, to assist intelligence agencies to do their job. But one might imagine that in some cases, if the work is unpaid anyway, people may decide to do it for themselves instead of working for an agency that benefits from the results. One does not have to be a Marxist to understand that many would loathe this kind of alienation from what they produce. Treverton does see possibilities for amateur intelligence that may compete with official agencies – why not, in the 'age of the amateur'? (Keen 2007; Reynolds 2006: 92). Such a private initiative has existed since October 2011: Open Briefing (see www.openbriefing.org). What will be the consequences for established intelligence agencies if such private endeavors produce better results than they do? Treverton recommends seeking help as a key to reshaping intelligence. That is both a noble and humble approach, but hardly one that seems to square with the public notion that intelligence agencies are there to come to the rescue by supplying the right information at the right moment.

Another question regarding the distinctive position of intelligence agencies is generated by the identification of new types of threat. If, for instance, climate change and pandemics result in security threats, how great will the distinction then be between the work of the Intergovernmental Panel on Climate Change and the World Health Organization on the one hand and that of intelligence agencies on the other?

Changes in the task and value environments

In the contributions to this volume, much is said about future threats and very little about future opportunities. This seems to be another illustration of the fact that intelligence studies continue to have a defensive bias, stressing worst case scenarios instead of looking for brighter skies such as future economic opportunities, new political alignments or less expensive means of collecting intelligence.

An aspect which some of the authors, such as David Omand, Jennifer Sims and Greg Treverton, do mention is the growing impediment to develop a cover or a legend as a result of biometrics, geolocation and the traces one leaves in the social media. This impediment for offensive intelligence operations is rightly seen as an opportunity for enhanced counterintelligence. However, it remains unclear whether an impediment amounts to the same as an impossibility (Lis 2010; Lefebvre and Porteous 2011; Fitsanakis 2012). Another important question facing the intelligence community is whether secrecy will survive for ever. Sir John Sawyers, the current head of MI6, certainly seems to think so. In a speech for the Society of Editors in London in October 2010 he was adamant that 'secret organizations need to stay secret ... without secrecy, there would be no intelligence services' (Hughes and Stoddart 2012: 626–627). On the other hand, Don Burke, the CIA architect of Intellipedia, predicted already in 2008 that in fifteen years secrecy would be a thing of the past (Spaulding 2010; American Bar Association 2011). Both the vulnerability of secrecy and the increase in transparency have serious consequences for intelligence, since it has been seen by many as at least partly constituted by secret information (Center for the Study of Intelligence 2004: 10; Lahneman 2007: 8; De Graaff 2012a: 15–16; De Graaff 2012b: 11–12).

Changes in the definition and functions of intelligence

One of the main difficulties in looking at the future is that intelligence itself is not a constant. Even though some, such as former DCI Richard Helms, have described it as the second oldest profession (Hitchcock 1991: 306; also Knightley 1986), intelligence has, as both David Omand and Wilhelm Agrell point out, reshaped and reinvented itself several times in the past, for instance, around 1900 and in the 1940s. What is to be expected from intelligence in the future? How will it reconstitute itself once more? In the past many authors have drawn a clear dividing line between information and intelligence. The question is whether the information revolution will pass without leaving any traces on the intelligence process. It is unlikely that many scholars of intelligence would think so. Many intelligence professionals already have to cope with the so-called 'CNN effect' of traditional journalism or the speediness of 'new journalism' via social media, and the literature on the significance of this is extensive (Ott 1993: 141; FitzSimmonds 1995: 287; Medina 2002: 26; Bodnar 2003: 14–15, 55–58; O'Connell and Tomes 2003: 25; Steiner 2004; Center for the Study of Intelligence 2004: 3, 5, 20; Andrus 2005; Davis 2005: 27, 29, 32; Johnston 2005: 107; Teitelbaum 2005: 10, 205, 208; Treverton 2005: 30–31; Faddis 2008: 3; Goodman 2008: 355–356; Steele 2009: 133, 137, 142–143; Williams 2011). Will intelligence agencies maintain early warning as one of their core functions, only to find out that others are almost always faster at reporting looming disasters or at indicating opportunities? Or will they shift the current balance between timeliness, accuracy and trustworthiness by putting more emphasis on the validation of news and knowledge, as Wilhelm Agrell and others predict (Rathmell 2002: 99; Medina 2002: 26; Barger 2005: 19; Betts 2007: 5–6)?

One of the strong points of this volume is the emphasis it puts on new forms of international collaboration between intelligence agencies. The descriptions of intelligence cooperation in EU institutions by Jelle van Buuren en Björn Fägersten show that the age-old adage of 'quid pro quo' no longer regulates intelligence cooperation the way it did in the past. Communities of interest and multilateral working relationships are gaining a foothold as trust is established. The question arises, however, what the implications are for intelligence and security agencies if they are no longer the guardians of national sovereignty. Whereas on the one hand new circumstances ask for closer international cooperation (Herman 2010: 116; Lahneman 2011: 100), the experience with the politicized intelligence process leading up to the invasion of Iraq convinced some countries that they should have their own intelligence capability independent from their American and British partners (Report 2010).

New threats, new forms of international cooperation, closer public scrutiny, greater transparency and an increasing demand from the public for legitimacy may also reintroduce the question of for whose benefit intelligence agencies actually operate. A distinction can be made on whether they work for the state or for the incumbent government. In the United States they represent the interests of 'we, the people,' while in Germany they protect the constitution. Do these ultimate ends add a specific meaning to their daily working processes? Or will such points of departure exactly become more significant as a result of future developments? Will the ultimate goal of intelligence and security agencies in the future ´risk society´ no longer be the protection of the interests of the state but the protection of the interests of its citizens and society, as Omand seems to imply here and elsewhere (Omand 2012: 154)? This last competence would seem to conflict with concerns about the growing powers of intrusion of intelligence agencies into private spheres, the pervasiveness of alert and alarm systems, or the undeclared warfare by intelligence agencies using drones for targeted killings in remote parts of the world. Intelligence and security organizations are then not the great protectors but the originators of an intelligence or surveillance state, as Omand and others recognize (Schaar 2007; De Koning 2008; Landau 2010; Chesterman 2011). Will the intelligence community then become one of the big players in the game of social and political risk transfer from one citizenry to the other? As Jelle van Buren indicates in this volume, that would then increase the need for forms of accountability that transgress national boundaries.

Future working processes

Even if none of the above ever materializes, one could wonder what the impact of technological revolutions will be on the 'throughput' of intelligence systems. What for instance do new tools for translation, data gathering, retrieval and visualization imply for intelligence working processes? Are they worth the effort and the cost, or do they create ever more haystacks in which it is harder to find the needles that hurt? Is old-fashioned analytic tradecraft just as good? In his contribution here, Mark Lowenthal appears nostalgic for the Cold War era when the amount of data was still manageable.

Meanwhile Arthur Hulnick questions whether a better study of alternative analytic methodologies is necessary, pointing out that previously such exercises using stricter criteria were more time-consuming and did not bring better results. Are intuition and imagination then just as good (Medina 2002: 28; Colby 2007; Russell 2007: 119–148; Bar-Joseph and McDermott 2008; Marrin 2009: 205–206; Hedley 2009: 220–224; Agrell 2009: 113–114)? Both Hulnick and Omand argue that the intelligence cycle model does not aptly describe the working processes in the world of civilian intelligence. Hulnick consequently recommends replacing it with a more realistic matrix model in which collection, research and analysis, counterintelligence and covert action operate simultaneously. This is more a recommendation for the present rather than the future, although he certainly has a point (shared with Omand) that in the electronic era decision-makers will act increasingly upon raw intelligence rather than wait for a finished product, and that the conversion from raw into finished intelligence may become increasingly auto-mated (Warner 2012: 146). Again, as was true for the collection of intelligence, it is remarkable how little attention the contributors overall devote to future changes in tradecraft. It may be that they do not want us to know what they know, or simply that they do not know it themselves. However, obvious questions present themselves, such as: Will the increasing importance of open sources intelligence negatively affect the importance of other sources? Or will Humint become more important as the most promising way to gain intelligence about the intentions of an increasing number of super-empowered or super-enhanced groups and indi-viduals with an ever-growing capacity to destroy or disrupt? Will Humint opera-tions become more dangerous in an arena filled with non-state actors than they were during the Cold War? Finally, has the technological advantage enjoyed by several intelligence agencies over the rest of society during the Cold War now been undermined by a more democratic distribution of technology? (Berkowitz and Goodman 2000: 43–45; Berkowitz 2003: 67–74; Barger 2005: 116; Zegart 2007: 11; Rossmiller 2008: 139–141).

The output

Perhaps the greatest challenge of the future pertains to the output and especially the dissemination of the intelligence product. If Gregory Treverton and others are right that current and future intelligence organizations are becoming (or at least should be) less engaged with solving puzzles and more involved with addressing mysteries or so-called 'wicked problems' for which no easy solutions present themselves (Treverton 1994; Davis 1994: 7–15; Steiner 2004; Treverton 2009: 16–21; Moore 2011: x), this will have major consequences for the place of intelligence in democratic society. This will have a far greater impact than the form in which finished intelligence will be presented, another 'revolution' that Treverton addresses. Intelligence analysts and their representatives will no longer solely present facts on the numbers of long-distance missiles, the newest gadgets in submarines, or changes in the line of succession within an opaque gerontocracy in a foreign power. Intelligence agencies of the future are not likely to be, as Sir David Omand predicts, primarily knowledge management organiza-tions (Omand 2012: 156), but instead they will become sense-makers. 'Suddenly the ability to make sense of information is as valued a skill as collecting it', Richard Fadden, Director of the Canadian Security and Intelligence Service (CSIS), stated in a recently publicized speech (Wheaton 2012). Intelligence ana-lysts will become sense-makers defining opponents for government and the public at large as terrorists, insurgents, a social movement, religious fanatics, cunning Machiavellists or irrational radicals. They will produce the metaphors and the graphs that will make cyber attacks understandable. Instead of present-ing reality they will be shaping it (Codevilla 1992: 19–23; Berkowitz and Goodman 2000: 99; O'Connell and Tomes 2003: 27; Fishbein and Treverton 2004; Treverton 2005; George 2007; Agrell 2009: 93; Treverton 2009: 16, 22, 27–28, 33–36; Bean 2011: xii; Moore 2011). Analysts will have to become communicators, in the process engaging with decision-makers who themselves make more use of open source intelligence. Sherman Kent's dividing line between intelligence and policy, established at the beginning of the Cold War, will become obsolete because making sense is itself a policy act (Bean 2011: 11). Hulnick discusses the relevance of this Kentian tradition in his contribution to this volume, indicating that some American authors are beginning to question whether it remains sound practice. Decision-makers and intelligence analysts will have to sit together to construct reality, not *re*construct it. Monologue will have to be set aside in favour of dialogue (Turner 2006: 173–174; Davis 2009: 178, 183, 186–187; Treverton 2009: 9–11). The knowledge-based domain of the intelligence analyst and the value-based domain of politicians and other decision-makers will tend to fuse. They will write the narratives that give individual facts a place and a context, in doing so making them understandable. No longer will intelligence only have a support function in relation to policy, but analysts will be involved in actually shaping policies together with others through an iterative process of sense-making (O'Connell and Tomes 2003: 24). Although such a situation seems to be developing almost naturally out of the evolving task environment of the intelligence community, it remains to be seen whether its value environment is ready for such a step. Will it be acceptable to a democratic society that its dominating perceptions and decisions are shaped by intelligence analysts who partly base their insights on information that is not transparent? How can legitimacy be created for government based on a continuous and intense interaction between intelligence and policy (the scenario that Treverton predicts)? It may lead to closer parliamentary and public scrutiny, but one should recognize that this is not necessarily a guarantee against politicizing intelligence. On the contrary, one could say.

The choice between adaptation and obsolescence

The so-called contingency approach in organization studies states that once an environment is known, it is clear what structure an agency needs. A rather static environment in which there are few actors or in which actors are clustered requires a more bureaucratic organization compared to a turbulent environment with (in principle) no limits to the number of actors or the connections they may create. Environmental complexity has to be mirrored by organizational complexity (De Graaff 1997: 326). The trick is to achieve this without enhancing the number of bureaucratic levels, which would worsen organizational inertia. If organizations do not timely adapt they may end up in the maelstrom their environment creates for them instead of staying in control. Organizational studies champion more fluid, horizontal organizational structures for present-day and future intelligence organizations, 'flat hierarchies', as David Omand calls them, and 9/11 created a cry for fusion centres (Kindsvater 2003: 33–34; Taylor and Goldman 2004: 419–421; Green 2005; Treverton 2005: 27–29; Posner 2006: xviii, 169; Thompson 2006; Turner 2006: 128; Jones 2007; Cole and Chiego 2009: Treverton 2009: 104–109, 113, 188–192, 200–206; Chapman 2010:

385–386; Olcott 2010). Nevertheless, new techniques favour micromanagement and top-level control, as could, for instance, be observed at the time of the Abbottabad raid when the US top-level decision-makers were closely watching the raid from their Situation Room in the White House.

In his contribution to this volume, Mark Lowenthal seems rather pessimistic about the ability of the intelligence community to function as a learning, adaptive institution. Other authors have also been rather sceptical about the ability of bureaucratic agencies to adapt to a different playing field. Within the CIA the joke did the rounds that the only way to defeat al-Qaeda would be to convince its leadership to adopt the bureaucratic structure of the CIA (Faddis 2008: 49). The question then is: Who will adapt faster in a world where not size but speed brings the decisive advantage? (Brand 2000: 14–15). It is a question to be answered by the future, a future that may be foreseen a little better, as I hope to have shown, by using a systemic approach.

Bibliography

Agrell, W. (2009) 'Intelligence Analysis after the Cold War – New Paradigm or Old Anomalies?', in G.F. Treverton and W. Agrell (eds), *National Intelligence Systems: Current Research and Future Prospects*, Cambridge: Cambridge University Press.

Aid, M. (2012) *Intel Wars: The Secret History of the Fight Against Terror*, New York: Bloomsbury Press.

American Bar Association Standing Committee on Law and National Security, Office of the National Counterintelligence Executive, and National Strategy Forum (2011) *No More Secrets: National Security Strategies for a Transparent World*. Online. Available: www.virginia.edu/cnsl/pdf/no-more-secrets.pdf (accessed 3 March 2013).

Andrus, D.C. (2005) 'The Wiki and the Blog: Toward a Complex Adaptive Intelligence Community', *Studies in Intelligence*, 49. Online. Available: www.cia.gov/library/center-for-the-study-of-intelligence/csi-publications/csi-studies/studies/vol. 49no3/html_files/Wik_and_%20Blog_7.htm (accessed 3 March 2013).

Bamford, J. (2004) *A Pretext for War: 9/11, Iraq, and the Abuse of America's Intelligence Agencies*, New York: Anchor.

Bar-Joseph, U. and McDermott, R. (2008) 'Change the Analyst and Not the System: A Different Approach to Intelligence Reform', *Foreign Policy Analysis*, 4: 127–145.

Barger, Deborah G. (2005) *Toward a Revolution in Intelligence Affairs*, Santa Monica, CA: RAND Corporation. Online. Available: www.rand.org/content/dam/rand/pubs/technical_reports/2005/RAND_TR242.pdf (accessed February 28, 2013).

Bean, H. (2011) *No More Secrets: Open Source Information and the Reshaping of U.S. Intelligence*, Santa Barbara, CA: Praeger.

Berkowitz, B. (2003) 'Failing to Keep Up With the Information Revolution', *Studies in Intelligence*, 47: 67–74.

Berkowitz, B. and Goodman, A. (2000) *Best Truth: Intelligence in the Information Age*, New Haven, CT/London: Yale University Press.

Blair, D.C. (2010) *Annual Threat Assessment of the US Intelligence Committee for the Senate Select Committee on Intelligence*, Washington, DC: Office of the Director of National Intelligence. Online. Available: www.au.af.mil/au/awc/awcgate/dni/threat_assessment_2feb10.pdf (accessed 3 March 2013).

Bodnar, J.W. (2003) *Warning Analysis for the Information Age: Rethinking the Intelligence Process*, Washington, DC: Joint Military Intelligence College.

Brand, S. (2000) *The Clock of the Long Now: Time and Responsibility*, New York: Basic Books.

Center for the Study of Intelligence (2004) *Intelligence for a New Era in American Foreign Policy*, Report of the conference held in Charlottesville, Virginia, 10–11 September 2003, Washington, DC: Central Intelligence Agency. Online. Available: www.fas.org/irp/cia/product/newera.pdf (accessed 3 March 2013).

Chapman, R.D. (2010) 'Intelligence Reinvented', *International Journal of Intelligence and Counterintelligence*, 23: 384–393.

Chesterman, S. (2011) *One Nation under Surveillance: A New Social Contract to Defend Freedom Without Sacrificing Liberty*, Oxford: Oxford University Press.

Codevilla, A. (1992) *Informing Statecraft: Intelligence for a New Century*, New York: Free Press.

Colby, E.A. (2007) 'Making Intelligence Smart', *Policy Review*, 144. Online. Available: www.hoover.org/publications/policy-review/article/5843 (accessed 3 March 2013).

Cole, R.T. and Chiego, C. (2009) 'A Season of (Info)Sharing: An Empirical Assessment of Intelligence Reform', University of Georgia. Online. Available: http://juro.uga.edu/2009/papers/rocky_cole_chris_chiego.pdf (accessed 13 November 2012).

Davis, J. (1994) 'A Policymaker's Perspective on Intelligence Analysis', *Studies in Intelligence*, 38: 7–15.

—— (2005) 'Terrorism and Intelligence Reform', in D. Aaron (ed.), *Three Years After: Next Steps in the War on Terror*, Santa Monica, CA: RAND Corporation. Online. Available: www.rand.org/content/dam/rand/pubs/conf_proceedings/2005/RAND_CF212.pdf (accessed 3 March 2013).

—— (2009) 'Strategic Warning: Intelligence Support in a World of Uncertainty and Surprise', in L.K. Johnson (ed.), *Handbook of Intelligence Studies*, London/New York: Routledge.

De Graaff, B.G.J. (1997) *'Kalm temidden van woedende golven'. Het ministerie van Koloniën en zijn taakomgeving 1912–1940*, The Hague: Sdu.

—— (2012a) *Intelligence revolution. Dramatische verandering, ontsporing of gril?*, Breda: Nederlandse Defensie Akademie.

—— (2012b) *De ontbrekende dimensie: intelligence binnen de studie van internationale betrekkingen*, Utrecht: Universiteit van Utrecht.

De Graaff, B.G.J. and Wiebes, W. (1992) *Gladio der vrije jongens. Een particuliere geheime dienst in Koude Oorlogstijd*, The Hague: Sdu.

De Haan, J. and Rotmans, J. (2011) 'Patterns in Transitions: Understanding Complex Chains of Change', *Technological Forecasting and Social Change*, 78: 90–102.

De Koning, B. (2008) *Alles onder controle. De overheid houdt u in de gaten*, Amsterdam: Balans.

Faddis, C.S. (2008) *Beyond Repair: The Decline and Fall of the CIA*, Guildford, CT: Lyons Press.

Fishbein, W. and Treverton, G.F. (2004) 'Making Sense of Transnational Threats', *Sherman Kent Center Occasional Papers*, 3. Online. Available: www.cia.gov/library/kent-center-occasional-papers/vol.3no1.htm (accessed 3 March 2013).

Fitsanakis, J. (2012) 'Analysis: Biometric Passports, Iris Scanners, Worry Undercover Spooks', *IntelNews*, 13 April. Online. Available: http://intelnews.org/2012/04/13/01–969/ (accessed 3 March 2013).

FitzSimmonds, J.R. (1995) 'Intelligence and the Revolution in Military Affairs', in R.

Godson, E.R. May and G. Schmitt (eds), *U.S. Intelligence at the Crossroads: Agendas for Reform*, Washington, DC/London: Brassey's.

George, R.Z. (2007) 'Meeting 21st Century Transnational Challenges: Building a Global Intelligence Paradigm', *Studies in Intelligence*, 51. Online. Available: www.cia.gov/library/center-for-the-study-of-intelligence/csi-publications/csi-studies/studies/vol.51no3/building-a-global-intelligence-paradigm.html (accessed 3 March 2013).

Goodman, M.A. (2008) *Failure of Intelligence: The Decline and Fall of the CIA*, Lanham, MD: Rowman & Littlefield.

Green, A.W. (2005) *It's Mine! Why the US Intelligence Community Does Not Share Information*, research report, Maxwell Air Force Base, Alabama. Online. Available: www.au.af.mil/au/awcgate/saas/green.pdf (accessed 2 March 2013).

Hedley, J.H. (2009) 'Analysis for Strategic Intelligence', in L.K. Johnson (ed.), *Handbook of Intelligence Studies*, London/New York: Routledge.

Herman, M. (2010) 'Ethics and Intelligence after September 2001', in J. Goldman (ed.), *Ethics of Spying: A Reader for the Intelligence Professional*, Vol. 2, Lanham, MD: Rowman & Littlefield.

Hitchcock, W.T. (ed.) (1991) *The Intelligence Revolution: A Historical Perspective*, Proceedings of the Thirteenth Military History Symposium, US Air Force Academy, Colorado Springs, Colorado, 12–14 October 1988, Washington, DC: United States Government Printing Office.

Hughes, R.G. and Stoddart, K. (2012) 'Hope and Fear: Intelligence and the Future of Global Security a Decade after 9/11', *Intelligence and National Security*, 27: 625–652.

Johnston, R. (2005) *Analytic Culture in the U.S. Intelligence Community: An Ethnographic Study*, Washington, DC: Center for the Study of Intelligence.

Jones, C. (2007) 'Intelligence Reform: The Logic of Information Sharing', *Intelligence and National Security*, 22: 384–401.

Keen, A. (2007) *The Cult of the Amateur: How Today's Internet is Killing Our Culture and Assaulting Our Economy*, London/Boston, MA: Nicolas Brealey.

Kindsvater, L.C. (2003) 'The Need to Reorganize the Intelligence Community', *Studies in Intelligence*, 47: 33–37.

Knightley, P. (1986) *The Second Oldest Profession: The Spy as Bureaucrat, Patriot, Fantasist and Whore*, London: André Deutsch.

Krieger, W. (2009) 'US Patronage of German Postwar Intelligence', in L.K. Johnson (ed.), *Handbook of Intelligence Studies*, London/New York: Routledge.

Lahneman, W.J. (2007) 'Is a Revolution in Intelligence Affairs Occurring?', *International Journal of Intelligence and Counterintelligence*, 20: 1–17.

—— (2010) 'The Need for a New Intelligence Paradigm', *International Journal of Intelligence and Counterintelligence*, 23: 201–225.

—— (2011) *Keeping U.S. Intelligence Effective: The Need for a Revolution in Intelligence Affairs*, Lanham, MD: Rowman & Littlefield.

Landau, S. (2010) *Surveillance or Security? The Risks Posed by New Wiretapping Technologies*, Cambridge, MA: MIT Press.

Lefebvre, S. and Porteous, H. (2011) 'The Russian 10 … 11: An Inconsequential Adventure?', *International Journal of Intelligence and Counterintelligence*, 24: 447–461.

Lis, J. (2010) 'Will Biometric Passports Limit the Reach of Israel's Intelligence?', *Haaretz*, 19 February.

Marrin, S. (2009) 'Adding Value to the Intelligence Product', in L.K. Johnson (ed.), *Handbook of Intelligence Studies*, London/New York: Routledge.

Medina, C.A. (2002) 'What To Do When Traditional Models Fail? The Coming Revolution in Intelligence Analysis', *Studies in Intelligence*, 46: 23–28.

Meeuws, T.J. (2010) 'Geheime diensten van VS verzuipen in de data', *NRC Handelsblad*, 9 January.

Moore, D.T. (2011) *Sensemaking: A Structure for an Intelligence Revolution*, Washington, DC: National Defense Intelligence College.

O'Connell, K. and Tomes, R.R. (2003) 'Keeping the Information Edge', *Policy Review*. Online. Available: www.hoover.org/publications/policy-review/article/6410 (accessed 2 March 2013).

Olcott, A.C. (2010) 'The Challenges of Clashing IC Interests', *The International Journal of Intelligence and Counterintelligence*, 23: 623–635.

Omand, D. (2012) 'Into the Future: A Comment on Agrell and Warner', *Intelligence and National Security*, 27: 154–156.

Ott, M. (1993) 'Shaking up the CIA', *Foreign Policy*, 93: 132–151.

Posner, R.A. (2006) *Uncertain Shield: The U.S. Intelligence System in the Throes of Reform*, Lanham, MD: Rowman & Littlefield.

Rapport Commissie van Onderzoek Besluitvorming Irak (2010) Amsterdam: Boom.

Reynolds, G. (2006) *An Army of Davids: How Markets and Technology Empower Ordinary People to Beat Big Media, Big Government, and Other Goliaths*, Nashville, TN: Thomas Nelson.

Rossmiller, A.J. (2008) *Still Broken: A Recruit's Inside Account of Intelligence Failures, from Baghdad to the Pentagon*, New York: Presidio Press.

Russell, R.L. (2007) *Sharpening Strategic Intelligence: Why the CIA Gets It Wrong, and What Needs to be Done to Get It Right*, Cambridge: Cambridge University Press.

Schaar, P. (2007) *Das Ende der Privatsphäre. Der Weg in die Überwachungsgesellschaft*, Munich: Bertelsmann.

Shultz, R.H. (2005) 'The Era of Armed Groups', in P. Berkowitz (ed.), *The Future of American Intelligence*, Stanford, CA: Hoover Institution Press.

Spaulding, S.E. (2010) 'No More Secrets: Then What?', *Huffington Post*, 24 June.

Steele, R.D. (2009) 'Open Source Intelligence', in L.K. Johnson (ed.), *Handbook of Intelligence Studies*, London/New York: Routledge.

Steiner, J.E. (2004) 'Challenging the Red Line between Intelligence and Policy', Institute for the Study of Diplomacy, Georgetown University. Online. Available: www7.georgetown.edu/sfs/isd/pdfs/redline.pdf (accessed 2 March 2013).

Taylor, S.A. and Goldman, D. (2004) 'Intelligence Reform: Will More Agencies, Money and Personnel Help?', *Intelligence and National Security*, 19: 416–435.

Teitelbaum, L. (2005) *The Impact of the Information Revolution on Policymakers' Use of Intelligence Analysis*, Santa Monica, CA: RAND Corporation.

Thomas, D. (2008) 'U.S. Military Intelligence Analysis: Old and New Challenges', in R.Z. George and J.B. Bruce (eds), *Analyzing Intelligence: Origins, Obstacles, and Innovations*, Washington, DC: Georgetown University Press.

Thompson, C. (2006) 'Open-source Spying', *New York Times*, 3 December.

Treverton, G.F. (1994) 'Estimating Beyond the Cold War', *Defense Intelligence Journal*, 3: 5–20.

—— (2005) *The Next Steps in Reshaping Intelligence*, Santa Monica, CA: RAND Corporation.

—— (2009) *Intelligence for an Age of Terror*, Cambridge: Cambridge University Press.

Turner, M.A. (2006, revised edn) *Why Secret Intelligence Fails*, Washington, DC: Potomac Books.

Warner, M. (2012) 'Reflections on Technology and Intelligence Systems', *Intelligence and National Security*, 27: 133–153.

Wheaton, K. (2012) 'Top 5 Things Only Spies Used To Do (But Everyone Does Now)', *Sources and Methods*, 2 July. Online. Available: http://sourceandmethods.blogspot. be/2012/07top-5-things-only-spies-used-to-do-but.html (accessed 28 February 2013).

Williams, C. (2011) 'Google Effect Means Spies Work Harder, Says Ex-GCHQ Chief', *Daily Telegraph*, 12 November.

Zegart, A.B. (2007) *Spying Blind: The CIA, the FBI, and the Origins of 9/11*, Princeton, NJ: Princeton University Press.

2 The future of intelligence

What are the threats, the challenges and the opportunities?

Sir David Omand

The international security environment for Western nations today has changed from that of the late twentieth century. Threats are perceived as emanating from so-called non-state actors, terrorists, proliferators, organized criminals and cyber hackers, as much as from potential state aggression. Globalization of communications has sensitized social attitudes to issues such as famine and disease, international human rights, migration and immigration. Technology has continued to transform our lives and has raised new concerns over personal privacy in a digital age. Such profound changes are having their impact on our intelligence agencies as much as on any other sector of society, and they are likely to continue shaping the future of intelligence communities over the next twenty years (Omand 2010).

A first question intelligence studies should ask therefore is whether we will still mean the same thing in twenty years' time when we speak of 'intelligence' or 'secret intelligence' as we mean today when we use those terms, just as the situation twenty years ago was very different, with the Cold War just over and the explosion in open sources of information through the internet still to come. Those now in charge of our intelligence communities had their formative experiences in a very different world of information scarcity rather than overload.[1]

There is, however, a simple truth at the heart of intelligence work. The most basic purpose of intelligence today remains the same as it was in the sixteenth century when Sir Francis Walsingham set up Europe's first effective espionage network: to help improve the quality of decision-making by reducing ignorance. In his case it was to uncover and exploit the machinations of the Catholic monarchies against his Protestant sovereign Queen Elizabeth I. That purposeful definition applies to all forms of intelligence today. A further important distinction may then be made: *secret* intelligence is simply achieving that purpose in respect of information that other people do not want you to have, from which flow all of the characteristic moral hazards associated with the world of intelligence so beloved of fiction and film.

By what alchemy is raw information to be transmuted into intelligence? There are a number of unique features about this process that deserve to be highlighted by intelligence studies in examining future challenges.

First, the basic purpose of intelligence is, as stated, to help improve the quality of decisions, not to guarantee that result. Intelligence very rarely deals in certainties, and it will continue to be incomplete, fragmentary and sometimes wrong. But the argument in favour of intelligence work is that used systematically and sensibly it will improve the odds on a decision being the best possible in the circumstances, whether by a National Security Council, foreign policy official, border policeman or military commander. The overall outcome will therefore likely be better than if the decisions had been made using hunch or instinct, valuable as these are, or just by the toss of a coin. This is similar to investment analysts, who on any one day may see their portfolio fall below the market due to some unwise purchases, but over time the good analysts will generate returns for their funds better than a single market index. Like investment fund managers, intelligence analysts are well advised to be very chary of 'too good to be true' offers or even of deliberate deceptions.

Second, the definition of intelligence purpose refers to 'decision-making' and thus to actions people want to take and outcomes they want to see. Intelligence in war has always been used to guide action, from rounding up enemy agents to identifying targets for air attack. Today we see a concentration on intelligence for action in peacetime too, often for urgent action. The demand for what is often referred to as 'actionable' intelligence is now a notable feature of tactical intelligence in counter-insurgency, counter-terrorism, counter-proliferation and counter-narcotics work. Much of the intelligence analysis supporting the current US drone counter-terrorist programme has to be capable of generating results in minutes, rather than hours or days. Nevertheless, seminal moments such as the US special forces assault on the hiding place in Pakistan of Osama Bin Laden in 2012, or the interception of the freighter *BBC China* carrying nuclear weapons materials to Colonel Ghaddafi's Libya in 2005, would not have been possible without literally years of patient intelligence effort beforehand.

Third, the reference to needing to acquire information that other people are trying to prevent you from knowing is the source of the moral hazards associated with the intelligence business. Secret intelligence cannot be obtained without using techniques that overcome the will of the person with the secrets. Traditionally, agents must be recruited (including those inside terrorist or criminal networks, with all the risk of ending up colluding in wrongdoing), private communications must be intercepted (with all the risks of intrusion into privacy) and liaisons maintained with countries overseas (sometimes with very different attitudes to the human rights of the individual and to international law). Facing moral hazard is inseparable from the process of acquiring secret intelligence. That inconvenient fact could be ignored by most governments running intelligence operations during the twentieth century. The twenty-first century is, however, witnessing a profound shift from the old paradigm of the 'secret state' (Hennessy 2002) in which intelligence activity was secret and unacknowledged, to that of the 'protecting state' (Omand 2007: 97) in which intelligence agencies and their activities are bound by legislation and parliamentary oversight. Intelligence is no longer an ethics-free zone.

Fourth, it is now a notable feature of our world that it is next to impossible to work, travel or communicate without leaving a digital exhaust behind us. The nature of the information being sought by security and intelligence agencies more than ever relates to individuals, so-called non-state actors, as opposed to governments and their agencies. The requirement is not just for access to traditional records such as immigration landing cards or personal bank accounts, but to digitized information that may contain data about individuals of potential interest – their location, movements, communications, finance and associations. Such information may be drawn from authorized access and exploitation of what I term PROTINT (by analogy with SIGINT and HUMINT), namely the protected personal information held in databases by governments and their agencies and by private companies, both here and overseas, including social media. There are evident implications for privacy rights and unease over what methods should be judged acceptable in the production of such intelligence by ourselves and by our partners, and there is far from an international consensus on the matter. Such concerns on the part of the public tend to bleed into wider worries about fears of the 'surveillance society', the exploitation of modern technology by the state to store, access and mine data on individual citizens. The challenge for intelligence communities is how to increase public trust to avoid pressure on government to introduce rules and regulations that genuinely constrain operational activity that is necessary for public safety.

Finally, the world of national security and intelligence takes a strongly rationalist Enlightenment stance based on the assumption of human improvement: more information will lead to more intelligence and thus less ignorance. Hence there exists at least the potential for better-informed decisions to be taken that have a higher chance of leading to success and hence to better outcomes. The steps connecting these statements are however not always obvious or straightforward.

As individuals, we use fresh information every moment to alter our assumptions about the risks involved in decisions, from crossing the road to proposing marriage. We do not always do so by extracting all the information content available to us: faulty peripheral vision and emotions of love (and hate) alike can temporarily blind us. There are many links in the chain of events that bring intelligence to the policy-maker or decision-taker, and each link has its own weaknesses.

Critical points in the intelligence chain

First, there have to be 'data points' to be accessed in the first place (either as observations in the real world or as digital information in the virtual world of data in motion or at rest). Of course, clever intelligence agencies can sometimes coax reluctant 'data points' to the surface through sting operations to draw out terrorists or narcotics dealers, or make use of the modern equivalents of other traditional tradecraft such as cutting landlines in war to force the enemy on to the airwaves.

Second, the relevant intelligence agencies have to be 'pointing their aerials' in the direction of the signals to be detected. This is a non-trivial requirement for all but the largest nations. Not every potential target can be covered, intelligence officers cannot be posted in-country in every region of interest, not every data stream can be intercepted and made comprehensible, and not every square metre of global interest can be monitored from the air or space. Thus a key link in the chain is represented by the directing function that sets meaningful priorities for the intelligence community, while at the same time providing the spare resources for the intelligence community to undertake its most crucial function of warning of the unexpected and unwelcome surprise that may have featured on no one's priority listing.

Third, intelligence agencies have to have the people, skills and technology to access the information, process it and validate it through a process akin to historiography (thus screening out attempts at deception for malice or gain, or information that simply represents wishful thinking), and all in a timely enough fashion. Increasingly, success in that endeavour requires the active operational cooperation of domestic and overseas services as the targets in a globalized world criss-cross that increasingly blurred boundary between home and overseas. Success also requires active cooperation between technical and human intelligence operations. A feature of recent years is also the fact that individual nations, even the US, will not be able to access all the sought-after information by their own means. Crucial information will reside in the hands of overseas intelligence services (or will be accessible to them, for example, through PROTINT sources) with which it is then necessary to maintain friendly liaison. In some cases these overseas services have very different ethical conceptions from our own, increasingly a moral hazard of working with them.

Fourth, the intelligence analysts have to recognize and interpret the information for what it is, and assess the significance of the validated intelligence correctly, piecing together an incomplete jigsaw puzzle, made more difficult since, in intelligence work, there is no picture on the lid of the box to guide the analyst. This is sometimes misleadingly referred to as the 'joining up the dots' problem. But dots can be joined together to make a surprising number of different patterns, some of which may be highly tempting if misleading, especially if they pander to the paranoia of the policy-maker or appear to bolster their case for more resources. Professor R.V. Jones, the Second World War founder of scientific intelligence, warned analysts of this tendency with an epistemological dictum that he called Crabtree's bludgeon: 'there is no set of mutually inconsistent observations for which some human intellect cannot conceive a coherent explanation, however contrived'. The field of intelligence studies is littered with examples, many tragic, where dots were connected wrongly (Iraq and weapons of mass destruction) or not at all (9/11), or where the picture was pieced together by the analysts only to be rejected by the relevant intelligence chief as inconsistent with prevailing wisdom (Yom Kippur, 1973).

Fifth, the customers for intelligence have to receive the reporting in a secure and timely way. Intelligence studies can show examples of correctly assessed intelligence warning arriving too late to be of use. A complicating factor for the modern world of intelligence is the plurality of customers for secret intelligence, not least when the target set expands to include terrorists, organized criminals and proliferators. For example, among the actions that may be prompted by intelligence may be an airline refusing to carry a suspect, a border official refusing admission, a customs officer searching a vessel before it sails, a diplomat seeking UN agreement for the freezing of a suspect's assets, a trade official refusing an export licence, a police service raiding a suspect safe house, or searching for an arms dump or hidden explosive device. Circles of trust have to be developed outward from the originating agency to include the other parts of the intelligence community and their overseas liaisons, government departments and agencies, law enforcement, and industry (noting what was said above about the critical national infrastructure). The means of communication between the intelligence world and its plurality of trusted customers now needs to be fast, digital, reliable and ultra secure, and increasingly have the bandwidth to transmit not just text but also voice and high-resolution moving images.

Sixth, the customers for intelligence have to understand and accept the significance of what they are being told. A welcome cannot be guaranteed for the bearer of bad tidings, especially when the intelligence tends to show that some external situation has arisen affecting national interests that will necessarily divert the government from being able to devote as much attention to its most cherished domestic policies, or that a policy or military operation was misconceived and is failing in its purpose (as in Bosnia in 1992–1993). In such circumstances, a natural reaction is to ask for further work to be undertaken to clarify the reporting, or to commission a second opinion. The well-understood phenomenon of cognitive dissonance may be observed when what is being reported is clearly wholly inconsistent with the model of reality being followed by the leader or leadership team (witness the fall of Singapore in 1942).

Finally, customers have to make the right judgements on what actually should be done on the basis of the intelligence – and have the means to do something about it. Secret knowledge is not always comfortable, especially when the source is highly sensitive and has to be protected, so that the intelligence cannot therefore be used as the public justification for anticipatory action. For military commanders today, intelligence can be provided in a way that gives unparalleled real-time situational awareness using fusion and virtual reality visualization tools that would have been unimaginable to the field commanders under Generals Montgomery or Patton. That said, the caveat about needing the means to do something with the intelligence will remain a constant of warfare. As the military historian John Keegan has so clearly described in his writings on intelligence, in the end, the clash of arms is determined by factors that Clausewitz would have understood (Keegan 2003). The battle for Crete in 1941 is perhaps the classic and tragic example that even the best intelligence (in that case from Enigma decrypts of German air force communications) cannot always win battles if there is insufficient force under the hand of the commander.

At each link in the above chain, well-known cognitive weaknesses may appear to delay or distort connections that need to be made: intelligence studies literature is full of discussion of group think, mirror imaging, transferred judgements, confirmation bias and similar hiatuses (Heuer 1999). These weaknesses can apply to both analysts and their customers alike.

Changing demands for intelligence

Having established some of these salient characteristics of intelligence work, it is possible to see how the demand for intelligence may be expected to change over the coming decades. A convenient starting point is to look at the demands of modern national security strategy, since most NATO nations are already engaged in rethinking what should be meant today by national security. National priorities and traditions in making policy for national security naturally differ, but three considerations appear to predominate in modern Western national security thinking. These are the adoption of a citizen focus, applying risk management methodology, and seeking better-informed decision-taking.

First, the citizen focus. Since the end of the Cold War, the prime objective of Western national security has shifted from concerns about the external defence of the national territory and the protection of the democratic institutions of the state (important as these remain), to a focus on the duty placed on government by the citizen to provide them with security. That is, a duty to try to protect society and its citizens, both at home and overseas, by mitigating or managing at least the worst effects of the most dangerous and disruptive of modern-day risks.

Once again, a number of consequences flow from this first observation. We find, for example, that both the British National Security Strategy (HM Government 2010) and the equivalent French Livre Blanc (Secrétariat Général de la Défense Nationale 2006) have similar lists of major modern threats, including of course terrorism and cyber attack, that could disturb the normal life of the citizen. Many such major risks have overseas roots, blurring the boundary between what is a domestic threat to be managed by the internal police and security services, and an external threat to be managed through diplomacy, defence and foreign intelligence. As already observed, the attention switches from the behaviours of states to those of non-state actors. Internal and external services have to develop deeper patterns of cooperation with each other, and with the armed services. Law enforcement and intelligence, with their very different histories and cultures, have to understand each others' needs in order to work harmoniously together.

This change to a citizen focus necessarily sweeps in all risks, including hazards due to natural causes as well as malicious threats. The UK National Security Strategy identifies four 'top-tier' risks, threats and hazards. Since the strategy was published in October 2010 all four risks have actually materialized, affecting the United Kingdom and friendly nations: international terrorism (such as the failed printer cartridge bomb plot of 2010); cyber attack (a continuing persistent threat driven by espionage and criminal gain); international military crises (Libya, 2011) and major accidents or natural hazards (Fukushima, Japan, March 2011).

When the electric light goes out it could be the result of bad weather, accident or hostile action such as terrorism or cyber attack. What concerns the citizen is whether the disruption can be predicted and prevented, or at least how resistant the systems supporting normal life are to any form of disruption. Thus the concept of national resilience enters the lexicon of the national security planner, as does the concept of the critical national infrastructure, that set of facilities, systems, sites and networks necessary for the delivery of the essential services upon which the daily life of the community depends. Today, most of that infrastructure in an advanced economy is in the ownership, or at least the operational control, of the private sector. This means that industry has to work with and take advice from the intelligence and national security community. In the United Kingdom the Centre for the Protection of the Critical National Infrastructure[2] has been established as part of the security service MI5, precisely in order to enable the intelligence community to work closely with the commercial operators of that infrastructure.

A second feature of the planning of modern national security is a logical consequence of this citizen focus. The driving logic behind it has become that of risk management. This is especially so now that national security has the wider responsibility of maintaining public confidence that risks are being satisfactorily managed (thus maintaining a collective psychological state) as well as creating the objective reality of freedom from attack and foreign invasion. Of course, the search for risk avoidance through collective defence and deterrence remains as an insurance policy against the (re-)emergence of more traditional state threats. People need to *feel* sufficiently safe domestically to justify investment, to be prepared to travel, indeed to leave the house in the morning to get on with ordinary life and to live it to the full even in the face of threats such as terrorism and hazards such as pandemics. Our adversaries – and the international markets – must know we have the confidence to defend ourselves against all possible vectors of attack. A feeling of insecurity is highly corrosive for a healthy society. In this sense it is justifiable to define modern national security as a state of confidence on the part of the public that the major risks are indeed being managed, in ways consistent with our values, to a level where normal life can continue. A glance at those nations not fortunate enough to enjoy this sense of collective confidence in security will reveal just how damaging a situation they are in, where even international efforts to provide much-needed humanitarian assistance is frustrated by lack of security on the ground.

The third step in the argument follows on from this: national security depends more than ever on effective pre-emptive intelligence to allow the identification, anticipation and management of risk upstream. This throws increased weight on better-informed decision-making by government and thus on the work of the intelligence community.

That said, there is always a residual uncertainty that cannot be insured against or otherwise managed away. Efforts to eliminate all uncertainty can do more harm than good, since the law of unintended consequences often applies. In particular, governments can, in their pursuit of intelligence and security, run the risk of compromising freedom of movement and of speech, the rule of law, and civic harmony. Indeed, an important ingredient in public security in a democracy is confidence in the government's ability to manage risk in ways that respect human rights and the values of society.

Governments ideally need to be prepared to act as dangers begin to become clear, but preferably *before* the dangers become present. They must therefore convince their public that they are justified in investing in security measures in anticipation, and in order to act upstream of impending danger. The public will expect to be given a proper justification for sacrifices, whether in terms of lives brought into hazard and resources spent on security, or the occasional inconvenience of security measures or invasion of privacy. That is why British govern- ments now regularly publish a national risk matrix along with the national security strategy, setting out the principal threats and hazards facing society that are being addressed by government security policy. The matrix shows the two principal dimensions of risk: likelihood of occurrence and impact should it happen, with a third dimension, national vulnerability to the risk, folded out of sight largely for security reasons.

As NATO has recognized in its new strategic concept (North Atlantic Council 2010), increasingly in modern society it will be too late to wait until the adversary is at the gate or even right inside the city – as was seen on the streets of Mumbai in November 2008 – before taking action to prevent, protect and prepare. Some potential risks, such as rogue states armed with nuclear weapons or terrorists armed with a dirty bomb, would be so potentially destructive of confidence in urban life (or indeed in civilization itself) that they demand preemptive action. In different ways, the consequences of other risks, such as those likely to flow from resource stress due to global climate change, equally require that governments anticipate the potential impact on our security and act now to avoid or mitigate future consequences.

If there is to be acceptance of that fundamental proposition, then clearly greater media and public understanding is needed of what is *really* involved behind the scenes in 'securing the state', distinguishing it from what is simply popular cinematic or television fantasy. There is a valuable role for intelligence studies in demystification.

Modelling intelligence

With good intelligence there is some hope that major risks can be anticipated, within the limits of the knowable, allowing government to decide in sufficient time whether to act to try to reduce the risk, to act to reduce society's vulnerability to it, or in some cases sensibly to decide to leave well alone. This task of helping to improve decision-making through reducing ignorance is of course the very purpose of intelligence.

Anticipation also places a great responsibility on the intelligence of those who are to provide strategic notice of emerging risks. It places even more weight on the wisdom of those who have to decide whether and how to act upon such warning. Machiavelli offered an infallible rule: 'A Prince who is himself not wise cannot be well advised' (Machiavelli 1991: 127).

A valuable service that intelligence studies can provide is to help model the intelligence process in ways that reflect the reality of how twenty-first-century intelligence may be expected to function in support of such a modern definition of national security (Omand 2010). The traditional intelligence cycle (Herman 1996) stands in need of reinterpretation in an age where the users of intelligence often interact with those involved in collection in ways more reminiscent of the detective investigating a crime than a Cold War analyst piecing together the adversary's order of battle. In addition, rather than the collection of intelligence from traditional secret sources, it is the real-time access to digitized data that may hold the key.

A traditional way of modelling intelligence knowledge, drawn from its application to military affairs, is to make a distinction between estimates of capabilities and of intentions. Capabilities can be quantified: how many strategic nuclear delivery vehicles, how many armoured divisions, their size, equipment, training level and state of readiness, how many modern war planes with which missile systems, and so on. Capabilities take time to build, and good intelligence about them (although always subject to errors in estimation) is unlikely to change quickly. On the other hand, intentions concerning the use of those capabilities can change in a twinkling of a dictator's eye. Stick to capabilities and leave intentions to the diplomats is a piece of advice often given to many military intelligence officers.

Another related way of modelling intelligence knowledge is the classic distinction between secrets and mysteries popularized by Professor R.V. Jones. Secrets are facts about the world that objectively exist somewhere, if only the intelligence officers are clever enough to find a way of accessing them. Their estimates of these secrets (especially if they are well guarded) are likely, as always, to be incomplete and hedged with uncertainty. Yet in principle they are knowable, unlike the mysteries concerning what may happen but has not yet. Whether the rogue state intends actually to test a nuclear weapon or the dictator aims to invade the neighbouring state may not yet even be known to the dictator himself, but intelligence analysts still have to make estimates of likelihood. Clearly, secrets and mysteries are two different epistemological categories, with the risk that for the latter the intelligence analyst can stray from prediction to prophesy. We can also add the category of complexities, where the estimate of likelihood in question depends on the analysts' assessment of what may be the impact on the situation of steps being taken by their own or allied governments to defuse the situation, such as an ultimatum or imposition of counter-proliferation sanctions. Many modern intelligence estimates therefore have a similarity to the net assessments of the Cold War.

The secrets/mysteries/complexities model still has utility in reminding analysts to be extra careful about what they think they really know when making a stab at what the future may bring, and also to include assumptions about the efficacy of own-side policies. Estimates of modern national security risks may, however, be better captured by a different four-level model drawn from contemporary philosophy of science (Deutsch 2011), using the following categories: situational awareness, explanation, prediction, and strategic notice.

The primary use of intelligence, and by far the greatest in terms of volume of effort involved, will continue to be what I term 'building situational awareness' to answer questions of 'what, where, who?' without forgetting to be explicit about the degree of uncertainty that may be attached to the answers. What such specific intelligence can do is help to build up awareness of a domain of interest to the policy-maker, military commander, defence technologist or senior police officer.

A second essential dimension in using intelligence in supporting decision-making is, however, in building an explanatory theory of past and present behaviour, answering the questions 'why and what for?' Such explanatory theories are important for understanding, and more importantly not misunderstanding, the behaviour of foreign states, for example, whether military deployments should be taken as indicators of defensive or offensive intent, and what the motives of non-state groups such as insurgents or terrorists may be.

Good intelligence assessment has explanatory value in helping deepen real understanding of how a situation has arisen, the dynamics between the parties and what the motivations of the actors involved are (as they, not we, see them), and thus how they themselves may be perceiving our side's moves. Providing such satisfactory explanation requires a deep knowledge of the country concerned, the languages, personalities, local cultures, history, commerce and topography. Developing expert analysts capable of such deep understanding represents a major challenge for all intelligence communities.

The third dimension of intelligence judgement is both potentially the most valuable and the most fraught, and that is prediction, answering the questions 'what next?' or 'where next?' Prediction is the desired end product of much intelligence activity. It could be fundamental to grand strategy, such as estimates of the likelihood of conflict over the South China Sea, or of tactical significance, such as the identification of an intended target of an insurgent or terrorist attack that can trigger anticipatory security action to save scores of lives.

Prediction need not be a 'point estimate' but could also be the forecasting of a limited range of outcomes that would still usefully narrow down the options for the policy-maker. It could be a predictive assessment based not on specific intelligence reporting but on judgements made about a developing situation that extends the explanatory into the predictive. Much of the intelligence studies debate about intelligence assessments has tended to focus on the instances of failure to predict sufficiently (if at all) the discontinuities of war, when active deception or high levels of secrecy had to be penetrated. In the case of failure to predict revolutionary change (such as Iran in 1979 and Berlin in 1989), what is likely to matter more is the 'feel' the analyst has for the interactive dynamics of the developing situation rather than any specific secret intelligence. It cannot be emphasized too strongly, however, that having a satisfactory explanation of events is a necessary precondition to producing well-founded predictive assessments.

A fourth, separate, category is needed in this model of modern intelligence, and that is the important element of 'strategic notice' of possible future risk-related developments (hazards as well as threats, and threats that might develop from hazards), especially where these may invalidate the explanations and predictions being made by the analysts.

Strategic notice will be needed, for example, of potential relevant developments in the fields of technology (such as the further development of bio- and nanotechnologies or of quantum computing), in diplomacy (such as the development of potential new alliances or groupings of nations), in nature (such as the effects of global warming on scarce resources) or in other aspects of security (such as the possible development of new violent ideologies) or prospective shifts in public and international attitudes to security.

Strategic notice in the form of a simple list of conceivable future possibilities is however of only limited use, in the same way that corporate risk registers which provide a catalogue of all the disasters that may occur are only a building block for a sensible risk management process. What is required at this level of thinking about security is a deep understanding of the phenomena in question, and their roots, causes and possible future development, expressed in ways that will help the policy staffs to develop options for government. One of the most important benefits of good strategic notice is in enhancing the ability of government to commission full intelligence assessments or longer term scientific and other research to illuminate the phenomena. This should be done systematically as a cross-government exercise. Open sources come into their own here, including academic intelligence studies.

To provide 'strategic notice' is not necessarily to predict that future (or in particular its timing) but to provide the advance notice that allows intelligence, diplomatic and scientific effort to be cued to look for signs that those potentialities are becoming realities. Without strategic notice (for example, of terrorist interest in new unconventional attack methods), it is less likely that the intelligence system will be geared to bring together data drawn from different agencies, or stovepipes within agencies, for the analyst to assess as a whole.

Without the quartet of situational awareness, explanation, prediction and strategic notice, intelligence analysts are less likely to generate in their minds the right set of possible hypotheses, and therefore very much less likely that they will share the data and join up the correct dots that are appearing into a genuine new pattern of threat.

Looked at in this light, current and future organizational reforms in response to the standard criticisms of intelligence performance may not bring as much improvement as reformers hope, since there is an irreducible level of uncertainty about intelligence work (Jervis 2006). Post-mortem inquiries such as those into 9/11, 7/7 and Iraqi Weapons of Mass Destruction will usually reveal mistakes and poor processes that can be improved, but it does not follow that these were responsible for the warning and intelligence failures.

One of the implications of such thinking is that the intelligence community needs to build data management systems so that hypotheses may be run across different domains and patterns of interest identified for further, more traditional investigation. Simply complaining that the different intelligence, police and security authorities 'failed to join up the dots' misses the point. We need analysts to be actively researching a hypothesis and testing explanations against the evidence, successively improving their models, not passively waiting for a pattern to emerge. We need hunters, not gatherers.

Historians now write about the twentieth century as 'the century of intelligence' in which states developed formal institutions called secret services and used them to spy ruthlessly on each other. By the end of the century most states had ended up avowing their existence publicly, establishing widespread overseas liaisons with each other, and attempting to regulate and oversee their activities by judges and parliamentarians. This chapter has described two of the forces that caused this reshaping of the intelligence community. The first was the shift from the Cold War secret state to the modern protecting state with its different demands for intelligence. The second was the way in which societal attitudes themselves have developed what has been called the end of deference towards authority, a reduced tolerance of risk (and a propensity to look for someone to blame, or sue, when things go wrong), and above all the rise of 24/7 mass media and social networking. These changes are not reversible, but further developments are to be expected over the coming years, especially stemming from the third shaping force that is science and technology.

It may well be that there will not be comparable scientific and technological revolutions around the corner that will have as transformative an effect on intelligence work as the scientific revolutions of the twentieth century that brought radio, radar, solid state electronics, satellites, computers and the internet, although new generation search engines and the semantic web will allow greater exploitation of open sources. Probably the biggest revolution going on now is in the bio-sciences, so we may expect new man–machine interfaces, the ability to access virtual reality representations of operating environments, and other ways of fusing information to transform the work of the intelligence officer.

What is certain is that all the effective intelligence agencies of the future will be knowledge management organizations *par excellence*. Such organizations tend to have flat hierarchies to encourage innovation and creativity, to have the minimum of regulations, to have the agility to adapt and put together teams at very short notice, and to use all the experience and talent from within and outside the organization: in short, the opposite of a late twentieth-century peacetime government department. I have high confidence that the United Kingdom's intelligence agencies have the message and the capacity to reinvent themselves to meet new circumstances, and I hope that will be true for all our allies and partners. I also believe that the public is beginning to understand better the essential role intelligence plays, for all its inherent limitations, in keeping us in relative security in a troubled world.

Notes

1 James R. Clapper, 'How 9/11 Transformed the US Intelligence Community', *Wall Street Journal*, 7 September 2011.
2 The CPNI website may be accessed at www.cpni.gov.uk/about/cni/.

Bibliography

Deutsch, David (2011) *The Beginning of Infinity*, London: Allen Lane.

Hennessy, Peter (2002) *The Secret State*, London: Allen Lane.

Herman, Michael (1996) *Intelligence Power in Peace and War*, Cambridge: Cambridge University Press.

Heuer, Richard J. (1999) *The Psychology of Intelligence Analysis*, Washington, DC: CIA Center for the Study of Intelligence.

HM Government (2010) *A Strong Britain in an Age of Austerity: The National Security Strategy*, London: Cabinet Office.

Jervis, Robert (2006) 'Reports, Politics and Intelligence Failures: The Case of Iraq', *Journal of Strategic Studies*, 29: 3–52.

Keegan, John (2003) *Intelligence in War*, London: Hutchison.

Machiavelli, Niccolo (1991) *The Prince*, London: Penguin.

North Atlantic Council (2010) *New Strategic Concept*, Brussels: NATO.

Omand, David (2007) 'Reflections on Secret Intelligence', in P. Hennessy (ed.), *The New Protective State*, London: Continuum.

—— (2010) *Securing the State*, London: Hurst.

Secrétariat Général de la Défense Nationale (2006) *Livre blanc: Défense et Securité Nationale*, Paris: La Documentation Française.

3 The future of intelligence

Changing threats, evolving methods

Gregory F. Treverton

Nature of the threat

It is widely acknowledged that the nature of the threat, hence the intelligence target, has changed dramatically, from nation-states to non-state actors as the primary target. Yet the implications of that shift reach much further than is recognized. Nation-states are geographic, in that they are fixed in space (they have 'addresses'). As important, they come with lengthy 'stories' attached; and intelligence is ultimately about helping people adjust the stories in their heads to guide their actions. Without a story, new information is just another empty fact. States, even ones as different from the United States as North Korea, are hierarchical and bureaucratic. They are a bounded threat. Many matters of interest about states are material and identifiable: tanks, missiles, massed armies (Treverton 2009a).

Terrorists (as individuals, networks and organizations) are different in every respect. They are small targets, as was Osama Bin Laden, and a single suicide bomber can cause large-scale mayhem. They are amorphous, fluid and hidden, presenting intelligence with major challenges simply to describe their structures and boundaries. Not only do terrorists not have addresses, they aren't just 'over there' – they are 'here' as well, an unpleasant fact that impels nations to collect more information on their citizens and residents and to do so with minimal damage to civil liberties. Terrorists also come with little or no story attached. More than a decade after 9/11, we still debate whether al-Qaeda is a hierarchy, a network, a terrorism venture capitalist operation, or an ideologically inspired cause. No doubt it contains elements of all four, but that hardly amounts to a story.

Cold War intelligence gave pride of place to secrets – information gathered by human and technical means that intelligence 'owned'. In contrast, an avalanche of data is available on terrorists. The addresses of the 9/11 hijackers were available in Californian motor vehicle records. But the sheer volume of data, plus the lack of a story, means that gathering information on terrorists necessarily involves 'mining' or other processing of large quantities of information. The hardest terrorists of all to pin down are the near 'lone wolves' such as US Army major Nidal Hassan, the Fort Hood killer of 2009 (Jenkins 2010).

Another difference is that terrorists constantly adapt to their adversaries. As former US Secretary of Defense Harold Brown quipped about the US–Soviet nuclear competition, 'When we build, they build. When we stop, they build' (Platt 1989: 80). While the United States hoped to influence Moscow, intelligence would suggest that it would not. The Soviet Union would do what it would do regardless. The terrorist target, however, is utterly different, shaping its capabilities according to identifiable vulnerabilities. The 9/11 suicide bombers did not hit on their attack plan because they were airline buffs. They had done enough tactical reconnaissance to know that fuel-filled jets in flight were vulnerable assets and that defensive passenger clearance procedures were weak. Thus, to a great extent, *we* shape the threat; it reflects our vulnerable assets and weak defences. This interaction between 'us' and 'them' has very awkward implications for US intelligence, especially those agencies with foreign missions such as the CIA that have traditionally been prevented from doing domestic intelligence.

The last major difference between transnational targets (especially terrorists) and state targets like the Soviet Union may be the most important of all. In principle, the fight against terror is an intelligence fight. In the Cold War, strategy did not depend much on intelligence. Now it does. If the goal is prevention, not deterrence, then there is enormous pressure on intelligence to reach into potential adversaries, their organization, proclivities and capabilities. How can intelligence achieve that? Table 3.1 lays out the difference, in slight caricature, between Cold War state threats and post-Cold War transnational threats.

Puzzles and mysteries

Table 3.2 lays out the spectrum from puzzles to mysteries to complexities (Treverton 1994, 2007; Nye 1994). When the Soviet Union would collapse was a mystery, not a puzzle. No one could know the answer. It depended, and was contingent, on innumerable factors. Puzzles are a very different kind of intelligence problem. They have an answer but we may not know it. Many of the intelligence successes of the Cold War involved puzzle-solving about a very secretive foe: Were there Soviet missiles in Cuba? How many warheads did the Soviet SS-18 missile carry?

Puzzles are not necessarily easier than mysteries – consider the decade it took to finally solve the puzzle of Osama Bin Laden's whereabouts – but they do come with different expectations attached. Intelligence puzzles are unlike jigsaw puzzles in that we may not be very sure that we have the right answer – the US raid on Osama Bin Laden in 2011 was launched, participants in the decision claimed, with the odds that Bin Laden was actually in the compound no better than six in ten. But the fact that there is in principle *an answer* provides some concreteness to what is expected of intelligence. By contrast, mysteries are those questions for which there is no certain answer. They are necessarily contingent; the answer *depends* not least on the intervention, be it policy or medicinal practice. Often, the experts (whether intelligence analysts, doctors or policy analysts)

Table 3.1 From Cold War targets to the era of terror targets

	Old: Cold War	*New: era of terror*
Target	States, primarily the Soviet Union	Transnational actors, also some states
'Story' about target	States are geographic, hierarchical, bureaucratic	Non-state actors come in many shapes and sizes (limited story)
Location of target	Mostly 'over there' (abroad)	Abroad and at home
Consumers	Limited in number (primarily federal, political, military)	Enormous numbers in principle (state, local and private)
'Bounded-ness'	Relatively bounded (and in the case of the Soviet Union, ponderous)	Much less bounded: terrorists patient but new groups and attack modes appearing
Information	Too little: dominated by secret sources	Too much: broader range of sources, though secrets still matter
Interaction with target	Relatively little: Soviet Union would do what it would do	Intense: terrorists as the ultimate asymmetric threat
Form of intelligence product	'Answer' for puzzles (best estimate with excursions for mysteries)	Perhaps 'sense-making' for complexities
Primacy of Intelligence	Important but not primary: deterrence not intelligence rich	Primary: prevention depends on intelligence

Source: adapted from Treverton (2009b).

Table 3.2 Intelligence puzzles, mysteries and complexities

Type of issue	*Description*	*Intelligence product*
Puzzle	Answer exists but may not be known	The solution
Mystery	Answer contingent, cannot be known, but key variables (and a sense for how they combine) may be identified	Best forecast, perhaps with scenarios or excursions
Complexity	Many actors responding to changing circumstances, not repeating any established pattern	'Sense-making'? Perhaps done orally, involving intense interaction of intelligence and policy

Source: adapted from Treverton (2009b).

find themselves in the position of trying to frame and convey essentially sub-jective judgements based on their expertise.

'Complexities are mysteries-plus' (Snowden 2002).[1] Large numbers of relat-ively small actors respond to a shifting set of situational factors. Thus, they do not necessarily repeat behaviour in any established pattern and are not amenable to predictive analysis in the same way as mysteries. These characteristics describe many transnational targets – small groups forming and reforming, seeking to find vulnerabilities, thus adapting constantly and interacting in ways that may be new. Indeed, a definition of wicked problems suggests the challenges for intelligence, and in particular the 'connectedness' of the threat with our own actions and vulnerabilities:

> Wicked problems are ill-defined, ambiguous and associated with strong moral, political and professional issues. Since they are strongly stakeholder dependent, there is often little consensus about what the problem is, let alone how to resolve it. Furthermore, wicked problems won't keep still: they are sets of complex, interacting issues evolving in a dynamic social context. Often, new forms of wicked problems emerge as a result of trying to understand and solve one of them.
>
> (Ritchey 2007)

To be sure, puzzles remain important for intelligence: consider Osama Bin Laden's whereabouts. With time and experience, some of the complexities associated with, for instance, terrorist targets are being reconstructed as mysteries. Still, the increase in complexity (hence uncertainty) is underscored by analogies with two other areas of science: medicine and policy analysis. The analogies between intelligence and medicine are striking. In both cases, experts – doctors or intelligence analysts – are trying to help decision-makers choose a course of action. The decision-makers for intelligence are policy officials, and for medicine, patients or policy officials. In both cases, the 'consumers' of the intelligence may be experts in policy or politics but they are not experts in the substance of the advice, still less in how to think about uncertainty. Both sets of experts are often in the position of trying to frame 'mysteries'.

Warnings of war aim to turn mysteries into puzzles in a Bayesian way.[2] Whether the Warsaw Pact would attack Western Europe was a mystery. What intelligence as warning did was construct indicators, such as the movements of troops out of garrisons. These indicators became warning lights: the more of them that began to turn red, the more likely an attack. The process was explicitly Bayesian – that is, the probability of attack was adjusted with additional information.

A similar Bayesian approach might address some aspects of terrorism warning. If a group of concern is identified – a big if – and if the fear were that it might seek to build and use a chemical, biological or nuclear weapon, then the paths to those weapons might be 'mapped', looking for steps that were important, unique – that is, indicative of weapon development – and detectable. The complicating factors are, first, that there are many possible chemical and biological weapons, so the paths to follow only proliferate; and second, many important steps, such as acquiring laboratory equipment, are hardly unique to building weapons.

These dilemmas mean that looking for steps and thus indicators that rank higher in 'uniqueness' is critical. Carefully inspecting a building can be terrorist surveillance, but it can also be simply tourism or curiosity. For reasons of uniqueness, traditional warning was hard to extend to more political and economic issues. Many political indicators, for instance, might be relevant for foreseeing a coup or other sudden change of government but be at best ambiguously related to that warning. They were not, in the sense of Bayesian analysis, very unique. If a step or indicator has few applications other than a terrorist attack it is highly unique, and likewise many applications indicates reduced uniqueness. Uniqueness tends to trump simple importance, since a step that is important but not very unique is of limited use to intelligence. For instance, acquiring laboratory equipment is very important in almost any process of producing biological weapons, yet that action ranks low in uniqueness. Possible purchasers of laboratory equipment range from students, to hobbyists, to an enormous range of legitimate businesses.

For indicators, visibility is also critical. Something that cannot be monitored by intelligence is not very useful as an indicator. The decision by an opponent's general staff to launch preparations for an attack would be a wonderful warning but is not likely to be very visible. For that reason, espionage, which may or may not be available on any given day, generally cannot be counted on for warning; it is a business involving 'targets of opportunity'. Is there some way in which a particular indicator manifests itself so that it could be recognized or searched for? The answers will differ across phases and tasks. Much terrorist planning, for instance, will be invisible to intelligence until long after the fact, left in terrorist staging areas, or available only with luck (e.g. seizing a computer). By contrast, acts of recruitment may be more visible, along with some kinds of training. In the biological weapons example, acquiring laboratory equipment is very important but not very unique. Moreover, it is also, in general, not very visible. If, by contrast, a group suspected of being terrorists recruited a biologist, that may be more unique *and* more visible.

With a Bayesian approach, the intelligence problem becomes an assessment of conditional probabilities. Against a prior suspicion that a group may engage in terror, does each available indicator increase that suspicion or diminish it? Each additional observation made with respect to an individual or group provides additional information – like additional flips of the coin – permitting analysts to sharpen their assessments of whether that person or group is more likely to engage in terror or not.

Ideally, intelligence would focus on indicators that were both very indicative of terror as opposed to some other more benign activity, and very visible. Unfortunately the world frustrates such convenience, since it offers few indicators comparable to large troop movements on the central front during the Cold War. Most will be like acquiring laboratory equipment in the bio-weapons example, perhaps important but not useful for intelligence because they are low in uniqueness and visibility. By contrast, acquiring a microbiologist is more detectable and more unique, though still not high on either scale.

Both uniqueness and visibility depend on the context, and policies can increase both, especially visibility. In terms of context, if the framework were applied not to an industrial society like the United States or Britain, but instead to a poor region of the world with only a limited industrial base, even the acquisition of laboratory equipment might acquire some uniqueness. Similarly, large purchases of fertilizer might carry more uniqueness if made in a large city rather than in a rural agricultural area, although this might not be very visible in either location.

Similar considerations may also apply to visibility. Transactions that are buried among thousands or millions of others in rich countries – thus obscuring the signal with enormous noise – might stand out more in poorer countries. That may be true whether the activity were observed in surveillance or detected by signals intelligence (SIGINT), and may apply to a wide range of indicators from simple international travel, which is much rarer to and from poor regions, to possession of materials that could be used to produce weapons.

Cold War confidence-building measures (CBMs), a policy instrument, increased uniqueness more than visibility. Large troop movements would have been visible in any case, but CBM limitations on out-of-garrison activity implied that any activity over the limit was on its face threatening. Policies can also make some of the steps along paths to terrorism more visible. For instance, in 2007 the US Nuclear Regulatory Commission moved to tighten procedures for getting licences to acquire radioactive materials after US Government Accountability Office investigators posing as West Virginia businessmen obtained a licence in twenty-eight days using nothing more sophisticated than a telephone, a fax machine and a rented post office box. The move sought to make acquiring radioactive materials more transparent.

Conveying uncertainty

The terrorism warning example drives home the point that uncertainty cannot be eliminated, only assessed and then perhaps managed. This is more and more obvious when the analytic task moves away from warning (especially very tactical warning) towards dealing with more strategic and forward-looking mysteries for which the analysis begins where the information ends and uncertainty is inescapable. In framing this task, it is useful to compare Carl von Clausewitz with his lesser-known contemporary strategist, Antoine-Henri, Baron de Jomini (Friedman and Zeckhauser 2012). Jomini, a true child of the Enlightenment, saw strategy as a series of problems with definite solutions. He believed that mathematical logic could derive 'fundamental principles' of strategy, which if followed should mean for the sovereign that 'nothing very unexpected can befall him and cause his ruin' (Jomini 2007: 250). By contrast, Clausewitz believed that unpredictable events were inevitable in war, and that combat involved some irreducible uncertainty (or 'friction'). He characterized war as involving 'an interplay of possibilities, probabilities, good luck and bad', and argued that 'in the whole range of human activities, war most closely resembles a game of cards' (von Clausewitz 1976: 85–86).[3]

Intelligence, perhaps especially in the United States, talks in Clausewitzian terms, arguing that uncertainty, hence risk, can only be managed, not eliminated.

Yet Jomini casts a long shadow over both war and intelligence. In fact, intelligence is still non-Clausewitzian in implying that uncertainty can be reduced, perhaps even eliminated. That theme runs back to Roberta Wohlstetter's classic book about Pearl Harbor, which paints a picture of 'systemic malfunctions' (Wohlstetter 1962). There were plenty of indications of an impending attack, but a combination of secrecy procedures and divided organizations prevented them from being put together into a clear warning. If, though, the dots had been connected, to use a recently much-overused phrase, the attack could have been predicted. So, too, the US report on 9/11 imposes a kind of Wohlstetter template, searching for signals that were present but not put together (National Commission on Terrorist Attacks 2004). The perception of linearity is captured by the formulation 'the system is blinking red'. Table 3.3 summarizes the differences between the Jominian and Clausewitzian approaches.

The Jominian approach pervades how analysis is conducted and taught. Most assessments, like US National Intelligence Estimates (NIEs), provide a 'best' estimate or 'key judgements'. They may then set out alternatives or excursions, but the process tends to privilege probability over consequences, when in fact it is the combination of the two that matters to policy. This emphasis on 'best bets' also runs through familiar analytic techniques such as the analysis of competing hypotheses (ACH). This points to the question 'competition for what?' The usual answer is likelihood. Indeed, the original description of ACH, in the now-classic book by Richard Heuer, explains its goal as being to determine 'Which of several possible explanations is the correct one? Which of several possible outcomes is the most likely one?' (Heuer 1999: 95).

A true Clausewitzian approach would rest, instead, on three principles. First, confidence and probability are different; thus there is no reason not to be explicit about probabilities, even with low confidence. Second, content of information matters as much as reliability; so, again, important information should not be excluded simply because it is deemed unreliable. Third, and perhaps most importantly, consequence matters in evaluating information and in constructing alternatives; thus consequential possibilities should not be relegated to the sidelines simply because they are judged unlikely.

Table 3.3 Jominian vs. Clausewitzian intelligence

Jominian	Clausewitzian
Goal is to eliminate uncertainty	Goal is to assess uncertainty
There is a 'right' answer	'Fog of war' is inescapable
More information and better concepts narrow uncertainty	Single-point high probability predictions both unhelpful and inaccurate
Large uncertainty indicates shortcomings in analysis	Better analysis may identify more possible outcomes

Source: adapted from Treverton (2009b).

The resulting product would, in effect, lay out a probability distribution, involving not multiple answers but rather a single distribution. If consequence were deemed as important as likelihood, intelligence would, in effect, produce a probability distribution in which consequential outcomes would receive attention not just as excursions, even if their probability was low or could not be assessed very clearly. In looking at 379 declassified US NIEs, Friedman and Zeckhauser found but one example of this style of analysis. A 1990 NIE, 'The Deepening Crisis in the USSR', laid out on a single page four different 'scenarios for the next year' in a simple figure (Friedman and Zeckhauser 2012: 832). Each was explained in several bullet points, and then assessed as a 'Rough Probability'. The scenario deemed most likely was presented first but was not given any more discussion than the others. The NIE thus neglected neither probability nor consequence. It conveyed no sense that one scenario should be thought of as 'best' or 'correct'; nor did it require readers to parse the meaning of concepts like 'significant', 'serious' or 'important' (even if those were elaborated on in a glossary, as is now the practice for NIEs). In the end, it allowed readers to decide for themselves which possibilities deserved pride of place.

Yet the question of whether busy senior policy-makers would sit still for a Clausewitzian approach is a fair one. The easy answer would be to try it as an experiment for a handful of estimates on issues that are both important and very uncertain. A hint of an answer was provided by Stephen Hadley, President George W. Bush's national security adviser. A November 2007 NIE on Iran's nuclear intentions and capabilities provoked a firestorm of controversy when its 'key judgements' were declassified and released. The first clause seemed to undercut not only any argument for military action against Iran but also the international campaign for sanctions against the country that the Bush administration had targeted. The President called the opening 'eye-popping', all the more so because it came 'despite the fact that Iran was testing missiles that could be used as a delivery system and had announced its resumption of uranium enrichment' (Bush 2010: 418).

Based on that experience, Hadley made the intriguing (and Clausewitzian in spirit) suggestion that for the several most important, and uncertain, issues a president faces, intelligence might present its assessment in ways different from the 'we judge with medium confidence' format. Imagine, for example, a pie chart representing all the United States would like to know about an issue. Different slices might be different sizes based on judgements about how important they are. In this case, the 'is Iran weaponizing?' slice would have been significant but smaller than the 'is it enriching?' piece, since the latter paces the country's nuclear programme. The slices may show clearly how much US intelligence knew about that piece. The weaponization slice would have indicated good information on that score.

The promise of transparency

Information technology is enabling new forms of collaboration within intelligence but also outside it: witness wikis and crowd sourcing. Those same developments are opening up the question of what intelligence's products – or, to put it more openly, 'outputs' – should be. For instance, the content of social networking media, like Facebook or Twitter, is more and more a matter of images, not words. Traditionally, intelligence has thought of pictures as a way to tell a story. Now those images *are* the story. Moreover, what is 'publication' in an era when anyone can publish, and a publication is no longer a commodity with a 'use-by' date? Social networking media are both a cause and a metaphor for the transparency that is rolling across both intelligence and policy science. They are the very antithesis of the way intelligence has been practised previously. Intelligence has been closed and passive; social media are open and active.

It is the combination of new media and new devices, smartphones and their kin, that are causing this revolution. Twitter grew by 1,500 per cent in the three years before 2010, and it now has, by its own statistics, about 175 million users. Facebook reached 500 million users in mid-2010, a scant six years after being created in a Harvard dorm room. The iPhone and other 'smart' handsets let users gain access to the internet and download mobile applications, including games, social networking programs and productivity tools. These same devices also allow users to upload information to network-based services for the purpose of communication and sharing.

The dominance of images, not words is plain with Facebook but is increasingly the case for Twitter as well. Making use of a traditional computer required literacy, but the same is not true of a smartphone. Apparently, these kinds of images can be powerful in shaping public opinion, and perhaps policy outcomes, both domestically and internationally, even if most of the posited effects are still anecdotal. Consider the effects of the pictures from Abu Graibh, or the YouTube video of a US helicopter strike apparently killing civilians in Baghdad in 2007.[4] Compare those with the leak through WikiLeaks of 92,000 US military documents pertaining to Afghanistan.[5] If the latter seemed to have less impact, that was probably largely because the main story lines – collateral damage and Pakistani complicity with the Taliban – were familiar (the former in part because of previous images). But the documents were just that: words; thus a quintessential newspaper story and not images that might go viral on the web.

Characterizing the future world in which social media are the leading wave demonstrates how dramatic the change will be for intelligence. That future world will be one of ubiquitous sensing and transparency. For the former, think of those closed-circuit TVs (CCTVs), which number 1.85 million in Britain, or one for every thirty-two inhabitants. Transparency will be driven by those ubiquitous sensors and their location awareness, by the increasing computational power of devices, and by increases in communication and connectivity. 'Converged sources' has been a buzzword for nearly a generation but only became a reality in recent years with the smartest of smartphones, not to mention the iPad and its kin. These personal mobile devices indicate who their users are; where and when they are, have been and will be located; what they are doing, have been doing and will be doing; with whom or what they are interacting; and the characteristics of their surrounding environment.

At the same time, threat signatures and footprints will continue to shrink – notice the challenge of attributing cyber attacks. Background noise will continue to rise. Given current technology, for instance, because of the huge volume and low reliability, Twitter is useful for intelligence analysis only in two circumstances: when information about what is happening is in short supply so that Twitter can supplement it (as was the case during the Mumbai attack of 2008); and when there is no other source of 'public opinion' (as in the aftermath of the 2009 Iranian presidential elections). Finally, these technological capabilities will continue to proliferate as cutting-edge research and technology go global. If it is not always that the bad guys can do everything the good guys can; the gap between the two cannot safely be counted on to be very large.

Perhaps because of their newness, it is not clear how important social networking media will be in organizing, for instance, anti-government groups. In Iran and other countries, they have been the latest IT innovation in organizing in a line that runs from Ayatollah Khomeini's audio cassette speeches smuggled in in the 1970s, through to the fax machines that played a role in Eastern Europe's transitions in the 1980s. In crisis periods, such as that following the Iranian elections, social media had the attractions of speed and relative anonymity from government retaliation, but they also carried the challenge of validating who was real and who was not (and who was a government agent).

On the operational side, ignoring social media can be done only at the peril of endangering the cover, and perhaps the lives, of intelligence officials. If twenty-somethings are not on Facebook or Twitter, they only become 'conspicuous by their absence'. They may as well advertise 'I work for intelligence'. Tomorrow, if not already today, if officials are undercover, they have to live that cover in virtual worlds as well as physical ones. They have to be prepared to move quickly from one medium to another. Indeed, 'official' cover as it has been practised by the United States and many other nations is already an artefact of the past, though intelligence organizations have not yet quite realized it. All the elements of transparency – from biometrics through geolocation – mean than any cover will be fleeting, with the possible exceptions of intelligence operatives who really live their cover, being and not just pretending to be businesspeople or some other professional, and never coming close to any government establishment. The technologies don't just apply to the future either. They also capture the past, for instance, as names, passport numbers, and perhaps biometrics like fingerprints that were collected at borders are digitized and thus made searchable in the present and future.

On the analytic side, if the challenges of a huge volume and low reliability are already plain, so are some of the possibilities. Social media have the potential to become a repository for collected information, in the process enabling amateur intelligence analysis. Already, the founder of Greylogic, a noted expert on cyber warfare and a consultant to the US intelligence community, has launched a trial balloon on Twitter – called Grey Balloons – seeking volunteers who might spend a few hours per week, unpaid, to help intelligence agencies do their jobs, especially in connecting the dots.[6] Intelligence has long fretted about competition from professionals like CNN, but now may find itself competing with amateurs for the attention of its customers. It may be asked to vet and validate amateur intelligence efforts, and it may be required to allocate its resources to fill in the gaps not covered by amateur efforts.

Social media are important in and of themselves, but they are also at the cutting edge of broader changes that are enveloping intelligence. Social media are active, not passive. They completely blur the distinctions that have been used to organize intelligence – among collector, analyst and operator, or between producer and consumer. They completely upset existing notions about what intelligence's 'products' are. Coupled with smartphones, they will turn any human being into a geolocated collector and real-time analyst. They offer enormous promise, but also carry large risks and obstacles. Small wonder, then, that a study of social media for the US National Geospatial Intelligence Agency (NGA) found:

> enthusiasm mixed with concern. Clear guidance is sparse. Measurement of any benefits these technologies may have brought is not well documented; at the same time there is little quantification of their potential negative impact – instead, a mixture of hand waving and hand wringing.
>
> (Flores and Markowitz 2009: 3)

In a study of uses of social media by US intelligence agencies by the RAND Corporation, a conversation with one of the managers of Intellipedia – a highly classified wiki internal to the US intelligence community – was more positive about the possibilities even as he demonstrated how far from reality those possibilities are. He recognized that it is interaction that drives the possibilities – from asking questions on Twitter to more specific 'crowd sourcing'; that is, posing issues for and explicitly seeking help from fellow netizens. A convert, he would take the logic of social media to its conclusion and have the CIA out there, openly, as the CIA, asking questions and seeking help. 'Sure,' he said in an interview with this author, 'we'd get lots of disinformation. But we get plenty of that already. And we might find people out there who were prepared to help us.' Seeing this as help is a key to reshaping intelligence.

Notes

1 The term is from Snowden (2002). His 'known problems' are like puzzles and his 'knowable problems' are akin to mysteries.
2 The provenance of Bayes theorem is complicated, but an English preacher, Thomas Bayes, is generally credited with publishing it in 1763. It has come to describe both an inclination and a process to update subjective probabilities in light of new evidence.
3 For a nice comparison of Clausewitz and Jomini, see Calhoun (2011).
4 The video is available at www.youtube.com/watch?v=5rXPrfnU3G0 (accessed 4 February 2013).
5 For excerpts and analysis, see the *New York Times*, 26 July 2010.
6 See Jeffrey Carr's Twitter site at http://twitter.com/greyballoons (accessed 4 February 2013).

Bibliography

Bush, George W. (2010) *Decision Points*, New York: Crown Publishers.

Calhoun, Mark T. (2011) 'Clausewitz and Jomini: Contrasting Intellectual Frameworks in Military Theory', *Army History*, 80: 22–37.

Clausewitz, Carl von (1976) *On War*, trans. Michael Howard and Peter Paret, Princeton, NJ: Princeton University Press.

Flores, Robert A. and Markowitz, Joe (2009) *Social Software – Alternative Publication @ NGA*, Harper's Ferry, VA: Pherson Associates.

Friedman, Jeffrey A. and Zeckhauser, Richard (2012) 'Assessing Uncertainty in Intelligence', *Intelligence and National Security*, 27: 824–847.

Heuer, Richard (1999) *The Psychology of Intelligence Analysis*, Washington, DC: Center for the Study of Intelligence.

Jenkins, Brian Michael (2010) *Stray Dogs and Virtual Armies: Radicalization and Recruitment to Jihadist Terrorism in the United States Since 9/11*, OP-343, Santa Monica, CA: RAND Corporation. Online. Available: www.rand.org/pubs/testimonies/CT353.html (accessed 4 February 2013).

Jomini, Baron H. de (2007) *The Art of War*, Charleston, SC: BiblioLife.

National Commission on Terrorist Attacks Upon the United States (2004) *The 9/11 Commission Report*, Washington, DC. Online. Available: www.9–11commission.gov/ (accessed 4 February 2013).

Nye Jr., Joseph S. (1994) 'Peering into the Future', *Foreign Affairs*, 77(July/August): 82–93.

Platt, Suzy (ed.) (1989) *Respectfully Quoted: A Dictionary of Quotations Requested from the Congressional Research Service*, Washington, DC: Library of Congress.

Ritchey, Tom (2007) 'Wicked Problems: Structuring Social Messes with Morphological Analysis', *Swedish Morphological Society*. Online. Available: www.swemorph.com/pdf/wp.pdf (accessed 4 February 2013).

Snowden, Dave (2002) 'Complex Acts of Knowing: Paradox and Descriptive Self-awareness', *Journal of Knowledge Management*, 6: 100–111. Online. Available: http://cognitive-edge.com/uploads/articles/13_Complex_Acts_of_Knowing_paradox_and_descriptive_self-awareness.pdf (accessed 1 March 2013).

Treverton, Gregory F. (1994) 'Estimating Beyond the Cold War', *Defense Intelligence Journal*, 3: 5–45.

—— (2007) 'Risks and Riddles', *Smithsonian*, June. Online. Available: www.smithsonianmag.com/people-places/presence_puzzle.html (accessed 1 March 2013).

—— (2009a) *Intelligence for an Age of Terror*, Cambridge: Cambridge University Press.

—— (2009b) 'Approaching Threat Convergence from an Intelligence Perspective', in Magnus Ranstorp and Magnus Normark (eds), *Unconventional Weapons and International Terrorism: Challenges and New Approaches*, London: Routledge.

Wohlstetter, Roberta (1962) *Pearl Harbor: Warning and Decision*, Stanford, CA: Stanford University Press.

4 Is the US intelligence community anti-intellectual?

Mark M. Lowenthal

For many years now, both the US intelligence community and its many critics – both well intentioned and not – have struggled to find ways to improve intelligence analysis. I have constantly tried to remind people that intelligence analysis is, at its core, an intellectual activity. What I have meant by this is the fact that most of the important things that go on in intelligence analysis happen in the minds of the analysts. No amount of tinkering with organizational charts, or inventing new analytical tools or succumbing to the latest 'buzzword' of the month – picture a crowd of wise black swans blinking at the tipping point – will change this. Yet having made this plea about the intellectual basis of intelligence analysis and still believing in it, we must also face the very strong possibility that the US intelligence community is also somewhat anti-intellectual.

The origins of US (and British) intelligence in the twentieth century

Although this chapter is primarily about US intelligence, it is worth noting that our British colleagues share an intellectual basis in their activities. We usually date modern US intelligence from the creation of the position of Coordinator of Information in 1941, but it is possible to go back a further in time for intellectual antecedents. In September 1917 Colonel Edward House, President Woodrow Wilson's policy adviser, established a study group to prepare materials for the coming post-war peace negotiations. The Inquiry, as the group was known, was headed by Dr Sidney Mezes, a philosopher and president of the City College of New York (CCNY); Mezes was also related to House by marriage. Other notable members of the Inquiry were Isaiah Bowman, president of the American Geographical Society; journalist Walter Lippmann; and historians James Shotwell and James Truslow Adams. The actual influence of the Inquiry upon Wilson's positions and the eventual shaping of the Treaty of Versailles remain somewhat entertaining (the role of advisers at Versailles is well told in Nicolson (1939)). However, the concept was an interesting precedent.

Turning to the British intelligence establishment, the histories of Bletchley Park are replete with stories about absent-minded Oxford dons and 'boffins' (scientists and engineers) working away to decrypt the German Enigma codes

(McKay 2011; Hinsley and Stripp 2001). Similarly, the US Office of Strategic Services, created in 1942, had a strong academic component. Harvard historian William Langer led the Research and Analysis (R&A) branch, which was staffed with 900 scholars. As the CIA's Center for the Study of Intelligence notes, OSS R&A officers included seven future presidents of the American Historical Association, five future presidents of the American Economic Association and two future Nobel Laureates.[1] In the post-war intelligence community, Langer set up the CIA's Office of National Estimates. He was assisted and then succeeded by Yale historian Sherman Kent, who had been chief of R&A's Europe-Africa Division. Kent, viewed by many as the father of CIA intelligence analysis, would remain at the CIA until 1967.

The effect of the Soviet target

Former Secretary of State Lawrence Eagleburger once noted that 'it is wrong to be nostalgic about the Cold War'.[2] True enough, although in retrospect it seems to have been a much simpler time in terms of world affairs and the management of intelligence, the prospect of nuclear Armageddon notwithstanding. Still, the nature and longevity of the struggle with the Soviet Union also fostered a strong intellectual undergirding to intelligence.

Several factors drove this. First, the struggle lasted for over four decades, providing both the opportunity and the necessity of developing in-depth expertise. Even at the outset of the Cold War, US policy-makers were prepared for a long struggle. George Kennan, in his seminal papers espousing containment, thought the contest would last for fifteen years. Kennan was obviously wrong by a factor of three but even a fifteen-year intense contest is a long one, especially for a democracy. Moreover, most of the premises Kennan made about Soviet behavior had less to do with the fact that they were communists than long-standing factors of Russian history, clearly an intellectual approach. Second, the Cold War struggle embraced all aspects of national life: political, military, economic, social, cultural and ideological. This again required a broad and integrated view of relationships and of what constituted the successful use of power in all of its forms. Finally, the struggle was, after 1950, global in nature, requiring ongoing knowledge about distant places that would otherwise have been easily ignored. Two new academic fields evolved. One was Soviet Studies, which was in several respects very different from Chinese Studies or German Studies, or even Russian Studies. It was more than area or cultural expertise, given the importance of ideology. In many ways it was like tracking a religious movement, replete with true believers, schisms and apostates. The other field was Strategic Studies, the Strangelovian world of nuclear exchanges and throw weights, some of which would have come into being given the fact of atomic weapons but clearly given added importance by the bipolar power struggle. Indeed, Strategic Studies provided a path for academics to take an active role in defence policy on a scale and at a depth never seen before. Thus, there was a strong intellectual component to intelligence during the Cold War.

What happened?

Several factors have led to what I call the budding anti-intellectualism of intelligence. The most obvious was the victorious conclusion of the Cold War. Soviet studies became antiquarian and strategic studies seemed quaint at best. We were not at 'the end of history', but much that had preoccupied us for almost half a century had gone away. We had not entered a period of universal peace (parts of Europe, for example, became increasingly violent following the Soviet demise) but the issues that mattered most to policy-makers and thus to intelligence were smaller and more numerous. There was no more central focus or one overwhelming issue. In this more scattershot world a new premium was put on 'agility' in intelligence, meaning the ability to shift resources (largely meaning analysts) from hotspot to hotspot as the need arose. In this fire-fighting mentality there has been much less ability to build up the kind of knowledge or expertise that characterized Cold War intelligence – although even this in-depth knowledge did not give many the foresight to see the coming end of the Cold War itself. US intelligence leaders talked frequently about 'velocity and volume', suggesting that speed was all and that the volume of data probably precluded attempts to truly master it. Indeed, in the face of supposedly overwhelming data we went from mastery to looking for the needle in the haystack.

A second crucial factor was the change in the analytical workforce. US intelligence had grown during the Reagan administration, after which the budget went flat and thereafter lost ground to inflation. There was a series of demographic shifts. First, many positions either went unfilled or were lost entirely during the period between 1989 and 2001. Former Director of Central Intelligence (DCI) George Tenet has stated that 23,000 positions were lost across US intelligence during that period. Second, as we reached the end of that period, some of the people hired in as part of the 1980s expansion began to retire, further hollowing out the force and also taking their expertise with them – with no one to whom they could pass it on. In truth, the intelligence community has never been very good at capturing and passing on expertise in a systematic manner, but the ongoing demographics made the problem worse. Third, as the workforce surged in the aftermath of the terrorist attacks in 2001, we took on thousands of analysts with no intelligence training, many of whom had other intellectual shortcomings which I will discuss below. As a result the overall balance of the workforce between experienced veterans and inexperienced novices was thrown badly out of kilter.

One final result of these workforce changes was a shift in how US intelligence dealt with pressing issues. We entered a period of 'analytical triage', again moving from pressing issue to pressing issue with fewer analysts who had less experience and who were given little time to learn about a topic before they were asked to move on. Now, granted, there were some exceptions to this. We did have analysts who began studying al-Qaeda, for example, long before anyone on the outside knew who they were. We did have pockets of more senior analysts who had been on their briefs for longer periods of time. Nevertheless, these began to stand out like islands in an archipelago and not as a general approach to intelligence issues.

Two other factors also helped foster the anti-intellectual shift. One has been the nature of the wars we have been fighting. Iraq and especially Afghanistan, as well as the efforts against terrorists, have been very tactical in nature. We have increasingly impressive amounts of data (vice knowledge) about terrorists, but we really have not had an overarching grand strategic concept to guide us as we did during the Cold War. Instead, we have fought these subnational groups as subnational groups: picking them off; interdicting them when we can; intercepting cash flows. No one would argue that these are not useful activities, but they turn on very tactical, highly operational intelligence. This is very different from building a body of expertise upon which these tactical operations can be informed.

The final factor is what I would call the 'PDB effect'. The President's Daily Brief goes back to the Kennedy administration (1961–1963) but the PDB's overwhelming importance in US intelligence stems from the George W. Bush administration (2001–2009). Bush, as is well known, not only wanted a daily briefing but insisted that DCI George Tenet be present each day. This not only represented a change from Bush's predecessor Bill Clinton, who was less rigorous about the daily intelligence briefing, but also from all past practice, as no previous president had required the DCI to be present for each daily briefing. Access to senior policy-makers is immensely important for intelligence officers, so Bush's request represented a gain from the sporadic access under Clinton. In addition, Tenet simply could not refuse the president's request. However, one consequence of this greater access and the greater emphasis on the PDB meeting was that it elevated the PDB in the minds of many CIA analysts (the PDB was still a CIA product up until the advent of the Director of National Intelligence in 2005).

As I have written elsewhere, the PDB is a somewhat overrated activity (Lowenthal 2009: 116). Yes, it is important to have access to the president. However, the PDB itself consists of intelligence that is *non-urgent* enough to wait for the morning briefing. For example, according to press accounts President Barack Obama was briefed at 3.55 a.m. about the North Korean shelling of Yeonpeong Island in 2010 as there were concerns about a more general war breaking out on the Korean peninsula (Reuters 2010). Moreover, the PDB tends to emphasize current intelligence issues which do not necessarily engage as much in-depth expertise, although this expertise is immensely useful in writing any intelligence. The format is restrictive, the longest articles tending to be no more than a page or two. Presidents Bush and Obama have both used the morning briefing for 'deep dives' on given topics, but the daily feeding of the 'briefing beast' is very different from the steady building of expertise and knowledge.

The anti-intellectualism of the intelligence community

What does it mean to be an intellectual? According to Merriam-Webster, an intellectual is someone who is given to study, reflection and speculation, and is engaged in activity requiring the creative use of the intellect.[3] I think this sounds very much like what we want intelligence analysts to be, at least in the ideal.

Here, then, are some of the reasons why I think the intelligence community is anti-intellectual. Some of these reasons may be unwitting but that does not ameliorate their effect. The main reason I would cite is the lack of value that the community places on education and training. Yes, almost every major agency has a schoolhouse of some sort, but once employees are past the entry stage ongoing training and education remains sporadic and haphazard. This being the case, professional education and training is therefore very uneven from agency to agency. The main emphasis has always been on-the-job training, which is a good thing but is hardly sufficient. The US Army remains the ideal here, with education and training an ongoing and continuous experience throughout an officer's career. How do we account for the difference? Simply put, culture: the Army values education and training, and the intelligence community does not. The usual excuse within intelligence agencies as to why they allow few such opportunities is that they are too busy. Yes, they are. But busier than the Army? Unlikely. Instead, in intelligence agencies we have what some of us used to call the Ben-Hur approach to personnel management: chain them to their desks and tell them to keep time with the guy with the drum.

Moreover, education and training in the intelligence community is not tied to career development. Indeed, it would be difficult – if not impossible – to tie education and training to career development in intelligence as we barely have that concept in hand, beyond entry, middle and high. Finally, to cite the military again, one of their goals is 'to train how we fight'. The intelligence community talks a great deal about integration and collaboration but it really does not train that way. There is a still nascent (after more than six years) National Intelligence University designed to train across the intelligence community but, in truth, training takes place predominantly within individual agencies.

The second reason I would cite is the rather steady decline of the intelligence community as a learning institution. What does it mean to be a learning institution? Turning once again to Merriam-Webster, learning is defined as, first, knowledge or skill acquired by instruction or study, and second, modification of behavioural tendency by experience. I would argue that the intelligence community falls short on the first but is better on the second, although not in an organized manner. The key issue in learning is to capture that which you have learned. This should be done systematically and continuously. Again, this tends not to be the case with intelligence agencies. The usual excuse, once more, is time pressure and the ongoing rush of issues. This is undoubtedly penny-wise and pound-foolish. US intelligence would be better off, once again, in following the lead of the Army, which has the Center for Army Lessons Learned (CALL). CALL's mission is to collect, analyse, disseminate and archive a variety of operational data rapidly, 'in order to facilitate rapid adaptation … and conduct focused knowledge sharing and transfer that informs the Army and enables operationally based decision making and innovation'.[4] To be fair, there is a rudimentary lessons-learned capability within the office of the DNI, but this office remains woefully undermanned and has nowhere near the same central role that CALL has for the Army.

My final argument is that we do not value knowledge because we no longer systematically develop knowledge. To some extent this again reflects the greater number of pressing issues (as opposed to the old single dominant issue) and the tendency to push analysts from one crisis to another. The intelligence community was not the sole fount of expertise on the Soviet Union but its capabilities in this area went quite deep. It is difficult to find similar reservoirs of knowledge (as opposed to talent) today. Here we must make a cautionary note: even though knowledge is highly preferable to ignorance, even deep knowledge will not entirely preclude making analytical mistakes or, on occasion, being surprised.

Knowledge is like sound: it requires a source, propagation and reception. Knowledge must not only be created but preserved so that it can be transmitted. However, if one is engaged in day-to-day tactical episodes, such knowledge-building becomes much more difficult. There is little time to learn and to absorb as one moves from one intellectual fire-fight to another. There has been some progress made in the preservation of knowledge, or at least the amassing of all disseminated analyses, in the Library of National Intelligence. Whether analysts use this as a regular resource as they craft new analyses is an open question. The one area of knowledge that consistently fails to be preserved is the knowledge held by retirees. It is rare for anyone to think about asking a senior analyst who is about to retire to sit down with junior analysts and pass along what he has learned, words of wisdom or career advice. This invaluable resource is allowed simply to walk away.

One final aspect that leads to anti-intellectualism are the analysts who have been (and are still) hired since 2001. What follows are some general observations, not true in each individual case but true often enough to be of concern. First, they are the first generation to be raised on the internet. They are very good at finding discrete packets of information but less skilled at the broader vision of context, flow and especially precedent. If the baby boomers were the 'Me Generation' then this group might be called the 'Now Generation'. They live almost entirely in the present and have little reference to the past, even the recent past. Their research skills beyond the internet are largely non-existent and their ability to communicate in writing appears to have been severely crippled by the extreme telegraphy of text messaging and Twitter. Having spent so much time multitasking and jumping from task to task in rapid fashion, they appear to have a similar view of their careers. They would like to move from issue to issue as each new issue attracts them, rather than focus on one issue long enough to develop the expertise that is really needed. I would compare this to viewing their careers as an endless buffet rather than as a series of eight-course meals in which each course must be properly digested. Finally, too few of them exhibit any historical or cultural knowledge: if it did not happen in their lifetime it is, by definition, uninteresting.

Solutions

Rather than allow this to be a dreary jeremiad, here are some steps the intelligence community could take to restore a necessary degree of intellectualism.

First, even though most of us believe that intelligence is a profession, we need to treat it as a profession both in and out of government. This means having a serious discussion about what it means to be an intelligence professional in terms of skills, expertise and career expectations. It also means thinking about what a progression of skills looks like across an analyst's career. Some of this will be general and some will have to allow for the fact that as an analyst becomes more specialized and finds his or her niche, or niches, degrees of specialization will take place. Having done that, we should develop a curriculum of education and training that carries across a career and then allow the analyst the necessary opportunities to take part in this curriculum – not as exceptions but as an essential part of his or her professional development. Indeed, there should be more rewards for education and training, and more penalties for those who avoid it.

Second, we should be serious about the need for a coherent and well-integrated lessons-learned capability, instead of the lip-service one we have now.

Finally, and most importantly, we must create incentives for the building of knowledge and expertise. The excuse of being too busy not only rings false but is also a very short-term and self-wounding decision. In part, a decision to invest more time and energy into building knowledge means making choices about what is important and what is less important. The more important areas will receive the greater investment. This has always been a fact of life in intelligence, along with the recognition that once-unimportant areas can and will suddenly rise to great importance overnight. Still, it should be possible to make some calculated investments in the areas where true depth of knowledge is most needed, and to begin incentivizing those areas now by placing sufficient emphasis on them so as to make them more attractive to analysts. Much is said these days about the 'knowledge worker', a term of which I am not fond. Regrettably, many of the definitions of the knowledge worker seem little different from how one would define a computer data specialist. If we in intelligence are serious about knowledge we should give serious thought to what it is, what it looks like and what it really takes to create, preserve and transmit knowledge. I would argue that this requires a shift away from the current emphasis on data and back to knowledge in its broader sense. This means a deeper understanding and a more comprehensive approach and commitment to the concept of knowledge within intelligence agencies and in the various academic programs that focus on training intelligence analysts.

We spend a great deal of time discussing what we want intelligence to be but precious little putting those thoughts into action. If we want highly educated, well-trained and deeply knowledgeable analysts, we will have to build them ourselves. They will not simply show up at our doorsteps. It is time, like the military, to educate and train the way we intend to fight.

Notes

1 'The Office of Strategic Services: Research and Analysis Branch', available online at www.cia.gov/news-information/featured-story-archive/2010-featured story-archive/oss-research-and-analysis.html (accessed on 24 January 2012).
2 Eagleburger gave a speech in September 1989, for which he was later accused of being nostalgic about the Cold War, which he denied (see Friedman 1989).
3 See www.merriam-webster.com/dictionary/intellectual (accessed on 8 February 2013).
4 See CALL's website at http://usacac.army.mil/cac2/call/about.asp (accessed on 10 July 2012).

Bibliography

Friedman, Thomas (1989) 'U.S. Voicing Fears That Gorbachev Will Divide West', *New York Times*, 16 September.

Hinsley, Sir F.H. and Stripp, Alan (eds) (2001) *Codebreakers: The Inside Story of Bletchley Park*, Oxford: Oxford University Press.

Lowenthal, Mark M. (2009, 4th edn) *Intelligence: From Secrets to Policy*, Washington, DC: CQ Press.

McKay, Sinclair (2011) *The Secret Life of Bletchley Park: The WWII Codebreaking Centre and the Men and Women Who Worked There*, London: Aurum.

Nicolson, Harold (1939) *Peacemaking 1919*, New York: Harcourt, Brace and Company.

Reuters (2010) 'U.S. Vows Unified Response to N. Korea', available online at www.reuters.com/article/2010/11/23/us-korea-north-usa-idUSTRE6AM48720101123 (accessed on 8 February 2013).

5 The future of the intelligence process

The end of the intelligence cycle?

Arthur S. Hulnick

Introduction

As students of intelligence will know, I have long argued that the intelligence cycle model, taught almost everywhere as an appropriate and accurate depiction of how intelligence systems function, is, in fact, neither appropriate nor accurate (Hulnick 2007). The cycle model seems to have its origins in the growth of intelligence systems in the Second World War, and has been taught both in the US and in other countries ever since.[1] This has created some serious problems as intelligence officers complete their training and start working in the field. Nothing works in the ways they have been taught to expect. I usually differentiate between military intelligence systems, which seem to be somewhat more attuned to the intelligence cycle, and civilian governmental systems, which are not. The intelligence system that comes closest to the cycle model lies in the private sector, although intelligence literature rarely mentions this.

In the civilian government world, policy-makers rarely give good direction to intelligence managers, and they certainly do not give specific requirements for intelligence collection. This means that intelligence managers have to translate what little direction they receive into more specific requirements, usually based on gaps in the existing intelligence database. In military systems, requirements for collection may be driven by specific operations, contingency planning, or even weapons procurement, and thus may provide more detail for intelligence units. Military intelligence systems in battlefield conditions may approach the intelligence cycle model even more closely as commanders deal with tactical situations that require specific intelligence inputs. In the private sector, because managers usually hire intelligence professionals to deal with specific issues, the requirements for intelligence collection are often agreed on a contractual basis.

The intelligence cycle model does not specify how intelligence should be collected, but we know that there are three main categories of collection systems. Open sources usually make up the bulk of the material to be tapped for intelligence, especially in civilian systems, while technical collection systems, including communication or signals intercepts and imagery, are increasingly prevalent in military intelligence. Both civilian and military intelligence collectors are users of human intelligence systems, from diplomatic or liaison contacts to espionage, and civilian intelligence agencies lay heavy emphasis on the value of human intelligence (Humint) (Hitz 2007).

In the private sector, espionage is supposed to be off limits, but there is increasing evidence that the use of such techniques are well known to private intelligence practitioners, perhaps because many of them have learned their trade in government intelligence agencies (Javers 2010). Private intelligence relies as well on technical sensors, which have become more readily available in the electronic age. The use of electronic search engines, while hardly comparable to signals intercepts, is a boon to private practitioners, and such programs as Google Earth give the private sector access to overhead imagery that was once reserved for specialized government agencies. Open source intelligence, of course, makes up the bulk of the material collected in the private sector, just as in government.

The cycle model suggests that intelligence collection drives the analysis process, but this is not usually the case in reality. In both civilian and military intelligence, analysts work from an enormous existing database. They do not have to wait for new inputs to meet the needs of intelligence consumers. Despite frequent calls by civilian politicians for more long-range intelligence analysis, most intelligence analytic output tends to have a short focus. This is caused by crises that disrupt long-range policy-making, and the increasingly short focus of government decision-makers as they deal with these crises (George 2011). Political leaders rarely have the time to read longer term analysis, and depend on their staffs to turn detailed products into something that can be absorbed quickly.

Still, intelligence managers push in-depth analysis, especially in regard to forecasts of the future, called 'estimates' in the US. These estimates are considered by intelligence professionals to be the premier product of intelligence analysis. Estimates can easily become politicized, especially if the judgements are revealed to the public. Even before the infamous estimate on Weapons of Mass Destruction during the George W. Bush administration in the US, estimates on Soviet capabilities and intentions sparked a debate when conservatives argued that the estimates undervalued Soviet strength. Now that the Cold War is over and we have learned more about the actual situation in Russia, we know that the US intelligence community's judgements were about right.

Intelligence analysts have been pressed to adopt more rigorous methodologies in their analysis, to avoid overlooking important but hidden items or ideas. The first push for structured analysis in this direction took place in the 1970s, but was not imbedded in the analysts' thinking. It was said at the time that they were too busy to adopt the more time-consuming use of methodologies that were pressed on them. Since then many new analysts and managers have apparently come into intelligence and are eager to try what did not work the first time. In military circles, longer term analysis is perhaps more readily used than in the civilian world, since contingency planning and weapons procurement require more far-reaching threat analyses. Of course, daily briefings and current analyses remain the main focus of intelligence production in the military, especially in regard to war fighting. Tactical intelligence during combat is an important part of military intelligence, and comes closer to the intelligence cycle model than the civilian sector. In fact, civilian decision-makers rarely rely on intelligence in making policy. This stands in sharp contrast to the intelligence cycle model, which suggests that policy is made only after intelligence products are delivered or, in intelligence jargon, disseminated. Nothing could be further from reality.

This is the part of the intelligence cycle model that has caused the most trouble. Analysts have all been trained to believe that the cycle actually works and that policy officials are waiting for the delivery of intelligence products before deliberating on policy. In reality, policy officials often have an agenda that has nothing to do with intelligence, and make decisions based on a variety of inputs. Their staffs often have access to the same intelligence inputs as intelligence analysts and are able to advise policy officials well before intelligence products are delivered.

When the intelligence products are finally delivered, they go most often to the staffs rather than to the principals. If the products agree with what the staffs have already concluded, then the intelligence is of little use. If the intelligence disagrees, then the staffs may either suppress the intelligence, or deliver the product to show how the intelligence stands at odds with what the policy officials wanted. It is not surprising that civilian policy officials often find intelligence to be unhelpful, inconvenient, or even insubordinate. A good illustration of this was the recent testimony of US Director of National Intelligence (DNI) James Clapper before the Senate. Clapper expressed the view that Colonel Ghaddafi of Libya would probably outwit the rebel opposition.[2] This brought immediate calls for Clapper's resignation because he was out of step with the White House on the issue. Of course, we now know that the DNI was quite wrong.

Interestingly, because the intelligence cycle model works very well in the private sector, the problems described above are not relevant. Private sector managers who have contracted for intelligence do want to wait for the deliverables. That is, after all, what they are paying for. This is in contrast to the civilian government sector, where intelligence officers are by tradition supposed to avoid offering advice about policy and withdrawing when policy discussions take place. This tradition of intelligence analysts absenting themselves from civilian policy discussions may be unique to the US. In many countries, the intelligence analysis units are not in the intelligence agencies at all, but rather in a separate office close to the chief of government. This is certainly true in both Canada and the United Kingdom.

This strict separation from policy discussions in the US has even involved the director of the CIA. Although some directors were close to policy officials and did not hesitate to give advice, others were criticized for this practice. While William Casey, both a CIA director and close confidant of President Reagan, became a member of the president's cabinet and thus a policy-maker, his successor, the judge William Webster, made clear that he would withdraw from policy discussions and would not be a cabinet member (Hulnick 2004).

As stated above, in the military, whether in the US or elsewhere, military intelligence officers at the command level (the J-2 in US parlance) are part of the commander's staff, as are the officers in charge of operations or other functions. The J-2 takes part in decision-making on an equal footing with the others. This is an even older tradition and seems to be common worldwide. In the US, some writers are beginning to question whether or not the practice of staying out of policy debates in the civilian sector is still relevant in the modern era (Kerbel and Olcott 2010).

Alternative to the intelligence cycle: the matrix model

My critique of the intelligence cycle model is not limited to the fact that it is not a good theory, even though it may meet the demands of the military and private sectors. The main failing is that it leaves out two of the key functions of intelligence: counter-intelligence (CI) and covert action (CA). Therefore I have argued that a better theoretical model is one that covers all the key functions of intelligence, from collection and analysis to CI and CA. Rather than depict these functions in a cyclical fashion, I suggest that they are rather parallel to each other and function most often in that fashion (Hulnick 2000). In thinking about the future, then, it would be best to consider each of the functions separately, since they do operate more or less independently of each other, while also considering how they connect.

My theory of intelligence, which I have called the 'matrix model', has so far not received much attention in the US. Instead, many intelligence scholars have continued to use the intelligence cycle model as if no other model existed. For example, in his most recent book on intelligence, Loch Johnson uses the cycle model in its traditional form (Johnson 2011). In his book on Dutch intelligence, however, Giliam De Valk cites the matrix model as one of three models useful in studying the intelligence process (De Valk 2005). The matrix model, I contend, is a much more realistic model of the intelligence process.

We begin with the collection function. All intelligence services whose mandate is foreign intelligence must have some way of gathering intelligence outside the country they serve. The US has the most complex system for fulfilling this function, but even in much smaller services the collection function is critical if it is to determine what activities abroad concern or threaten the nation. There are three key methods for gathering intelligence abroad: the acquisition of open sources, the use of technical sensors, and obtaining information from human sources. Although the functions have not changed much over time, the methods have, and they will probably continue to change even more in the future.

For example, open source intelligence, once focused largely on print and broadcast media, has become increasingly web-based (Steele 2007). The advent of electronic media provides almost universal access to news and developments to intelligence services that were once dependent on their respective overseas missions for exploiting local open sources. The downside of this development is that the proliferation of electronic media often overwhelms the collectors who gather this material. Various new methodologies for data mining have to be used to separate key information from the vast sources available. The rapidity of electronic collection of open sources gives collectors little time to determine what may be passed to other parts of the intelligence system, or to policy officials (Hulnick 2010).

Technical collection systems have also changed over time. During the Cold War only the most sophisticated and advanced intelligence systems could intercept communications or other electronic signals, mostly using satellites for the purpose. Now most intelligence systems can engage in cyber espionage – hacking is the more common term – to penetrate an adversary's communications. As increasingly advanced encryption systems are developed to protect communications, hackers glory in being able to break into those systems to steal data. Of course, governments can do this without much restriction, but this is technically illegal in private sector intelligence, and can lead to lawsuits when the hacking is revealed.

The world of imagery collection has undergone an even more radical change. When the US developed the first digital imagery system for overhead reconnaissance in the 1970s, it replaced the rather cumbersome film return systems that both the US and the then Soviet Union were using for spying from space. While digital space systems are still in use, many intelligence services have begun to rely on drone aircraft for imagery. Drone systems are much cheaper than space-based systems and are more flexible in terms of targeting. What is more, publicly available overhead imagery from such servers as Google Earth has allowed even the smallest intelligence services to become adept at imagery analysis. This trend seems likely to continue.

In addition to open sources and technical sensors, intelligence services have not given up on seeking human sources to obtain the kinds of intelligence electronic systems sometimes miss. Espionage has always been considered an essential part of intelligence collection, and most intelligence services should be able to carry out such operations, even if only focused on their neighbouring states. Espionage requires a level of training and experience, however, that may be missing in current systems. Recruiting and handling spies can be dangerous, and very often the spies are so-called 'walk-ins' or volunteers whose reliability is not so certain.

While military intelligence services have often sought to recruit and maintain an espionage network, there does not seem to be a great pay-off for such efforts, although there are some interesting historical examples of military spies. Rather, espionage seems best suited to the civilian intelligence sector for agencies such as the CIA or MI6. In the private sector, espionage is supposed to be off-limits, but we see increasing evidence that private business uses espionage to gather proprietary data, using techniques that would be familiar to government intelligence systems. People who are caught undertaking espionage on behalf of their governments may face severe penalties from other authorities, but in the modern era trading disgraced spies is more the norm. In the private sector, failed espionage operations usually result in lawsuits and embarrassment for the firm or individuals involved.

According to the intelligence cycle model, intelligence collection should trigger intelligence analysis. In reality, the reports that are generated reach policy officials at about the same time as intelligence analysts receive them in most systems today. According to my alternative matrix model, the analysis process works in parallel with the collection process. This reflects what actually happens in the real world. Intelligence analysis may function quite independently of the collection process, and analysts are able to evaluate events based on the existing database. New information that comes from the collection process may trigger or assist evaluation, but is not completely necessary in most cases.

Policy planners or business managers may begin to act on the so-called 'raw reports' without waiting for the analysis to take place. In the electronic era this happens quite rapidly, thus putting intelligence analysts at a disadvantage. Of course, analysts need not wait for new collection inputs to figure out the import of events and determine their meaning. There are two main issues in intelligence analysis that have not changed. The first is the challenge of evaluating the raw data from the collection system, or from the existing database. The second challenge is packaging the analysis into useful products for consumers (Betts 2007).

In the US there is a growing fascination with structured analysis, involving the use of algorithms to analyse data and forecast future outcomes of events. The idea is to force analysts to consider ideas they may otherwise overlook, or consider outcomes they may have ignored. This has been tried before in the 1970s, but with limited results. Analysts complained that they did not have time to use structured analysis because of time pressure. This pressure is now even worse than before. It is not clear that the use of structured algorithms will produce better analysis, but intelligence managers seem determined to apply these techniques.

From time to time, overseers of intelligence, including legislators responsible for oversight and outside observers, complain that there is too much emphasis on current or daily intelligence analysis and not enough on in-depth studies, long-range estimation and forecasting, but time pressure on both analysts and consumers means that daily intelligence in various forms will be more useful. Current intelligence is more easily produced and more readily absorbed by policy-makers. Consumers often admit that they have little time to read longer range studies and estimates. The result is that intelligence managers have to press analysts to create in-depth studies when the demand is not clear.

One issue which surfaces frequently in the US is the proper relationship between intelligence analysts and senior policy officials. According to tradition, intelligence analysts may provide their products to consumers, but without suggesting policy options or courses of action. Likewise, analysts should avoid becoming too close to the decision-makers they serve. These traditions are not always found elsewhere, but in the CIA these traditions date back to the earliest days of the agency. Only now are they being questioned as out of date or counterproductive.

In many countries, intelligence analysts are not located inside collection agencies but rather are established within policy-making units, or as stand-alone elements within the government. Further, prohibitions on giving policy advice or taking part in policy discussions do not exist. Perhaps the US will have to make some changes to the producer–consumer relationship to remain relevant in the modern era. The downside, of course, is that intelligence analysts will inevitably become enmeshed in partisan debates, but that may be better than becoming irrelevant.

This problem does not exist in military intelligence. As stated above it has long been common practice, perhaps dating back to the development of the military staff system, that the intelligence component of the staff (the J-2) is equal with other staff members, and does not shy away from joining in command decisions, even while delivering intelligence to the commander and staff. This practice is almost universal in application, and works at all levels where there is a staff intelligence officer. This practice may well serve as a model for setting aside the restrictions in the civilian system.

In the private sector, the issue of policy avoidance does not arise because executives want and expect advice from their intelligence people, whether they are part of the organization or from a consultancy unit. In all these cases, in order to be helpful, intelligence analysts must concern themselves with policy options, feasible policy solutions and the implementation of policy.

The intelligence cycle model suggests that policy-makers will wait for intelligence to be delivered before making decisions. This is rarely the case. The reliance on the cycle model over many generations has frustrated analysts who have been taught to expect decision-makers to wait for intelligence before making policy. Therefore, understanding the true nature of how intelligence is used would benefit intelligence analysts, and bringing them into the decision process would not only make intelligence more relevant but also more timely.

Counter-intelligence and covert action

As stated above, the intelligence cycle model ignores two very important functions in intelligence. The first of these is counter-intelligence: preventing adversaries (intelligence services or otherwise) from working against the state. Commonly referred to as CI, counter-intelligence has become much more broad in modern intelligence, now moving beyond countering espionage to include countering terrorism, subversion, organized crime, and other threats to the nation (Taylor 2007). It may include stopping the secret operations of a foreign intelligence service, or, in the private sector, preventing competitors and adversaries from stealing proprietary data.

In theory, the best ways to thwart hostile intelligence services, or other threatening groups, is to penetrate them by recruiting a spy on the inside. In reality, this rarely happens. Intelligence services train their people to watch out for recruitment efforts by adversaries and, looking back over recent history, penetrations of intelligence services have more often resulted from defections or 'walk-ins'. During the Cold War both the US and its allies and the Soviet system suffered from intelligence professionals volunteering to spy for the other side.

When they were caught, as most were, they were imprisoned, executed, or very often traded for those held by the other side.

Today, with the fragmentation in world order, spying 'for the other side' no longer seems relevant, although cases do surface from time to time. The focus of counter-espionage seems to have shifted to the private sector, where intelligence services have stolen proprietary secrets to benefit their domestic businesses. Yet the US Economic Espionage Act of 1996 was aimed, at its creation, at hostile intelligence services rather than at privately sponsored spies. A great deal of this kind of spying has shifted to cyber space, creating new challenges for counter-intelligence units and law enforcement.

Although penetration of a hostile intelligence service is the ideal, it is rarely successful. Instead, counter-intelligence services have had to resort to surveil-lance of adversaries in the hope of catching them during their operations. Sur-veillance may be carried out in the traditional form of physical surveillance, using teams of trained agents, or more commonly through the use of electronic methods. The aim is to identify the adversary agents, gather evidence of their operations, and then turn the information over to law enforcement to prosecute them. While most countries use a domestic or internal security service to identify the adversary agents, a separate law enforcement unit gathers evidence for prosecution.

This system does not apply in the US, where the Federal Bureau of Investiga-tion (FBI) combines intelligence and law enforcement in one agency. This has created some bureaucratic problems over the years, even though the FBI has an excellent track record in regard to identifying and stopping adversary operations by hostile intelligence services or by private intelligence operatives (Kessler 2002). After 9/11, politicians and others investigating the attack began to call for the creation of a domestic intelligence service along the lines of the British MI5. Instead the FBI made efforts, not entirely successful, to ramp up its intelligence branch. The debate about this issue remains current.

As many countries have learned, stopping terrorism is a serious challenge for security services. Because terrorist groups operate in small cells, they are almost impossible to identify, penetrate or place under surveillance. Terrorists may even be lone actors, an even more difficult target. We do know, however, that terror-ists almost always need some kind of support network to supply and finance their operations. Penetrating or placing under surveillance the support network may be more productive than aiming at the terrorists themselves. One method for dealing with this problem involves gathering forensic evidence after a ter-rorist attack to try to identify the support network.

Surveillance may be the best way to identify individual terrorist key actors. This was certainly the case in regard to finding and killing Osama Bin Laden. According to press reports, both physical and electronic surveillance were used to pinpoint his location, although it took several years to find him.[3] Once found, US Special Forces were able to penetrate his compound and kill him.

Because identifying terrorists is so difficult, the US has resorted to rather extreme and unpleasant defensive measures to try to prevent terrorist attacks.

Many countries have resorted to profiling to protect themselves against terrorism. Profiling means identifying physical characteristics or identifiable behaviours to seek out terrorists. In the US, profiling is considered politically unacceptable. At airports, security officials have adopted the practice of treating all passengers as potential terrorists, searching even the smallest children and the aged and infirm before they are allowed to fly. Protests against these practices are considered as suspicious and may result in penalties. Surely these practices must change. They waste resources, inconvenience passengers, and to date have not resulted in the identification of even one terrorist. Such draconian measures are only focused on air travel. Other kinds of transportation in the US receive little scrutiny.

The US has not suffered any serious problems with subversion in the modern era, but many countries that have devote intelligence resources to identifying subversive groups. Even deeply rooted democracies like the United Kingdom, Canada and France have had to fight off efforts to disrupt the government. In countries where democratic government is less firmly fixed, the fight against subversion often becomes the main issue for domestic security services. In dictatorships, intelligence services may find that protecting the regime in power by far outweighs any other demands. Penetrating subversive groups and placing key actors under surveillance are effective methods for countering subversion. More and more, subversive groups are using social media to rally their followers. The overthrow of the Egyptian regime is just the latest case where this played a role.

Whatever the target, it appears that the hybrid model of a domestic security service, such as the FBI in the US which combines investigation and law enforcement, is not as popular or effective as the models that separate the two functions. While there is little pressure in the US to adopt the British MI5 model, this issue may well arise again if there is another major terrorist attack. Meanwhile it appears clear that, whatever the organizational model, there will have to be a closer relationship between intelligence and law enforcement in countering threats from espionage, terrorism and global organized crime. The connection between intelligence and special operations forces seems much easier to manage.

Finally, we come to the second function that is ignored in the intelligence cycle, that of covert action, or secret operations (Johnson 2007). Traditionally, covert action has been used to help friends and allies, or to carry out security policy in such a way that the hand of the sponsoring country is hidden. The US has a long history of using covert action, dating back to the War of Independence when irregular military units fought against the British. Covert action reached a high point in the Cold War when the CIA and the KGB applied it to help allies and disrupt the enemy. Covert action can also be carried out by military forces, but civilian intelligence services seem best suited to such operations because they have the secret agents and clandestine resources at hand.

Covert action has not disappeared with the end of the Cold War. It was a critical element in the battle against the Taliban in Afghanistan, where covert operatives laid the groundwork for the insertion of regular military forces, and it has figured in other aspects of US security policy in the fight against terrorism. Yet covert action has come in for considerable criticism, especially the use of 'extraordinary renditions' in kidnapping and transferring terrorist suspects to partner countries for interrogation, often leading to abuse and errors. In order to prevent problems the US has established a rather rigorous oversight mechanism with Congress, so that presidents who order the use of covert action have to convince the intelligence oversight committees that their plans are sound.

Covert action may involve a so-called 'agent of influence', someone recruited not to steal intelligence but rather to aid friends and confuse the enemy. This may mean the circulation of false information. Increasingly, covert action refers to secret military operations, such as the kind that took out Osama Bin Laden. In order to carry out covert action, intelligence services have to develop a special cadre of professionals well trained for such operations. This may be more than many smaller intelligence services can manage.

Conclusion

What does the future hold for the intelligence functions I have described? Will they continue to be relevant in a world in which superpower relationships have shifted, and the problems of developing countries impact the more developed world? Some things seem clear. Political leaders will expect their intelligence services to be able to manage their key functions in support of policy, whether in a democracy or a dictatorship.

With this in mind, it is time for those who teach intelligence to abandon the inaccurate and misleading intelligence cycle model for something that more closely resembles real-world experience. This is especially true for the training of intelligence professionals who are being misled by the model's inaccuracies. Much has been written in the past decade about the various functions of intelligence, and more and more colleges and universities have developed courses on what was once the rather arcane world of intelligence. Perhaps it is time for the professionals to catch up with the state of intelligence education in our changing world, and consider the matrix model as a more accurate basis for understanding how intelligence processes are supposed to work.

Notes

1 Professor Kristan J. Wheaton has been trying to track down the origins of the intelligence cycle. See his blog post on 4 January 2011. Available at: http://sourcesandmeth-ods.blogspot.nl/2011/01/rfi-who-invented-intelligence-cycle.html (accessed 8 February 2013).
2 David E. Sanger, 'U.S. Escalates Pressure on Libya Amid Mixed Signals', *New York Times*, 11 March 2011, p. A10.
3 Mark Mazetti, Helene Cooper and Peter Baker, 'Behind the Hunt for Bin Laden', *New York Times*, 3 May 2011, p. A1.

Bibliography

Betts, Richard K. (2007) *Enemies of Intelligence: Knowledge and Power in American National Security*, New York: Columbia University Press.

De Valk, Giliam (2005) *Dutch Intelligence: Towards a Qualitative Framework for Analysis*, Rotterdam: Legal Publishers.

George, Roger Z. (2011) 'Reflections on CIA Analysis: Is It Finished?', *Intelligence and National Security*, 26: 72–81.

Hitz, Frederick P. (2007) 'The Importance and Future of Espionage', in Loch K. Johnson (ed.), *Strategic Intelligence Volume 2: The Intelligence Cycle*, Westport, CT: Praeger.

Hulnick, Arthur S. (2000) *Fixing the Spy Machine: Preparing American Intelligence for the 21st Century*, Westport, CT: Praeger.

—— (2004) *Keeping Us Safe: Secret Intelligence and Homeland Security*, Westport, CT: Praeger.

—— (2007) 'What's Wrong with the Intelligence Cycle', in Loch K. Johnson (ed.) *Strategic Intelligence Volume 2: The Intelligence Cycle*, Westport CT: Praeger.

—— (2010) 'The Dilemma of Open Source Intelligence: Is OSINT Really Intelligence', in Loch K. Johnson (ed.), *The Oxford Handbook of National Security Intelligence*, Oxford: Oxford University Press.

Javers, Eamon (2010) *Broker, Trader, Lawyer, Spy: The Secret World of Corporate Espionage*, New York: Harper Collins.

Johnson, Loch K. (2007) *Strategic Intelligence Volume 3: Covert Action: Behind the Veils of Secret Foreign Policy*, Westport, CT: Praeger.

—— (2011) *National Security Intelligence*, Malden, MA: Polity Press.

Kerbel, Josh and Olcott, Anthony (2010) 'The Intelligence–Policy Nexus: Synthesizing with Clients, Not Analyzing for Customers', *Studies in Intelligence*, 54: 11–27.

Kessler, Ronald (2002) *The Bureau: The Secret History of the FBI*, New York: St Martin's Press.

Steele, Robert David (2007) 'Open Source Intelligence', in Loch K. Johnson (ed.), *Strategic Intelligence Volume 2: The Intelligence Cycle*, Westport, CT: Praeger.

Taylor, Stan A. (2007) 'Definitions and Theories of Counterintelligence', in Loch K. Johnson (ed.), *Strategic Intelligence Volume 4: Counterintelligence and Counterterrorism*, Westport, CT: Praeger.

6 The future of counter-intelligence

The twenty-first-century challenge

Jennifer Sims

Counter-intelligence (CI) professionals in governments around the world should be on edge.[1] Over the past decade, economic, cultural and technological trends have been redefining national interests, the bounds of legitimate claims to sovereignty, and the role played by firms in interstate conflict. During 2011, for example, as the Eurozone was threatened by rising national debts, states traded sovereignty to solve public demand for services they could not afford. Global technology firms, looking to expand their market, turned away from government procurement to cultivate the burgeoning demand for connectivity in the civilian marketplace. Governments, looking for cheap access to innovation, engaged in industrial espionage to keep up. Arab populations used cell phones, Facebook and other social media to connect with fellow protestors, communicate with the international community, and coordinate actions in the popular uprising known as the Arab Spring. When the competitive environment changes this fast, governments have historically feared surprise, throwing intelligence services into hyper-drive. Modern trends are startling because they threaten the classic tool once used to address them: secrecy.

Indeed, of all the new twenty-first-century challenges for counter-intelligence, the new role played by information and communications firms may be the most interesting. Most of these firms have thrived on an internet culture that is progressive, liberal, and rooted in the notion of free information. They have also claimed to be apolitical, supplying the communications and organizational infrastructure for the Arab Spring as well as for counter-revolution. In practical terms, however, companies have taken sides. In Syria, for example, insurgents have begun using Google Map Maker, a crowd-sourcing program, to wipe names of the ruling regime's family members off streets and bridges. In their place, protestors have, with the approval of Google editors, inserted the names of their revolutionary heroes.[2] Protestors are not only changing online maps, they are tearing down street signs and raising their own. Google uses images of these changes to validate their new maps, thus legitimizing claims in international disputes based on popular opinion rather than sovereign will. In the Middle East, the effect has been to empower insurgents; in South Asia and in Latin America, it has inflamed irredentism.

Although such name-games may seem inconsequential, the implications are not. Certainly the Assad regime is taking the matter seriously. Syria's UN envoy,

Bashar al-Jafaari, has complained about Google's activities before the United Nations General Assembly, hinting at US government complicity. Google, in turn, has responded carefully, noting that it makes maps based on the input of 'many authoritative sources, including public and commercial data providers, user contributions and imagery references'.[3] Michael Hayden, former head of the US National Security Agency, has likened the role of these corporations to that played by the East India Tea Company or the Hudson Bay Company during the era of empires and discovery; such mega-companies enjoyed then, as they do now, measures of sovereignty and rights of self-defence. Yet these modern multinational companies are also new in a striking way: they constitute 'intelligence arms' for transnational interest groups and social movements challenging state authorities, and their self-protection constitutes a counter-intelligence capability potentially more powerful than that of any state or assembly of states. These companies could thus become, more than ever before, a special kind of power broker in international politics.

The example of Google in Syria is important because it highlights the need to think holistically about the future of counter-intelligence. If intelligence is about finding and using information to win contests, then counter-intelligence is all about defeating one's opponents' abilities to do so by blocking or manipulating relevant information (Sims and Gerber 2009). The first step for a national counter-intelligence analyst, then, is to understand the evolving nature of international contests, who the competitors are likely to be, and how their interests may converge, overlap or diverge. Google's role in politics – that is, in contesting power outside the marketplace – raises important questions. In which contests will multinational firms engage and with what purposes will multinational companies act? How will technological trends empower allies, enable adversaries, or even create new enemies? How are the dynamics of international politics changing and what will be the implications for the counter-intelligence community?

This chapter focuses on the implications of technological trends and addresses these questions in four steps. First, it reviews the conceptual foundations of counter-intelligence in order to distinguish them from those of positive 'intelligence and security. Second, it discusses the lessons and legacies of the Cold War in shaping modern counter-intelligence practices. Third, it discusses the technological and societal trends that pose particularly stiff challenges for counter-intelligence professionals. It concludes by summarizing the chief consequences of the challenges posed, and offers recommendations for practical steps to improve counter-intelligence in the coming decades.

The theory and historical practice of counter-intelligence

Methods of stealing, intercepting, hiding and revealing information have long been part of a statesman's or warrior's toolkit. For centuries, generals, kings and presidents have developed intelligence and counter-intelligence systems to gain advantages over their adversaries. Intelligence systems are not exclusive to

international relations; they may be found in almost every form of modern competition from NFL football and Silicon Valley to political campaigns. Just as
with other kinds of power, however, this tool of political or commercial warfare
can hurt its handler. Done poorly, intelligence operations can undermine
decision-making through delays, misinformation, propagated self-deception and
lost trust. To prevent damage and disruption, an intelligence service needs good
tradecraft, oversight and robust counter-intelligence. Of all these elements,
however, counter-intelligence is perhaps the least well understood.

The theory

The purpose of counter-intelligence is to gain advantages over competitors by
preventing them from acquiring decisive information. CI officers do more than
secure their own side's operations; they disrupt or manipulate opposing services'
efforts to collect, warn, advise and protect. Operations can range from simple
surveillance of an opposing service (defence) to influencing a target to act
against its own self-interest by distorting its appreciation of the situation it faces
(offence). To succeed, therefore, counter-intelligence requires strong positive
intelligence and security. It is, in this sense, the only intelligence function that
cannot stand alone. Understanding its connectedness to both security and positive collection is therefore crucial to an appreciation of the challenges counter-
intelligence officials will face in the future.

Counter-intelligence and security

Although the missions of counter-intelligence and security overlap, they are not
the same. Even practitioners sometimes mistakenly equate counter-intelligence
with information security. The latter mission involves keeping sensitive information protected, much as a jeweller might lock gems in a safe. The driving idea
behind security is the need to protect against loss. Security officials regard the
items they protect as having enduring value; their loss would necessarily hurt
their owner and benefit the thief. Anyone asked to secure valuable items might
reasonably build walls, buy guard dogs and set up alarms commensurate with
the value of the treasure they wish to retain. They might recruit sources to learn
how the prospective thieves are planning their next attack or who within the
bank or vault might become complicit in any future burglary. In the security
paradigm, the value of what is secured is assumed and adversaries are akin to
criminals. Counter-intelligence, on the other hand, is a discipline with a very different driving idea. Its purpose is to help one competitor develop and execute a
winning strategy against another – not necessarily to protect a given set of
information. For a counter-intelligence officer, the value of information will vary
as strategies develop and change. For example, formerly sensitive military plans
might be usefully passed to an enemy if they become obsolete and are thus more
disorienting than helpful. Such attempts to twist an opponent's mind for one's
own gain are examples of offensive counter-intelligence; for it to be effective,

security must be a subordinate goal and selectively applied. Operational security may, in fact, be purposefully weakened if the idea is to use vulnerability to distract an adversary from a more important effort.

Given such difference in the missions of security and counter-intelligence, officials in each discipline often feel threatened by the other. Security is easier to explain, understand and use, so it often dominates counter-intelligence in government efforts to secure intelligence advantage. Especially in democracies, security seems straightforward and honest, while counter-intelligence, with its emphasis on deception, seems devious and even unethical. Then there are the problems with measuring success: security seems to be working so long as there are no losses, but counter-intelligence seems to produce little unless spies are caught or sources questioned.[4]

Thought of in this way, counter-intelligence and security may occasionally be at odds with one another. Whereas security officials resist disclosures, counter-intelligence officers sometimes use them for a purpose. For example, in response to the needs of policy-makers, CI officers might suggest the release of secret information to establish the bona fides of potential double agents, or to shape the information environment to the disadvantage of opponents. After the US killed Osama Bin Laden, US government officials released information about certain aspects of the operation that had been highly sensitive and compartmentalized just days before, such as the way in which the compound was breached and the methods used for identifying and burying Bin Laden. They did so in order to influence the decisions of the Pakistani government as well as public opinion, especially in the Muslim world.[5]

Similar differences exist between security and CI professionals over classification policy. Whereas security officials will care little about public information, counter-intelligence officers may advise that, in certain circumstances, unclassified or 'open source' information be restricted or classified as secret if it could prove useful for an enemy. After the 9/11 attacks, for example, blueprints of major bridges, dams and other infrastructure across the United States were taken off the internet because officials recognized that these formerly public documents, while containing no government secrets up until that point, had new competitive value for terrorists.

In fact, when competition increases in intensity and perceptions of threats rise, incentives to withhold information will also be high.[6] Such far-reaching restrictions are not uncommon in wartime. Yet it is precisely during these more intense contests that good counter-intelligence experts will be on high alert for the dangers security may pose to the overarching strategic mission. For example, CI experts may argue *against* keeping a certain class of secrets because doing so may reveal their own government's strategies. During the Second World War the US government classified the formerly open scientific work of physicists recruited to the task of developing the atomic bomb. The disappearance of a whole category of formerly open research made sense from a security standpoint, but made no sense from a counter-intelligence perspective because it revealed to Soviet scientists that Washington had classified nuclear research as secret and presumably related to the war, leading one of those scientists to report his suspicions to Stalin. What seemed a 'no-brainer' for American security professionals was, from a counter-intelligence standpoint, a rather large mistake (Holloway 1994: 78–79).

Counter-intelligence and positive intelligence

Given the discussion above, it seems evident that positive intelligence and counter-intelligence professionals should share much in common: both collect, analyse and disseminate information for national security decision-makers. Both should act in concert with a strategic plan, with positive intelligence officers working to inform, while counter-intelligence officers work to degrade the information available to an opponent. The story of Churchill's decision not to act on knowledge, gained through decrypted signals, of the Nazi plan to attack Coventry during the Second World War, while apocryphal, illustrates the point. Decisions not to act on intelligence advantages may reflect a desire to preserve a source for a later day (Hinsley 1993). Security and counter-intelligence should help each other, in theory, because their work is synergistic. Espionage can obtain penetrations, revealing moles that CI officers seek to capture, while counter-intelligence reveals what an adversary is seeking, and thus can fill in gaps in the estimation of an opponent's intentions.

Yet proximity of missions can also lead to trouble among security, intelligence and counter-intelligence officials. Security experts empower positive intelligence and counter-intelligence by providing the tools of secrecy, but disempower both when they insist that secrecy cannot be selectively applied. Precisely because collection efforts reveal strategic inclinations, CI officers may also warn of the dangers of ill-considered concealment or revealing too much through intelligence sharing. If a government's security apparatus is guided more by perceived threat than strategic purpose, an opponent can manipulate it. Indeed, without guidance from strategists, security and counter-intelligence professionals cannot know what to hide from enemies or when those secrets might usefully be revealed. In their confusion, they may hide so much that they waste valuable resources, hobble their own side, or fail to notice what the enemy is trying to learn for the sake of achieving surprise. The more fluid the dynamics of competition, the more essential it will be that counter-intelligence officials, in close consultation with policy-makers, oversee the security aspects involved. If they do not, security efforts can actually pose an internal threat to the mission.

To understand how this might be true, consider a homeowner grappling with thieves (this is a common analogy used by CI officials to make their point). If the owner is interested only in securing his possessions, he will immediately repair a broken lock. If, however, he is interested in clearing the thieves out of the neighbourhood, he may leave a window ajar or a lock broken, allowing repeated thefts until everyone involved in the criminal effort is identified – provided, of course, that the price of what is lost does not become too high. In such instances, security can become a tool of deception, suggesting that security and

CI, while different missions, must work together, with CI in charge. Alternatively, if the homeowner is keeping better televisions, waffle irons and coffee makers in his garage than he has in his house, he may actually leave weak locks on the front door to encourage the thieves to steal the old stuff. In this way he can avoid the expense of hauling services and dumping charges as he works to fill his house with the latest gadgets. In fact, leaving the old gadgets protected, but only weakly so, can be a strategy for deceiving the thieves into believing that the best stuff is in the house, not the garage, even if the thieves know about the work underway there. Understanding the importance of selectively using lures and locks during times of rapid scientific or technological change, savvy strategists may decide to develop an advanced technology through maximized information flows among scientists rather than aiming for maximized secrecy. Much depends on how quickly and intensely a competition is crystallizing and how technologically capable an opponent is judged to be – all assessments in which intelligence and counter-intelligence officials must collaborate if the balance between defence and offence is to be wisely struck.

Yet, despite the theoretical logic of seamless intelligence and counterintelligence operations, practice has often diverged from the ideal, for good reasons. Especially in democracies, those who practise intelligence, counter-intelligence and security operate separately to some degree because those who spy and those who use the law to stop spying see their domestic missions so differently. More important, however, is the threat to democracy entailed in any optimized intelligence system that joins intelligence, legitimate force and the powers of arrest. Perfected ability to gain information dominance empowers those in power to keep it, to hide the mechanisms by which they do so, and to deceive those to whom they must be accountable. For this reason, joining powers to spy with the powers of arrest threatens the balance between the governed and the governors in democracies; those holding the powers of arrest and espionage must remain accountable to the people they serve, even as they fight adversaries infiltrating their homelands. Dictatorships are not, however, so constrained.

The practice: lessons and legacies from the Cold War: the US case

The natural tension that attends the relationships among security, counter-intelligence and intelligence has troubled democracies since the beginning of the Cold War, particularly in the United States, where a political culture of privacy and federal restraint runs deep and shapes the American way of life the state is designed to protect. Yet, at the same time, the Cold War represented for the US as well as its allies an existential threat that demanded a vigorous counter-intelligence response. This mix brewed aggressive approaches to intelligence within the NATO alliance that, larded with rules, political truces and bureaucratic boundaries, left a legacy of costs and benefits after the Cold War ended. On the positive side of the ledger, most NATO governments had institutionalized strong counter-intelligence functions, enforced espionage laws, and placed limits on domestic spying. Most legislatures had developed mechanisms for some measure of oversight. On the negative side, these same democratic govern-ments suffered from occasional intelligence and counter-intelligence over-reach and from gaps in counter-intelligence training and practice as agencies developed institutionally rigid views of their missions.

These trends were perhaps particularly evident in the United States. With the end of the bipolar strategic threat and the emergence of diverse transnational ones, US intelligence and counter-intelligence bureaucracies became ever more tightly wedded to existing counter-intelligence practices as they worked to defend their budgets in the post-Cold War environment. Although the Federal Bureau of Investigation (FBI) did recognize the upswing in industrial espionage and the new authorities it would need to counter it, the Bureau missed the domestic implications of the threat posed by terrorism – a threat against which major metropolitan police forces were already gearing up before 9/11. The efforts of the metropolitan police prior to 9/11, particularly in the Los Angeles area, readied the US for its network of Joint Terrorism Task Forces, headed by the FBI, after 9/11.

Of course, limits on collaboration among bureaucracies at the federal level also reflected political compromises, ethical standards and processes for account-ability deeply embedded in the national, Cold War consensus. These attitudes still shape, to a large degree, the rules of the road. To briefly explore these dynamics, it is useful to consider the US case, which has been perhaps the most telling in these regards. The history of US counter-intelligence also serves to highlight the problems democracies will face as they transition into the twenty-first century.

US counter-intelligence during the Cold War

The story of US counter-intelligence during the Cold War is mixed, but nonethe-less threaded with successes. Significant Soviet penetrations were eventually stopped, spies were caught, and, most importantly, the US and its allies won the strategic contest with the Soviet Union without engaging in a hot war (Warner and Fox 2009).[7] The US government built this CI system on the foundation of a newly institutionalized, centralized and empowered intelligence community and an older domestic counter-intelligence system shaped by the first FBI director, J. Edgar Hoover. Almost from the beginning, Hoover recognized the need for insti-tutionalizing CI processes, developing a strong body of law, and keeping opera-tions untainted by presidential political strategies that might corrupt the business of domestic surveillance. Yet the story of US counter-intelligence also reveals four troubling themes: the dominance of a defensive CI culture at the federal level; the subordination of strategic counter-intelligence to all other missions; mis-steps and mistrustful political discourse regarding domestic intelligence; and, partly as a result of the foregoing, tangled espionage laws and executive orders that confuse discussions of national purpose.

Defensive bias and policy disconnects

Although the Second World War demonstrated the utility of offensive counter-intelligence for winning wars, the end of the war entailed a spike in Soviet espionage that quickly led to defensive efforts to counter it on US soil. As the Soviet Union demonstrated its ability to infiltrate and steal US government secrets, the FBI aggressively pursued domestic counter-intelligence operations. Not surprisingly, the FBI interpreted its mission as defensive and security related: catching Soviet spies and protecting secrets. Enabled by new classification systems and tougher espionage laws, it pursued its mandate with vigour, prosecuting suspected spies, conducting mail-opening campaigns throughout the 1950s and infiltrating domestic groups involved in the Civil Rights Movement or protesting the Vietnam War. As a law enforcement organization, however, the Bureau did not regard its mission as political or policy oriented. Its purpose was to stop infiltration by communist agitators and operatives. The FBI measured success, quite reasonably, by the number of spies caught and prosecuted.

The Central Intelligence Agency (CIA), on the other hand, has traditionally regarded counter-intelligence as a two-fold mission involving operational security and strategy. James Jesus Angleton, the post-Second World War US counter-intelligence czar, had studied the Trust, a successful Bolshevik CI operation that eliminated monarchists after the revolution. He had direct experience with the Office of Strategic Services' counter-intelligence branch (X-2) that had worked with the British-run XX Committee to successfully deceive Hitler during the Second World War. This experience had convinced him of the power of offensive counter-intelligence as a tool of statecraft. During Angleton's tenure, the CIA and other US intelligence agencies developed sources and defectors to sniff out plants and provocateurs. Although most information on US and allied penetrations of the Soviet bloc still remains classified, the Justice Department did allege, following the capture of Aldrich Ames, that he had compromised at least ten 'penetrations' of the Soviet military and intelligence services. Similarly, the 2005 report of the post-9/11 WMD Commission hinted that CIA case officers targeted Warsaw Pact officials, deriving knowledge that led to 'a considerable number of successful counterintelligence investigations' (Warner and Fox 2009: 64).

Yet Angleton's personal experience with the deceit of Kim Philby, the principal British intelligence representative to the US and a Soviet spy who infiltrated MI6 and thus US intelligence agencies before being exposed, led him to suspect many of his colleagues. His fantastic conspiracy theories gradually tied the CIA's Soviet operations in knots. Although eventually forced out in the 1970s, Angleton left his mark. CIA management gradually came to view counter-intelligence less as an enabler of advantages, an aid to strategy, or a means to gain insights on competitors, and more as a separate discipline whose purpose was to catch spies or to voice scepticism on sources and methods. Steps to correct the problem were, in turn, stymied by politics. The Watergate crisis, during which an American president sought to harness intelligence services for his own political purposes, led to congressional investigations of intelligence over-reach. Revelations about how presidential prerogatives had been exercised through aggressive domestic intelligence initiatives, allegedly involving collaboration between FBI, CIA and city police forces in spying on domestic protestors, led to new restrictions on domestic intelligence activities, including warrantless wire tapping, mail opening and domestic source recruitment.

The decade of the 1970s thus became, for the US at least, the years of enabled oversight which bound the development of an ever more aggressive intelligence capability to rules designed to improve democratic accountability. These rules affirmed President Truman's declaration at the end of the Second World War that police forces would not engage in intelligence operations, affirmed the executive branch's constitutional authority to conduct domestic intelligence with justice department oversight, and led to procedures to ensure that counter-intelligence methods did not taint due process for domestic criminal investigations. A procedural 'wall' was thus established that seemingly required the separation of counter-intelligence activities from those of law enforcement, and constrained both in domestic cases.

Over time, the US intelligence community's counter-intelligence capabilities weakened even as oversight improved performance in other ways. Cuban deception campaigns disrupted CIA intelligence operations, and insider spies gained footholds within an intelligence community no longer grooming itself with aggressive, purposeful, counter-intelligence programmes (Latell 2012). The political cultures of the CIA, which trained and rewarded professional thieves and wheelmen, and the FBI, which trained and rewarded lawmen, grew increasingly apart. The CIA came to think of counter-intelligence as securing operations designed to break overseas laws; the FBI thought of counter-intelligence as a form of federal law enforcement. Offensive counter-intelligence was largely forgotten, so policy-makers began to equate CI with security. Analysts rarely thought of CI collection as useful to their assessments or of CI analysis worth reading as part of a collaborative process of estimation. The face of counter-intelligence for policy-makers became the guards, safes and classification stamps with which they had to cope each day – not the advisers who could inform them about what foreign intelligence services needed to know and thus how they might be influenced or their actions interpreted.

This polarization of the US intelligence community was exacerbated with each revelation of insider spying. The capture of the Walker ring and others in 1985, and later Aldrich Ames and Robert Hanssen, led to tighter restrictions on intelligence sharing as defensive security measures came to dominate the counter-intelligence agenda. Taking due note of the criticisms levelled by blue ribbon commissioners following the Ames fiasco which triggered a loss of agents overseas, senior counter-intelligence officials bore down harder on the problem of operational security, not strategic or even tactical advantage. All elements of the foreign intelligence community were affected by the repeated spy scares, and few agencies proved exempt from penetration or treachery. The capacity of strategic counter-intelligence to play a role in positive intelligence collection or to flag deceit waned in almost all intelligence agencies.

The most striking manifestation of the problem was in the CIA. According to one former deputy director of the agency with years of experience, there evolved a sense by the 1990s that once cases were referred to counter-intelligence officials, they were 'out of our hands'.[8] In other words, calculating the costs and benefits of case management was left to security- and defensive-minded counter-intelligence officials. Thus, the vigour and competence with which officials pursued their separate missions of security, intelligence and counter-intelligence worked to undermine joint purposes. Counter-intelligence analysis of adversaries' intelligence objectives did not flow naturally to those estimating these same adversaries' intentions. Yet, in one of the world's most sophisticated intelligence services, few seemed to notice the problem. Counter-intelligence professionals developed a deep, defensive bias that allied them more with security missions than with national security policy. Repeated failures, particularly against the Cuban target, fear of foreign dangles, and failed double agent operations rendered the discipline increasingly subordinate. Over time, disuse of strategic deception led to lapses in training for it, which in turn led to inabilities to recognize its use by others.

Failures caused by these gaps in collaboration among intelligence and counter-intelligence officials probably never outweighed counter-intelligence successes during the Cold War (although the documentary record is not complete, making final judgements impossible). It is nonetheless clear that these gaps began to bite deeply after the Cold War ended and transnational threats gathered momentum. The FBI, working with its own atrophied processes for identifying and prioritizing new threats and the domestic tools needed to meet them, was slow to develop new collaborative initiatives with the CIA, and slow to advise political leaders of the policy implications of what they did know. These gaps in intelligence and counter-intelligence performance caused serious problems for US policy-making in the 1990s, including slow recognition of the domestic threat posed by international terrorism and international organized crime. Despite growing recognition of transnational threats, the intelligence community only fitfully disseminated information to domestic entities, such as the Federal Aviation Authority, Amtrak and city police forces (though dissemination to industry in the face of growing threats from industrial espionage was a noteworthy exception).

Latent problems, which had long resided in the rigid allocation of responsibilities between federal law enforcement agencies and the national intelligence community, became salient on 9/11 and during its aftermath. Counter-intelligence contributed to failures prior to the First Gulf War, when Saddam Hussein's deceptions led to underestimation of his nuclear capabilities, and before the 2003 war, when Saddam Hussein's apparent attempts to deceive others caused NATO allies to over-estimate what he had. These 'failures' were, in part, the predictable result of a system designed to be slow to damage personal privacy, to give rights to those residing on US soil, and to hold espionage agencies accountable. Ironically, they are therefore also a reflection of its success. The system is, in a sense, designed to succeed both by thwarting adversaries and resisting the temptation to undermine the very democracy it is sworn to protect.

Indeed, in some ways, weaknesses in US counter-intelligence are necessary because of the symbiotic relationship between these vulnerabilities and one of the chief priorities: to avoid a national surveillance state. It is reasonable, then, to hope for laws that may guide us through the twenty-first century, a time when transnational threats are becoming more important. Unfortunately, the legacy of confusing US espionage laws and regulations is not helpful in sorting out how to strike the right balance between surveillance and privacy. Moving into the twenty-first century, the US counter-intelligence system, which is described and contained by a plethora of laws, is also dangerously entangled in them.[9] Most glaring are the differences in definitions of classified information (which cannot be released to the public), defence information (technically 'unclassified' but non-releasable), restricted data (separate restrictions relating to nuclear weapons), and formerly restricted data (historical data relating to nuclear weapons) that is actually, confusingly enough, still restricted.[10]

Laws laid down by the United States during a period of existential bilateral threat did not hamper action until terrorists armed with new technologies demonstrated their flaws. Now, the emergence of the cyber domain, where lawmaking is both risky and contentious, has left governments in a quandary and counter-intelligence agencies without adequate guidance. With the legal framework so confused, it is hardly surprising that countering threats has become ever harder, particularly when posed by insiders.[11] When the classification system is riddled with inconsistencies, insiders who seem to 'leak' from one agency's standpoint may simply be discussing federal policy from the standpoint of another. As the digital age increases the number of electronic secrets stacking up behind federal walls, the problem is likely to get worse before it gets better.

The performance of intelligence and counter-intelligence institutions in democratic polities is directly related to changes in information technology and the challenges these changes pose for democracies. It makes sense, then, to consider how technology is changing the ways in which advantages in information may be obtained and what these trends may portend for the future. Historians of international relations have observed that with every technological revolution has come an expansion of force and an adjustment in attitudes towards the state. What lies in store in the twenty-first century?

Technological trends and their implications

According to classical measures of power such as the distribution of population, resources and military might, the twenty-first century is arguably seeing a shift in strength from West to East, particularly China and India. But if information is power, then traditional measures of power may not capture the whole picture. For example, states with the most advanced information infrastructures may have an edge. Large corporations that manage the global information infrastructure may be becoming new power brokers, capable of allying with bands of insurgents on the one hand, or repressive governments on the other, depending on their profit motives. Power shifts may, in fact, be occurring not only among states but also within them. New technologies for data mining and artificial intelligence are improving the capacity of states to conduct surveillance and counter-insurgency, but photo- and video-equipped mobile phones, miniaturized microphones, and supporting internet software are also in the hands of the governed, empowering protest.

In this regard it is important to note that companies such as Apple see their profitability turning on private purchases, not governments. During the first quarter of 2012, iPhone sales by Apple grew by 35.1 million, contributing to Apple's $39.2 billion surge in growth during that period – three times what the company earned during the same period in 2011. Sales in China made up 20 per cent of that surge, compared to just 4.5 per cent the previous year. Whereas such a surge in connectivity might have positive socio-economic effects in a democracy, it has demonstrably destabilizing effects for repressive political systems.

In fact, growth in internet use may be a more important indicator of societal change than degree of penetration per se. Table 6.1 shows that, from 2000 to 2010, internet use in Africa and the Middle East grew over 2,000 per cent. Despite such rapid growth, these two regions are still the least penetrated by internet access, with only 13.5 per cent and 35.6 per cent of their respective populations able to go on line. China's relatively modest internet penetration (38.4%) and potential for explosive growth could thus pose challenges for Beijing,[12] especially because the state has forged no national understanding on the collection, control or use of citizens' information.

Herein lies the paradox. From a counter-intelligence standpoint, the growth of the internet has enabled governments to reach deeply into their own polities, monitoring citizens' locations and their online use. Yet, while this new capacity empowers unconstrained totalitarian states relatively more than democratic ones, making them potentially more dangerous, the pace of individual empowerment has generally been faster than the growth in governments' capacities to monitor, so that governing without the consent of the governed has become more difficult. As Kevin O'Connell and Randall Forster have observed:

> Solutions only governments once held – the ability to communicate globally with mobility; the power of mapping & geolocation; the instant surveillance tools of high quality sound, imaging, and video; the ability to plan and execute while geographically distant – (have) evolved from thousands of government systems to billions of personal unregulated devices available to anyone anywhere on the globe. Today, every traditional intelligence discipline has a 'seam' in the open world.
>
> (O'Connell and Forster 2011)

The message for policy-makers is that they need to connect with these newly enabled citizens; the message for counter-intelligence services is that governments will likely seek a deeper grip on their own and foreign populations than ever before, not through superior data, but through the interpretation of events for those whom they govern or hope to manipulate. Terrorists and other

Table 6.1 World internet usage and population statistics, 31 December 2011

World regions	Population (2011 Est.)	Internet users 31 December 2000	Internet users latest data	Penetration (% population)	Growth 2000–2011 (%)	Users % of table
Africa	1,037,524,058	4,514,400	139,875,242	13.5	2,988.4	6.2
Asia	3,879,740,877	114,304,000	1,016,799,076	26.2	789.6	44.8
Europe	816,426,346	105,096,093	500,723,686	61.3	376.4	22.1
Middle East	216,258,843	3,284,800	77,020,995	35.6	2,244.8	3.4
North America	347,394,870	108,096,800	273,067,546	78.6	152.6	12.0
Latin America/Carib.	597,283,165	18,068,919	235,819,740	39.5	1,205.1	10.4
Oceania/Australia	35,426,995	7,620,480	23,927,457	67.5	214.0	1.1
World total	6,930,055,154	360,985,492	2,267,233,742	32.7	528.1	100.0

Source: www.internetworldstats.com/stats.htm.

Notes
1 Internet Usage and World Population Statistics are for 31 December 2011.
2 CLICK on each world region name for detailed regional usage information.
3 Demographic (population) numbers are based on data from the US Census Bureau and local census agencies.
4 Internet usage information comes from data published by Nielsen Online, by the International Telecommunications Union, by GfK, local Regulators and other reliable sources.
5 For definitions, disclaimers and navigation help, please refer to the Site Surfing Guide.
6 Information in this site may be cited, giving the due credit towww.internetworldstats.com. Copyright © 2001–2012, Miniwatts Marketing Group. All rights reserved worldwide.

adversaries can reach deep inside states to turn the governed against themselves and their governors. New users are particularly likely to be unsophisticated in their appreciation for how the internet can be used to manipulate and monitor them and generate bias, making states undergoing rapid internet penetration particularly vulnerable to disruption. On the other hand, savvy governments enjoying the trust of the governed can rely on them for early warning and self-organization during crises. From this perspective, the shift of state power from West to East seems less certain and the risks of instability in the latter seem, in any case, rather grave.

To better understand the implications of the information revolution for counter-intelligence, it is useful to explore three related technological trends shaping the information environment in somewhat greater depth: big data and its processing; miniaturization and proliferation of sensors and platforms; and the evolution of the cyber domain. These technologies are shaping not only who competes in political contests both nationally and internationally, but also how they do so. Although all relevant technologies cannot be reviewed, a few examples will give a flavour of the changes underway.

Big data

In 2009, Richard Way of the *Guardian* newspaper captured the startling growth of the world's stockpile of digital information:

> At 487bn gigabytes (GB), if the world's rapidly expanding digital content were printed and bound into books it would form a stack that would stretch from Earth to Pluto 10 times. As more people join the digital tribe – increasingly through internet-enabled mobile phones – the world's digital output is increasing at such a rate that those stacks of books are rising quicker than Nasa's fastest space rocket.[13]

Way observed that, at this rate, the digital universe would double over the next eighteen months. Actually, in 2010, the globe produced 1.2 zettabytes and in 2011, 1.8 zettabytes (1.8 trillion gigabytes) of data,[14] mostly as a result of the spread of cell phones and personal computers to individuals using new 'apps' and sharing pictures and videos. EMC^2, the company that posted the data Way used for his article, explains why it thinks such trends are important: by 2020 digital data will have grown by 50 per cent, but the number of human beings managing it will grow by only 1.7 per cent.[15] Information managers are facing digital chaos, and companies such as EMC^2 want to help them gain control.

The implications for intelligence practice seem clear: if information is power, then those who master this digital chaos first, and derive meaning from it, will likely gain critical advantages. Intelligence professionals, whether in business or in service to the state, are therefore in a silent race to develop tools for mining and analysing growing volumes of swiftly moving information and then to use it to understand the competitive security environment and help policy-makers shape it in their favour. In the United States, the intelligence community runs an open source intelligence (OSINT) centre, which has sources in over 160 countries that report in over eighty languages.[16] The centre provides foreign source material to the public through the Commerce Department's National Technical Information Service's online World News Connection. This data-feed only becomes good intelligence, however, when the centre adds timeliness and attentiveness to provenance (examining where the foreign newspapers, government spokesmen, map-makers and best-selling authors acquired their information, and the motives they had for sharing it). Open information is rarely born pristine; much of it is offered and replicated with a purpose. It is, even if 'true', nonetheless biased. Open source counter-intelligence is necessary to reveal the intent behind the substance. For example, if a foreign government releases formerly classified documents, it matters whether the officials were forced to do so or did so purposely in an attempt to influence international events. For this reason, processing 'open source' information in competitive conditions requires scrubbing the data for its provenance, not just mining it for gems.

What makes the modern challenge particularly difficult is that the leaders in this open source race are in the private sector, where businesses have developed sophisticated tools for understanding the provenance of data, not just how to sift its great bulk.[17] Tying consumers' decisions to information is, after all, the essence of marketing, and it is fully legal. Thus the provenance of data on consumer choice is the essence of what companies want and what they are already getting to an ever more impressive degree. Large corporations, such as Google, Yahoo and Twitter, want to gain subscribers and win advertising dollars by an ever increasing refinement of the search function. They offer search engines to consumers with questions, and offer sellers increasingly detailed profiles of those consumers based on those searches. Programs for data mining and analysis allow companies to know their customers both intimately and collectively for the purpose of targeting them, and to sell that information to others. These programs are, in fact, becoming so good that Google customers have agreed to a breathtaking forfeiture of privacy in order to gain the advantages of easy access to the valuable information and the faster decision-making it provides. If companies processing this data agree to partner with states, powerful tools will be handed to intelligence and counter-intelligence institutions.

Among those tools are sensing systems developed for private use but with significant consequences for intelligence operations. Take, for example, biometric data. On the one hand, the increasing ability of employers and officials to track people by their heat signatures, irises or DNA may make counter-intelligence easier. Establishing false identities or multiple identities is becoming difficult if not impossible. On the other hand, the boon for CI has its offensive CI blowback: to the extent that guarding against foreign penetrations of one's own side requires penetrating the intelligence systems of adversaries, the difficulties of cover will likely require re-engineering offensive counter-intelligence operations as well. In the meantime, the multiplication of identity data, absent the artificial intelligence to process it, may leave some competitors swamped.

Cheap, miniaturized collection platforms and sensing systems

For many of the reasons discussed above, it is not clear that all states win in the big data world. The logic that makes business a winner in the evolution of big data and artificial intelligence is the same as the logic that says democracies will trump autocracies in the new information environment: people power. Since the biggest contributors to the surge in digital volume are individuals, these individuals can play sides in ways they were unable to do before. Human beings with iPhones can take pictures, write on-the-scene reports of battlefield developments, make videos, and upload all this media from any location covered by their service providers.

Such advances in privatized 'sensing' are important for intelligence for reasons beyond open source databanks. The development and miniaturization of new sensors and forms of communication are accompanied by the development and miniaturization of the platforms on which they ride. Sensors are thus going beyond the hostile environments of space and sea, to a rapidly expanding list of other formerly denied areas, such as inside nuclear reactors, into terrorists' caves, and across national borders in peacetime. It is thus getting harder to establish sanctuaries by detaching from the information grid. Terrorists avoiding traceable cell phones may not be able to avoid drones in Pakistan and Afghanistan. Yet drones can also be privately owned and the tables turned against the more powerful. In Texas, for example, a private citizen flying his own UAV photographed blood in the Trinity River from the Columbia Meat packing plant – a report that triggered a formal law enforcement investigation (Hill 2012). In Libya, insurgents used low-cost drones bought from Canada to watch Qaddafi's military movements during the insurrection. *National Geographic* captured the implications for privacy when it ran a cover story on the rapidly evolving efforts to miniaturize flying robots to the size of humming-birds. Aerial drones are simply flying robots, while land-based drones were sent into the Fukishimi Daiichi nuclear plant following the 2011 tsunami crisis. Mexican drug cartels have used sea-based drones to ferry illicit cargoes on to US soil for years.

The significance of 'big data' and miniaturized, inexpensive collection platforms for counter-intelligence is obvious: adversaries can learn much more about each other by spending much less than they once did. Will fighting this kind of information gathering be a fool's errand? In the language of classical intelligence warning: the noise will be increasing exponentially while the signals will be growing ever weaker. In such an environment, the race will be won by those who are agile, quick and adept at aligning platforms and sensors against targets. Nowhere is such alignment more obvious than in the cyber domain.

Cyber

Most discussions of cyber begin with the vulnerabilities of critical information infrastructure to hacking and other forms of attack. Counter-intelligence discussions usually cover the difficulties of tracking, intercepting and attributing such attacks. In essence, there are four critical challenges posed by the cyber domain (Hayden 2011):

> Firstly, the nature of the 'domain'. Although it is manmade, ownership of content is neither divisible nor attributable. Friendly and hostile data co-exist.
>
> Secondly, while entry fees to the domain are low, vulnerabilities once there are high. Defense is necessary but difficult to implement. In fact, states' efforts to protect or govern it could lower the value of the domain itself.
>
> In these conditions, the motives of commercial firms to defend their networks vary greatly, and may not be coincident with governments' interests in protecting national security. The conduct of firms could trigger war or prevent states from bringing it to an end.[18]
>
> In these circumstances, governments could become embroiled in new forms of industrial espionage as they seek to understand and map the threats that corporations pose for the state, both because of their vulnerabilities and their policies in cyberspace. These policies might prompt retribution against hardware located within state territory.

Distinguishing between cyber espionage and cyber attack will likely plague international conflict and its successful resolution for years to come. What constitutes an act of war in cyberspace? How are wars terminated if they can be prosecuted by private hackers with axes to grind?

Most of these issues and the problems they raise for counter-intelligence have been addressed at length elsewhere (Brenner 2011). What has been less appreciated is the role the integrity of cyber plays in *managing* information wars in the public domain and the role offensive counter-intelligence might play in that process. Joel Brenner, former director of the US National Counterintelligence Executive (NCIX), has explained that one of the foremost challenges of cyber espionage is its potential for peacetime use with wartime ends in mind. He points to the penetration of US networks by the Chinese for the purpose of robbing US industries of their intellectual property. To counter such espionage, the US needs to penetrate the networks of adversaries to see what is coming and to deflect or destroy the effort. Who, then, is the attacker? Both sides live in the networks of others to avoid surprise; yet one also exploits that pre-positioning for purposes of economic espionage, not simply defence. Telling the difference between the guard at the gate and the thief is impossible. In this silent war, in which objectives (resources, industry) can be achieved without battle, what matters is *control* of the cyber domain, not necessarily its destruction. Governments that can sort thieves and guards and act quickly to ally with private sector interests or release information at an adversary's expense will be best able to prevent losses and shape the way critical audiences react, influencing who wins and loses.

This last idea, which relates to deception, is perhaps the most frequently forgotten dimension of what is widely understood to be the threat from cyber operations. It is not just that states and hackers can burrow into information systems to damage, steal and disrupt; they do it to influence as well, sometimes for the sake of no one state's agenda but for the sake of 'free information' or some private cause. Leaked secrets, absent competitive context, offer the opportunity to gain advantages; open source information, as explained above, is never born pristine and can be competitively neutral in its significance, until one side or the other shapes meaning from it. Bradley Manning's treachery in leaking volumes of classified cables to Wikileaks was not driven by sympathy for any particular adversary. Manning probably didn't even know who would win or lose from his act. As the cables emerged in the public domain, counter-intelligence officials brought public criticism on the government with hopeless efforts to staunch the flow. Less attention was given to the equally important effort to manage how others sought to understand and use the information. An effective counter-intelligence response could have included silence on some issues, such as the authenticity of certain documents, and emphasis on others, such as the role US diplomats were playing in pressing dictators for democratic changes. To effectively manage such an effort, policy-makers needed to lead, with the willing involvement of counter-intelligence officials. To some extent this was done, but less by design than by default.

With technological advance, cyber deceptions are likely to grow, infecting not only how adversaries derive meaning from stolen data, but drive meaning into shared data. Intelligence wars entail influence operations; modern counter-intelligence must entail counter-influence informed by solid appreciation of open sources. Counter-intelligence as it exists now can do well in catching the perpetrator but fail utterly in managing spills and cyber poisons unless capacity for offensive counter-intelligence matches that of spy catching. And to manage narrative in the age of information, one needs not only an active and cooperative citizenry that trusts officials not to manipulate them, but the attentive participation of policy-makers who understand their role in managing the information environment and, most importantly, how to shape the *meaning* of events without lying about the facts. A counter-intelligence culture imbued with the missions of stealing and protecting truths is poorly equipped to work with policy-makers in such a world of grey. In any case, with people power becoming ever more important in managing international conflict – whether to induce panic from terrorist acts or to reduce it and hunt down the perpetrators – control of the integrity of cyber systems is a critical problem.

Twenty-first-century challenges

The modern counter-intelligence problem is complex, turning on computer and communications technologies, legal statutes governing their use, and the intent of adversaries to exploit them. Instantaneous communication is simultaneously a boon to information managers and so ubiquitous that advantages are hard to capture and retain for competitors. When new communications capabilities develop, they hit the market immediately, driven by a private sector with worldwide reach. Steps the US takes to ramp up the internal capabilities of intelligence agencies empower insiders to use expanded access for unauthorized purposes. At the same time, the digital revolution threatens to shackle governments with petabytes of new media, such as email, video and the like – secrets whose worth is as uncertain as are the consequences of their release and yet which will entail enormous effort and expense to store, review and declassify. In democracies, technology is charging ahead and the law is scrabbling to keep up.

Three consequences of these trends seem particularly important for counter-intelligence: the rise in insider threats, the importance of private sector collaboration, and the increasing imperative of streamlining laws governing the relationship between policing, policy and counter-intelligence. It seems sensible to conclude with a few brief remarks about each.

Insider spies

The first and perhaps most immediate consequence of the trends outlined above concerns the likely rise in insider espionage over the coming decade. With empowerment of the individual comes his mobilization for causes of all kinds: political, social, environmental, economic, military and criminal. Moreover, the capability to act decisively now travels with the person in the form of cell phones, secure, wireless lap tops, digital recording devices, cameras and the like. From a single location, an individual can connect with friends, participate in a poll, pay for parking tickets, buy movie tickets, order a book and read it instantaneously, 'go' to the movies or order dinner. The idea of acting decisively at any moment travels with people to their workplaces, and the connectivity with others of like mind encourages spontaneity, not caution. This social dynamic raises the risk of insider spying not so much because people are more easily recruited by foreign powers but because they are more easily disgruntled and able to act on that feeling.

A new era for science: direction finding in cyberspace and other countermeasures?

A second major challenge flowing from technological trends will be to build collaborative efforts between the government and scientific-industrial communities in the interest of national security. Such an effort would be nothing new. During the Second World War and the early Cold War, technology was also changing quickly. The US and its allies recruited patriotic scientists, such as R.V. Jones and Richard Bissell, to help them tackle the challenges of radar, rocketry and sophisticated direction finding. Such collaboration blossomed into the CIA's Science and Technology Directorate. A similar effort is needed now, with intelligence and counter-intelligence receiving attention in equal measure and the scientific minds coming more from industry than from the government or military services. Although the US system of federally funded research survives in the form of the Department of Energy Laboratory system, Defense Advanced

Research Projects Agency (DARPA) and its intelligence counterpart IARPA, these agencies cannot foresee the next new 'thing' in a rapidly evolving industry as well as the innovators can themselves. The key here will be to gain the trust of an industry that, in wanting to empower all customers, has little interest in aiding governmental efforts to discriminate among them or to increase their vulnerability to surveillance in any measure.

Law enforcement challenges

Finally, the twenty-first century is likely to be one in which transnational threats are accelerating, and law enforcement will be taking a larger place in the pantheon of national security agencies. This will be a difficult transition for states, such as the US, that have developed a law enforcement culture comfortable with catching spies but historically walled off from the larger intelligence enterprise. Domestic intelligence agencies, which have grown in size and mission since 9/11, have a new need for domestic sources and thus liaison with law enforcement, while the police will also expect better sharing of threats at the state and local level. As the technological capacities for surveillance increase, largely spurred by business and national security interests, the police will want to be 'first adopters' of those technologies suitable for the public domain. In states with good systems of law enforcement and intelligence oversight, the legitimacy of private sector surveillance will be settled early, making law enforcement relatively empowered to act in concert with domestic interest groups chasing lawbreakers of all kinds, be they slaughterhouses or terrorists. Carefully managed, law enforcement agencies can become ever more trusted interlocutors among citizens, businesses and state agencies involved in domestic intelligence. If mismanaged, however, they can evolve into the intelligence arms of excessively intrusive surveillance agencies, with consequential effects for governments struggling to maintain legitimacy with the governed. For this reason, perhaps, the power shift we see occurring from West to East may be too premature to call.

Notes

1 This chapter was prepared with support from the American Academy of Arts and Sciences and with the assistance of Ryan McKinistry and Alexandra Bellay, my research assistants at Georgetown University in early 2012.
2 Colum Lynch, 'Syrian Opposition Seeks to Wipe the Assad Name off the Map – via Google', *Washington Post*, 14 February 2012. Online. Available: www.washingtonpost.com/world/national-security/syrian-opposition-seeks-to-wipe-the-assad-name-off-the-map–via-google/2012/02/14/gIQAad5aER_story.html (accessed 28 January 2013).
3 Ibid.
4 To understand the measurement problem, it may be helpful to consider two views of the somewhat analogous mission of a librarian. In its most limited sense, the job of a librarian is to maintain track of books in order to keep them safe and available for users. Libraries might therefore measure their staff's success by assessing whether all the library's holdings are in proper order on the shelves. In a larger sense, however,

a librarian's mission is to serve a community of learners. Understood in this way, the number of books accounted for but *not on the shelves* would be positively correlated with success. In fact, overdue books might be less of a worry than books that are safe but never checked out. Counter-intelligence officers ought to differ from security officers in a similar way: the former should measure success in terms of the strategic purpose of those they serve, not the security of information per se. Security most certainly matters, because secrets or advantages lost cannot usually be regained; but, if security rules, the strategists may lose opportunities to go on the offensive or the flexibility they need to shape their opponent's perceptions.

5 Some CI experts noted that, though accidental, the loss of a helicopter during the operation had a salutary effect, because its easily photographed pieces served as publicly available proof that the operation had indeed taken place and that the US was involved.

6 A striking example comes from the Second World War, when cable and radio censorship included, among other things, '[t]he civil, military, industrial, financial, or economic plans of the United States, or other countries opposing the Axis powers, or the personal or official plans of any official thereof,' '[w]eather conditions (past, present, or forecast)' and 'criticism of equipment, appearance, physical condition or morale of the collective or individual armed forces of the United States or other nations' opposing the Axis powers (U.S. Cable and Radio Censorship Regulations $$1801–18(d), (g), (k), 7 Fed. Reg. 1499,1500 (1942), cited in Edgar and Schmidt 1973: 934). Press dispatches were excluded from this particular rule and were covered in another regulation.

7 Major failures have indeed happened, but successes are likely under-appreciated because of the sparse public record. What matters is which services 'won' overall. The official historians of the DNI and FBI note that more than seventy-two spies were successfully prosecuted between 1978 and 1985. The Senate's Select Committee on Intelligence, in its 1986 report *Meeting the Espionage Challenge*, revealed the (largely still classified) contributions of CIA counter-intelligence during the Cold War with hints of this kind:

> A major element in counterintelligence is offensive operations, especially efforts to recruit agents-in-place within hostile intelligence services and to induce defections from those services. The strategic payoff of agents and defectors can be immense as demonstrated by the exposure of Edward Lee Howard and the successful prosecution of Ronald Pelton.
>
> (p. 63)

8 Interview with a former DDCI, 11 July 2011.

9 US intelligence laws are riddled with semantic distinctions and conceptual gaps that make navigating the terrain of national security especially perilous. The underlying inconsistencies among the various provisions of US espionage laws have never been resolved. The creation of the US classification system and the US intelligence agencies followed the original Defense Secrets Act of 1911 by several decades. The 1911 Act was incorporated into the Espionage Act of 1917, which in turn has been amended several times. This law was in turn incorporated into 18 U.S. Code 793, which was modified in 1950 by the Internal Security Act. The last added 18 U.S. Code 794.

10 See the website of the Public Interest Declassification Board (PIDB) for more information on the current confusion concerning classification and declassification: www.archives.gov/declassification/pidb/index.html (accessed 19 December 2012).

11 In a widely cited article, Edgar and Schmidt (1973) exposed how bad the situation had already become by that time. As they wrote in the introduction to their now classic treatise:

> When we turned to the United States Code to find out what Congress had done, we became absorbed in the effort to comprehend what the current espionage statutes mandate with respect to the communication and publication of defense

information. The longer we looked, the less we saw. Either advancing myopia had taken its toll, or the statutes implacably resist the effort to understand. For the persistence of this problem, see Herbig (2008: 23).

12 China lags behind both Azerbaijan and Armenia (44.1 per cent and 47.1 per cent respectively) in internet use. See www.internetworldstats.com/stats3.htm.

13 'Internet data heads for 500bn gigabytes: World's digital content equivalent to stack of books stretching from Earth to Pluto 10 times', *Guardian*, 18 May 2009. Online. Available: www.guardian.co.uk/business/2009/may/18/digital-content-expansion (accessed 23 May 2012).

14 'Produced' here refers to information created and replicated as data 'in motion' on the internet.

15 See their website at www.emc.com/leadership/programs/digital-universe.htm (accessed 29 January 2013).

16 See their website at www.opensource.gov/ (accessed 29 January 2013).

17 See the website at http://reclaimdemocracy.org/walmart/2007/spying_operation.php (accessed 29 January 2013).

18 Google Maps is, for example, a new voice regarding the boundaries of states and even the naming of towns and roads. See John D. Sutter, 'Google Maps border becomes part of international dispute', CNN, 5 November 2010. Online. Available: www.cnn.com/2010/TECH/web/11/05/nicaragua.raid.google.maps/index.html (accessed 29 January 2013).

Bibliography

Brenner, Joel (2011) *America the Vulnerable: Inside the New Threat Matrix of Digital Espionage, Crime and Warfare*, New York: Penguin.

Edgar, Harold and Schmidt, Benno (1973) 'The Espionage Statutes and the Publication of Defense Information', *Columbia Law Review*, 73: 930–1087.

Hayden, Michael (2011) 'The Future of Things "Cyber"', *Strategic Studies Quarterly*, 5: 3–7.

Herbig, Katherine (2008) 'Changes in Espionage by Americans, 194'007', *Department of Defense Technical Report 08–05.*

Hill, Kashmir (2012) 'Potential Drone Use: Finding Rivers of Blood', *Forbes Magazine*. Online. Available: www.forbes.com/sites/kashmirhill/2012/01/25/potential-drone-use-finding-rivers-of-blood/ (accessed 29 January 2013).

Hinsley, F.H. (1993) *British Intelligence in the Second World War*, Abridged edn, Cambridge: Cambridge University Press.

Holloway, David (1994) *Stalin and the Bomb: The Soviet Union and Atomic Energy*, New Haven, CT/London: Yale University Press.

Latell, Brian (2012) *Castro's Secrets: The CIA and Cuba's Intelligence Machine*, Basingstoke: Palgrave Macmillan.

O'Connell, Kevin T. and Forster, Randall T. (2011) *Intelligence Integration Strategy: Realignment of Sources and Methods for 21st Century National Security*, prepared for the Office of the Director of National Intelligence/Deputy for Intelligence Integration (ODNI/DII).

Sims, Jennifer E. and Gerber, Burton (eds) (2009) *Vaults, Mirrors and Masks: Rediscovering US Counterintelligence*, Washington, DC: Georgetown University Press.

Warner, Michael and Fox, James (2009) 'Counterintelligence: The American Experience', in Jennifer E. Sims and Burton Gerber (eds), *Vaults, Mirrors and Masks*, Washington, DC: Georgetown University Press, pp. 51–68.

7 Analysing international intelligence cooperation

Institutions or intelligence assemblages?

Jelle van Buuren

Intelligence studies is a multi-disciplinary, specialist field of study, a niche that has emerged out of, among other things, the fields of strategic studies, international history, law and sociology.[1] Swedish intelligence scholar Wilhelm Agrell (2006: 635) has observed: 'there is no generally established theory of intelligence', while A.D.M. Svendsen (2009: 705–708) has remarked that 'the state of the discipline reflects its origin'. Some dimensions of intelligence studies are theoretically impoverished, while others have enjoyed substantial theory development. Svendsen describes the field as 'haphazardly theorized', which captures the ad hoc nature of the theorization efforts. He defends this 'picking and mixing' from different disciplinary and theoretical strands (a 'complex co-existence plurality') on the grounds that at least to some degree, this reflects what practitioners do in the real world of intelligence. In this chapter we will also be 'picking and mixing' from various theoretical and conceptual strands to look at the European cross-border cooperation of intelligence and security actors. Drawing on insights from governance theory, network theory and the 'practice turn' in social science (Schatzki *et al.* 2001), we will argue that the 'state-centric view' (Fägersten 2010) which dominates the literature on the history, functioning and future of European intelligence cooperation does increase our understanding of this phenomenon, but that it also obscures developments 'on the ground' which can be of equal relevance.

Although European intelligence cooperation is not a new phenomenon, it has been changing rapidly since the 9/11 attacks in the United States and the subsequent terrorist attacks in Madrid in 2004 and London in 2005. The European Union responded to the new terrorist threat with an 'unprecedented wave of policy interventions' (den Boer 2006: 83). New counter-terrorist agencies and structures were created on top of already existing structures, and the latter were furbished with new and special powers. With this 'plethora of initiatives' the EU reinforced the already 'crowded policy space' on counter-terrorism (den Boer 2006: 99). At the same time the cooperation with intelligence and security actors from outside the European Union also changed markedly; therefore it is perhaps better to speak of the 'internationalization' or 'globalization' of intelligence than to restrict the new developments to the European theatre. According to Aldrich (2009: 27), this 'black hole' of international intelligence cooperation has been expanding for more than a decade. The Global War on Terror has accelerated the scope and scale of international cooperation, ranging from clandestine operations to information exchange and an expanding network of intelligence liaison officers (Sims 2006; Svendsen 2008). This has resulted in a 'complex and blurred transnational sphere of counterterrorism' (den Boer *et al.* 2008: 103–104).

It was not only intelligence and security agencies that were affected by the changing international situation. Closer connections were forged between domestic police, security and intelligence services, eroding the distinction between what constitutes domestic and foreign. At the same time, the expanding role of private security providers blurred the distinction between what is public and what is private (Arthur 1996; Hoogenboom 2006; Voelz 2009). This 'blurring of borders' is captured in the notion of an emerging security continuum. This security continuum of internal and external security has created a novel situation whereby concepts and institutional arrangements traditionally aimed at internal security challenges (police, national and local information, and administrative authorities) become increasingly challenged to address matters previously reserved for the external security professionals (military and international police forces, foreign affairs officials, international legal agencies and diplomatic corps), while the latter are in turn required to deal with matters reserved for the former (Burgess 2009: 310). With a little variation of what Loader (2000: 326–328) has described for the field of policing, we can now speak of a development in which intelligence *by* government is supplemented with intelligence *through* government, intelligence *above* government and intelligence *beyond* government. The military are now also tasked with internal counter-terrorism measures and assistance in crisis situations; information on home-grown terrorism and radicalization is supplied by youth workers, school directors and police community officers; private security and intelligence companies are supplying risk and threat assessments for public agencies and companies; and surveillance operations are fed with data from a plethora of local, international, public and private actors.

Nodal governance

These developments, however, are not a phenomenon related exclusively to the intelligence community; nor are they the only response to the emerging networked world of terrorism. The governance of security has been radically transformed in recent decades. Established notions are based on the idea of autonomous, territorially bound nation-states in which state agencies like the police, border guards and intelligence services are responsible for the delivery of security. Today, we inhabit a world of multi-level, multi-centre security governance, in which states are joined, criss-crossed and contested by an array of transnational organizations and factors that operate via regional and global governmental bodies, commercial security outfits and informal networks (Wood and Shearing 2007: 3). One could think, for instance, of global private players like Control Risk or Stratfor, which deliver a range of security and intelligence products and services to both private and public parties and who work together with public intelligence agencies in informal or personal networks.

This has been termed the 'nodal governance' of security, consisting of a plurality of decision centres in which no clear hierarchy between centres exists; the core of the decision structures itself consists of networks; the boundaries of decision structures are fluid; and the actors include professional experts, and public and private actors (Goetz 2008: 262). Whether the state in this new fluid security amalgam is 'stripped of its commanding heights' (Neocleous 2007: 346), 'hollowed out' and is just one 'nodal actor' among many, or whether it continues to function as a kind of 'eminence grise', a 'shadow entity lurking off-stage' (Hawkins 1984: 190), is a subject of fierce academic debate (van Buuren 2010). Leaving this dispute aside for a moment, there seems to be agreement among scholars studying and researching changes in governance that nowadays we are facing the multiplication of auspices and providers of security (Shearing and Wood 2003: 406), and that security is not provided only by the institutions of the state, nor shaped solely by thinking and acting originating from the state sphere (Wood and Shearing 2006).

These insights from governance theory on the nodalization and hybridization of security (vertical and horizontal models of security governance and practices are combined together in more or less integrated modes of interaction), however, seem to be overlooked when it comes to the study of European intelligence and security cooperation. The story of this cooperation is commonly told from an institutional perspective, centring on treaties, structures, competences, legal powers and institutional developments (Bendiek 2006; Bossong 2008; Kaunert 2010; Monar 2007; Müller-Wille 2002; Zimmermann 2006). Typical questions that arise from this perspective would be as follows: What are the opportunities offered by the new Lisbon Treaty for intelligence cooperation? What will be the influence of qualified majority voting in the relevant European institutions? How relevant are the new powers of the European Parliament? How should we appreciate the new European External Action Service? Is the European Joint Situation Centre (van Buuren 2009) the embryo of a true European central intelligence agency?

It is not that these kinds of questions are irrelevant. More traditional theories and concepts from political science or public administration can be deployed to analyse and evaluate the development of cross-border intelligence structures, patterns of cooperation, conflicts of interest, bureaucratic turf wars, or the problem that agencies sometimes are reluctant to follow political directives. Fägersten, for instance, showed nicely how bureaucratic interests and conflicting bureaucratic cultures hindered the European police organization Europol in fulfilling the intelligence and counter-terrorist mandate which the political leaders of the European Union wanted it to have (Fägersten 2010). In his article, Fägersten criticizes the 'state-centric view on intelligence cooperation' which assumes that states are unitary and sole actors when it comes to the development of intelligence cooperation, and that state preferences are thus the key to understanding cooperative outcomes. The basic assumption behind the state-centric view

'is that states get what they want: if the strategic calculus is in favour of cooperation, then cooperation will occur.' However, states will in fact not always get
what they want, due to – among other things – bureaucratic cultural wars (Fägersten 2010: 500–501).

Although Fägersten criticizes the state-centric view, he himself seems unable
to escape what I would like to call the 'normative state-centric view'. At the end
of his article, Fägersten advises policy-makers to include bureaucratic perspectives at an early stage in the planning process, otherwise governments may find
themselves in 'the uncomfortable position' of not getting what they want (Fägersten 2010: 520). Although from a normative point of view this advice is understandable – we will return to this discussion at the end of this chapter – there
seems to be an underlying presumption that it is politics and policies that matter
and that shape the reality on the ground. The question then is: do they really?
One way or another, the presumption in much of the literature on European intelligence remains that the state – by invoking institutions, rules and policies – is, or
at least should be, the leading actor in the styling of intelligence cooperation. This
runs the risk, however, of confusing normative with conceptual matters and
thereby obscuring developments 'on the ground' that may be at least as important
for our understanding of the internationalization of intelligence. Studies into international police cooperation show that most of the EU policy instruments lack a
practical orientation and therefore have a limited effect on police practices. Block
(2010: 195) points at the cumbersome procedures and protocols for international
police liaison officers which reflect more administrative preoccupations with
sovereignty issues and internal organizational problems than the practical needs
of liaison officers engaged in cross-border cooperation. Studying international
police practices therefore seems to be a better way of becoming informed about
international police cooperation than studying in detail all kinds of institutional
and policy matters on the political and administrative level.

For this reason it is worthwhile to look at international intelligence and
security cooperation from a de-institutionalized perspective. Diplomats and
lawyers negotiating international treaties or policy-makers debating options
operate from different interests, insights and bodies of knowledge than specialists who have to design practical forms of international cooperation. It is one
thing to design a treaty, institutional arrangement or policy paving the way for
international intelligence and security cooperation; it is however quite another to
put these policies in practice while acknowledging the particularities of the intelligence cultures involved. At a time when scientists, politicians and policy-
makers are discussing the future of European intelligence and security
cooperation, the reality on the ground is that intelligence and security professionals *are* working together, they *are* exchanging information and analyses,
they *are* running cross-border operations, they *are* advising policy-makers and
politicians. So the more interesting question is: what is actually *happening* when
different intelligence and security actors are working together in different forms
and formats? Can we still understand these practices as the result and implementation of political preferences and policy decisions, as the result of structures and

institutions? Or are we witnessing a rise of practices with their own dynamics, their own language, their own symbols and their own content?

Intelligence assemblages

Acknowledging that institutions and policies cannot be the self-evident conceptual point of departure paves the way for the use of other concepts and theories that could shed light on the practices of internationalization of intelligence. A challenging way of addressing the reality of international and hybrid intelligence cooperation is by looking at it as 'intelligence assemblages', a concept that has also been used to study public–private security cooperation at the national (Schuilenburg 2008) and international level (Abrahamsen and Williams 2009), and surveillance practices (Haggerty and Ericson 2000). The concept of (intelligence) assemblages introduces a 'radical notion of multiplicity into phenomena which we traditionally approach as being discretely bounded, structured and stable' (Haggerty and Ericson 2000: 608). 'Assemblages' consist of a 'multiplicity of heterogeneous objects, whose unity comes solely from the fact that these items function together, that they "work" together as a functional entity' (Patton 1994: 158). The concept of assemblages refers therefore to self-organizing processes from below, from the bottom up. The concept of intelligence assemblages assumes that when different public, private, national and international actors work together, they produce a new reality, a new order, and give new meanings to this order. It also assumes that these new practices can no longer be understood or conceptualized by just looking at the parts from which they were initially constructed.

The emerging hybrid intelligence and security practices can be looked at in the same way. We should no longer try to understand and analyse these practices by referring to the different parts and the logic embedded in them, but understand them as something new: fluid and hybrid intelligence assemblages that produce order and meaning through self-organizing processes. These can no longer be understood or appreciated by only looking at the policies, interests, cultures, powers or motives that set them in place. An assemblage has its own dynamic, it is a self-organizing activity that cannot be reduced to its elements; its essence lies instead in the relationships between the elements that make up the assemblage. The concept of assemblages may therefore be understood as a radicalization of the notion of nodal governance. Not only is the state-centric view contested (as with the concept of nodal governance), but the different nodes – be it public or private or hybrid, be it national or international – are partly dissolved into a new reality, the essence of which cannot be analysed by only looking at its origins.

The notion of assemblages gives conceptual manoeuvrability to focus analyses of international intelligence and security cooperation on what exactly is happening inside these assemblages. This can examine the role security entrepreneurs play inside networks, or the importance of informal rules and cultures. Of course, it is a little bit tricky to use insights from network theory to analyse assemblages. Adherents of these theoretical strands will argue (correctly) that this comes close to comparing apples and oranges. Yet, as stated at the beginning of this chapter, this is a deliberate 'picking and mixing' from different theoretical and conceptual strands to offer new perspectives on European intelligence cooperation. We do not pretend to offer a hermetically sealed theory as the be-all and end-all of international intelligence cooperation.

Following Charles Tilly (1998: 456), networks are taken to be a 'continuing series of transactions to which participants attach shared understandings, memories, forecasts, rights, and obligations'. Within networks, a special role is reserved for what Bardach (1998: 29) has labelled the 'smart practices of creative craftsmen'. Creative craftsmen are characterized by two elements: creativity combined with public spiritedness. Bardach described the work of creative craftsmen as 'a polyglot crew of labourers constructing a house out of mis-shapen, fragile, and costly lumber on a muddy hillside swept by periodic storms' (1998: 29). Within formal European intelligence cooperation, William Shapcott, director of the European Joint Situation Centre (SitCen) from 2001 to 2010, may be seen as such a craftsman. Acknowledging that formal[2] multilateral intelligence cooperation is restrained by national agencies unsure how to transcend national borders while still serving national interests, Shapcott deliberately chose to let SitCen develop itself organically; that is, driven from below as a self-organizing entity aware of its limitations.[3] 'Sharing of intelligence in a multinational environment is something which you probably had to let come to you rather than go out and promote' was how Shapcott himself described it (House of Lords 2005: 54). He therefore rejected setting up formal information exchange mechanisms as was suggested by EU officials, and waited until agencies from the member states indicated that they wanted to start sharing sensitive information. It was only then that the 'empty shell' of SitCen was given an intelligence assessment function (House of Lords 2005: 54). SitCen therefore deliberately operated for years without any 'major policy documents or any major fanfare' in order to facilitate incremental and modestly pragmatic cooperation (House of Lords 2005: 56).

The figure of the creative craftsman resembles what others have called 'political entrepreneurs'. Political entrepreneurs, although constrained by structures, are capable of remaking and transforming structures, contesting norms, shifting identities and creating space for significant political change (Goddard 2009: 249). It is this process of building, integrating and destroying ties that lies at the heart of entrepreneurship. Switching processes alters network structures, leaving actors with a fundamentally different set of network ties and a changed set of issues, institutions and other actors involved in a political system (Goddard 2009: 250). In doing so, they create a whole new system of meaning that ties the functioning of disparate institutions together.

Entrepreneurs also alter ideas and identities; they can introduce norms that not only change behaviour but reconstitute identities and mobilize them across state boundaries (Adamson 2005). This is of course of special relevance for the study of international intelligence cooperation. Director Shapcott of SitCen, for instance, chose to combine the position of (national) intelligence specialist with that of intelligence liaison officer for his personnel. In this way each intelligence officer's input was guaranteed while at the same time national agency suspicions about what exactly was going on inside SitCen were overcome. By further identifying these specialists as 'seconded national experts' instead of appointing them as EU officials, the risk of these officers 'going native' – choosing EU institutions and interests above national interests – was mitigated. In so doing, a delicate balance between national and European interests was ensured, giving space for the important but difficult task of developing a 'culture' or 'identity' of formal European intelligence cooperation from the bottom up. Another example of this balancing act is the way in which SitCen treated the information it received from national agencies. This information, once received and assessed by SitCen, formally qualified as 'EU information' and could therefore be subject to EU policies giving member states equivalent right of access to each other's information. By maintaining the principle of originator control, SitCen could guarantee that no documents would be passed on without the permission of the member states that had contributed the information (House of Lords 2005: 57).

Network theory also offers opportunities to look into the hybridization of intelligence and security, as entrepreneurs have the ability to bridge cultural fragmentation by speaking 'multivocally' across networks (Padgett and Ansell 1993: 1263). Entrepreneurs can use language that may be interpreted coherently from multiple perspectives simultaneously. Because listeners occupy different structural positions, they interpret a broker's ideas through divergent cultural lenses and histories. As a result, any symbol, word or event can be read with contradictory, even mutually exclusive meanings. Entrepreneurs thrive on multivocal language: the more multivocal the entrepreneur's ideas, the more likely it is that they will be accepted and adopted across fragmented networks (Goddard 2009: 266). Within the European Union, for instance, a formal and institutionalized distinction between internal security and external security exists. The intelligence and security agencies of the member states put forward the idea that this distinction was artificial and counterproductive. Members of the Club de Berne, the informal cooperation mechanism of both intelligence and security services, therefore established the Counterterrorism Group (CTG) that levelled this 'artificial' distinction. There was however no institutional connection between the CTG and the EU. SitCen realized the importance of connecting with CTG, but from the perspective of diplomats and constitutional lawyers this was something close to an institutional nightmare. By constantly invoking the need for a 'comprehensive approach to terrorism' and arguing in policy and strategy papers for a 'global approach', SitCen slowly developed a reasonable discourse acceptable to actors responsible for both internal and external security.[4] This resulted in the acceptance of a small presence of CTG within SitCen, enabling the fusion of inputs from internal and external services (House of Lords 2005: 54–55).

To be sure, the altering of ideas, identities, cultures and even structures or institutions is not something that can simply be understood as the conscious result of strategies deployed by entrepreneurs to achieve a set of predefined goals. Just as the concept of assemblages prioritizes the inherently open and fluid multiplicity whose unity comes solely from the fact that these items function together, so network theorists underline that ideas that are introduced in networks often resonate in unpredictable ways. By deploying inventive ideas, entrepreneurs can produce autonomous and unanticipated structural effects in networks (Goddard 2009: 268). Helmke and Levitsky (2004: 725), in studying the role of informal rules, also underline that the 'rules of the game' which structure political life are informal, in that they are created, communicated and enforced outside of officially sanctioned channels. Informal rules and informal structures therefore shape the performance of formal institutions in important and often unexpected ways.

The logic of practicality

These reflections on the unpredictability of change and the essential non-functionalist character of assemblages offer a link to a final concept useful for analysing international intelligence and security cooperation: the 'logic of practicality'. This emphasizes the importance of common sense and practical knowledge in the daily business of actors operating in the international theatre. Practice theory tries to do justice to the practical nature of action by rooting human activity in a way that is not being reduced or explained a priori by concepts or theories. It does so by bringing background knowledge to the foreground of analysis (Pouliot 2008: 258). It recognizes that the work of intelligence and security professionals is an art and not a science. Whereas the scientific observer is inclined to interpret actions as the result of rational calculus, rules-driven behaviour or the result of policy preferences articulated at the political-administrative level, in actuality the same actions can derive from practical hunches acted upon under time pressure. 'One cannot reduce practice to the execution of a theoretical model.... Practice is what makes social reality possible in the first place' (Pouliot 2008: 261, 264). Using Scott's conceptualization of *mètis* (Scott 1998),[5] Pouliot points at the importance of local and contextual practical knowledge that can only be acquired through practices and cannot be centralized in a core doctrine or translated into deductive and abstract models. As practical knowledge it is learnt in and through practice, located within practices instead of behind them. It is in a way 'thoughtless', representing what others call common sense, experience, intuition, skill or craft (Pouliot 2008: 271).

Although Pouliot uses practicality in the context of international diplomacy, it seems to fit nicely into the world of international intelligence as well. In the 'habitus' of international intelligence, actors are informed by individual and collective historical trajectories (dispositions) that actualize the past in the present and that are made up of inarticulate, practical knowledge learned by doing (see Bourdieu 1990; Bourdieu and Wacquant 1992). Habitus is a grammar that provides a basis for the generation of practices related to a social configuration, or a field that is structured along relations of power, objects of struggle and taken-for-granted rules. The logic of practicality seems of importance for researching and analysing the internationalization of intelligence, because it reflects the practical modus operandi that thrives in security communities. The politics of intelligence is a practical one, with a 'pay as you go' culture in which the main producers will not relinquish their accustomed dominance to new multilateral organizations set up by the EU or anyone else (Aldrich 2004: 733). Pouliot points, for instance, at the key role 'trust' plays in security communities: 'a perfect example of an inarticulate feeling derived from practical sense... or informed by the logic of practicality' (Pouliot 2008: 279).

This chapter therefore proposes a more grounded approach to the study of European intelligence cooperation, or the internationalization of intelligence, informed but not determined by different theoretical and conceptual insights from different academic disciplines. The starting point is that the internationalization and hybridization of intelligence and security have initiated practices that fruitfully may be conceptualized as intelligence assemblages. These assemblages and especially their 'working' cannot be primarily understood as the conscious and rational result of political-administrative decision-making, institutional changes or policies (although institutions and policies of course have their effect on these practices).

It is also proposed that it is important to look closer at the role which intelligence entrepreneurs play inside these assemblages, and their potential to influence or change practices, cultures, discourses, operations, policies and even institutions. SitCen, administratively located in the Secretariat-General of the EU Council, was from the beginning careful not to become a formal part of the second pillar of the EU (external security) because the importance of working cross-pillar was understood. This fragmentation into different pillars, with their own powers, interests and cultures, in an important way determines the dynamics of the EU as a whole. SitCen noticed that the Ministers of Justice and Home Affairs (JHA, the third pillar) regarded it as something from the second pillar, covering foreign and security policy. As a result, SitCen devoted considerable time to persuading the JHA ministers that it also wanted to work for them, and that the JHA ministers should be co-owners of the project. Thanks to these efforts SitCen was capable of bridging the classical division between the pillars and was welcomed at JHA meetings. This was quite uncommon within the EU. In the words of Shapcott himself: 'I now go to a host of JHA committee meetings which I would never have dreamt of a long time ago' (House of Lords 2005: 60–61).

The entrepreneurs and the assemblages they are embedded in are guided and informed mostly by the logic of practicality, instead of the rules, norms, cultures and policy preferences from which they were initially constructed. In these assemblages different 'practicalities', informed by their public or private, national or international, and formal or informal habitus, collide with each other and merge into new, unforeseen logics of practicality. In particular, the domain of intelligence, characterized by informality, craftsmanship, creativity, discretion and unorthodoxy, seems pre-eminently suitable for approaches that make use of the logic of practicality. To clarify: if we take the logic of practicality seriously, we have to give more weight to what is happening in assemblages in order to understand the internationalization of intelligence rather than continue relying on approaches that centre around institutions, treaties, policy-makers and policies. The best way to appreciate possible futures for (European) intelligence and security cooperation is to look at the practices, order and meaning that are constructed from below by different intelligence assemblages. The developmental trajectory of SitCen illustrates this perfectly.

Obstacles

Various obstacles stand in the way of this approach. First, there is a scientific obstacle. As Pouliot (2008: 260–261) states, the 'godlike posture of modern science' has triumphed over practical knowledge, emphasizing formal and abstract representations of the world. This 'ethnocentrism of the scientist' (Bourdieu and Wacquant 1992: 69) replaces the practical relation to the world with the observer's theoretical relation to practice. The dominance in modern science of quantitative research, statistical causality, model building, generalization and abstract theorizing 'from above' ensures that a turn towards 'practice' will not be without controversy.

Second, an obstacle can be situated at the normative level. The centrality of state institutions, politics and the political-administrative level in most analyses of the internationalization of intelligence is closely linked to normative assumptions about the primacy of politics, the rule of law, and good-governance issues like transparency and accountability. Researchers may feel that international intelligence relations should be approached primarily from that perspective. Without denying the enormous importance of these issues, it is argued here that it cannot be a sound argument to approach developments from the perspective of how they *should* be, rather than how they *are* in practice. For instance, if we look at issues of accountability and transparency, there seems to be a general agreement among scholars that the internationalization of intelligence will irrevocably lead to major problems (Svendsen 2009: 703). Existing mechanisms of accountability and transparency are insufficient in coping with the internationalization of intelligence (see e.g. Born 2007). Insisting on accountability and oversight mechanisms that are closely tied to formal national or European structures only means that too much energy is spent on strengthening the door of a stable from which the horses have long since bolted (Loader 2002: 296). Therefore it may be more fruitful to divert attention to different kinds of nodal accountability, no matter how diffuse these nodes currently are. For instance, Richard Aldrich, while acknowledging that intelligence agencies have been cast in the unwelcome role of the 'toilet cleaners of globalization' which can therefore never be 'soft enough to please the human rights lawyers', also points at an emerging informal counter-surveillance network of activists and pressure groups and an emerging culture of 'regulation by revelation' (Aldrich 2009: 29, 36, 53–55). He expects that global civil society, including journalists and human rights watchers, will play an increasing role in informal oversight and accountability.

Second, it is important to look more closely into the forms of accountability, transparency and ethics that originate from intelligence assemblages. Much of the literature on accountability and transparency seems to assume that practitioners in the field are more prone to cowboy-like behaviour and to going rogue than those at the political-administrative level. This seems to be a biased view. To give one example, operatives from the Dutch intelligence and security service exercised restraint in exchanging information with their counterparts in Portugal during the 1960s and 1970s when they became aware that Marxists mentioned in their security reports were being executed by the Portuguese regime by literally throwing them off cliffs into the sea. Some Dutch security officers therefore refused to provide information on critics of the Salazar regime who were resident in the Netherlands, so long as there was no guarantee that this information would never be transmitted to the Portuguese service (Hoekstra 2004: 41–42, 53–54). Apart from restraint exercised by intelligence practitioners themselves, however, it is noteworthy that recent scandals, notably the practices of rendition, torture and other violations of basic civil and human rights by the US, were initiated, directed and approved at the highest political levels (see e.g. Human Rights Watch 2010). It would give a false impression of events to suggest that the moral high ground in intelligence is exclusively populated by politicians and policy-makers. It is the opinion here that all actors engaged in hybrid intelligence and security practices should be made aware of the ethical issues involved, including – or especially – those at the highest political levels.

Third, there is of course a huge practical problem in researching intelligence cooperation from a grounded approach. Research into intelligence and security is an inherently difficult enterprise given the extreme levels of secrecy that, out of dire necessity, political expediency, power games, or by default, are the rule inside the intelligence community. No easy solutions are available to solve this problem. It calls for courage from both the academic world as well as the intelligence community to make such solutions possible. Historical studies into practices of international and hybrid intelligence and security cooperation are a logical point of departure for further research. The approach proposed here is not without its difficulties, but it nevertheless offers an improvement on more established models. At a time when different institutions are wrestling with their role, function and legitimacy in a new, hybrid, horizontal or 'flattened' world, practitioners are dealing with it on a daily basis. They cannot simply wait for the political level to come up with some magic formula to reconnect the vertical, compartmentalized world of politics with the horizontal and hybrid world of practices. Solutions, innovations, ideas and practices from below produce order and meaning through self-organizing processes originating from assemblages. If we really want to understand the internationalization and hybridization of intelligence and want to see a glimpse of the future, assemblages are the locations we should have a closer look at in the present.

Notes

1 The author would like to thank Peter Keller for his commentary and assistance in understanding and illustrating practices of European intelligence cooperation.
2 Informal cooperation between national intelligence and security services is the favoured model. This is form-free cooperation in which national interests and cultures prevail and some of the characteristics of intelligence cooperation – third-party rule, confidentiality – are being guaranteed. For the same reason, bilateral cooperation occurs more often than multilateral cooperation. An example of informal multilateral intelligence cooperation is the Club de Berne in which most European agencies cooperate.
3 Modesty seems to be an underestimated value in international cooperation. Newly established EU agencies show a tendency to overstrain their voices in underlining their importance, thereby only provoking resistance from the national agencies they have to work with. This was one of the problems Europol faced, as its officials later admitted (van Buuren and van der Schans 2003: 81, 109).
4 Between 1993 and 2009 internal security was the 'third pillar', Justice and Home Affairs (later Police and Judicial Cooperation in Criminal Matters), while external security was the 'second pillar', Common Foreign and Security Policy.
5 By *mètis* Scott refers to 'a rudimentary kind of knowledge that can be acquired only by practice and that all but defies being communicated in written or oral form apart from actual practice' (Scott 1998: 315).

Bibliography

Abrahamsen, R. and M.C. Williams (2009) 'Security Beyond the State: Global Security Assemblages in International Politics', *International Political Sociology*, 1: 1–17.
Adamson, F.B. (2005) 'Globalisation, Transnational Political Mobilisation, and Networks of Violence', *Cambridge Journal of International Affairs*, 18: 31–49.
Agrell, W. (2006) 'Sweden and the Dilemmas of Neutral Intelligence Liaison', *Journal of Strategic Studies*, 29: 633–651.
Aldrich, R.J. (2004) 'Transatlantic Intelligence and Security Cooperation', *International Affairs*, 80: 731–753.
—— (2009) 'Global Intelligence Co-operation versus Accountability: New Facets to an Old Problem', *Intelligence and National Security*, 24: 26–56.
Arthur, H.S. (1996) 'The Uneasy Relationship between Intelligence and Private Industry', *International Journal of Intelligence and CounterIntelligence*, 9: 17–31.
Bardach, E. (1998) *Getting Agencies to Work Together. The Practice and Theory of Managerial Craftmanship*, Washington, DC: Brookings Institution Press.
Bendiek, A. (2006) *EU Strategy on Counter-terrorism. Steps towards a Coherent Network Policy*, SWP Research Paper, Berlin: SWP.
Block, L. (2010) 'Bilateral Police Liaison Officers: Practices and European Policy', *Journal of Contemporary European Research*, 6: 194–210.
Boer, M. den (2006) 'Fusing the Fragments. Challenges for EU Internal Security Governance on Terrorism', in D. Mahncke and J. Monar (eds), *International Terrorism. A European Response to a Global Threat?*, College of Europe Studies No. 3, Brussels: Peter Lang, pp. 83–111.
Boer, M. den, C. Hillebrand and A. Nölke (2008) 'Legitimacy under Pressure: The European Web of Counter-terrorism Networks', *Journal of Common Market Studies*, 46: 101–124.
Born, H. (2007) *International Intelligence Cooperation: The Need for Networking Accountability*, NATO Parliamentary Assembly, Reykjavik, 6 October.

Bossong, R. (2008) *The EU's Mature Counterterrorism Policy – A Critical Historical and Functional Assessment*, LSE Challenge Working Paper.

Bourdieu, P. (1990) *The Logic of Practice*, Stanford, CA: Stanford University Press.

Bourdieu, P. and L.J.D. Wacquant (1992) 'The Purpose of Reflexive Sociology', in P. Bourdieu and L.J.D. Wacquant (eds), *An Invitation to Reflexive Sociology*. Chicago, IL: University of Chicago Press, pp. 61–215.

Burgess, J.P. (2009) 'Cooperation and Conflict. There is No European Security, Only European Securities', *Cooperation and Conflict: Journal of the Nordic International Studies Association*, 44: 309–328.

Buuren, J. van (2009) *Secret Truth. The EU Joint Situation Centre*, Amsterdam: Euro-watch. Online. Available: www.statewatch.org/news/2009/aug/SitCen2009.pdf (accessed on 11 February 2013).

—— (2010) 'Private Security Ethics. Reintroducing Public Values', in M. den Boer and E. Kolthoff (eds), *Security Ethics*, The Hague: Eleven International Publishing, pp. 165–188.

Buuren, J. van and W. van der Schans (2003) *Keizer in Lompen. Politiesamenwerking in Europa*, Breda: Papieren Tijger.

Fägersten, B. (2010) 'Bureaucratic Resistance to International Intelligence Cooperation – The Case of Europol', *Intelligence and National Security*, 25: 500–520.

Goddard, S.E. (2009) 'Brokering change: networks and entrepreneurs in international politics', *International Theory*, 1: 249–281.

Goetz, K.H. (2008) 'Governance as a Path to Government', *West European Politics*, 31: 258–279.

Haggerty, K.D. and R.V. Ericson (2000) 'The Surveillant Assemblage', *British Journal of Sociology*, 51: 605–622.

Hawkins, K. (1984) *Environment and Enforcement: Regulation and the Social Definition of Pollution*, Oxford: Clarendon Press.

Helmke, G. and S. Levitsky (2004) 'Informal Institutions and Comparative Politics: A Research Agenda', *Perspectives on Politics*, 2: 725–740.

Hoekstra, F. (2004) *In dienst van de BVD. Spionage en contraspionage in Nederland*, Amsterdam: Boom.

Hoogenboom, B. (2006) 'Grey Intelligence', *Crime, Law and Social Change*, 4: 373–381.

House of Lords (2005) *After Madrid: The EU's Response to Terrorism. Report with Evidence*, London: Stationery Office.

Human Rights Watch (2010) *'No Questions Asked'. Intelligence Cooperation with Countries that Torture*, New York: Human Rights Watch.

Johnston, L. and C. Shearing (2003) *Governing Security. Explorations in Policing and Justice*, London: Routledge.

Kaunert, C. (2010) 'The External Dimension of EU Counter-terrorism Relations: Competences, Interests, and Institutions', *Terrorism and Political Violence*, 22: 41–61.

Loader, I. (2000) 'Plural Policing and Democratic Governance', *Social and Legal Studies*, 9: 323–345.

—— (2002) 'Governing European Policing: Some Problems and Prospects', *Policing and Society*, 12: 291–305.

Monar, J. (2007) 'Common Threat and Common Response? The European Union's Counter-terrorism Strategy and its Problems', *Government and Opposition*, 42: 292–313.

Müller-Wille, B. (2002) 'EU Intelligence Co-operation. A Critical Analysis', *Contemporary Security Policy*, 23: 61–86.

Neocleous, M. (2007) 'Security, Commodity, Fetishism', *Critique*, 35: 339–355.

Padgett, J.F. and C.K. Ansell (1993) 'Robust Action and the Rise of the Medici, 1400–1434', *The American Journal of Sociology*, 98: 1259–1319.

Patton, P. (1994) 'MetamorphoLogic: Bodies and Powers in A Thousand Plateaus', *Journal of the British Society for Phenomenology*, 25: 157–169.

Pouliot, V. (2008) 'The Logic of Practicality: A Theory of Practice of Security Communities', *International Organization*, 62: 257–288.

Schatzki, T.R., K.K. Cetina and E. von Savigny (2001) *The Practice Turn in Contemporary Theory*, New York: Routledge.

Schuilenburg, M (2008) 'The Dislocating Perspective of Assemblages. Another Look at the Issue of Security', *Open*, 15.

Scott, J.C. (1998) *Seeing Like a State: How Certain Schemes to Improve the Human Condition Have Failed*, New Haven, CT: Yale University Press.

Shearing, C. and J. Wood (2003) 'Nodal Governance, Democracy, and the New Denizens', *Journal of Law and Society*, 30: 400–419.

Sims, J.E. (2006) 'Foreign Intelligence Liaison: Devils, Deals, and Details', *International Journal of Intelligence and CounterIntelligence*, 19: 195–217.

Svendsen, A.D.M. (2008) 'The Globalization of Intelligence Since 9/11: The Optimization of Intelligence Liaison Arrangements', *International Journal of Intelligence and CounterIntelligence*, 21: 661–678.

—— (2009) 'Connecting Intelligence and Theory: Intelligence Liaison and International Relations', *Intelligence and National Security*, 24: 700–729.

Tilly, C. (1998) 'Contentious Conversation', *Social Research*, 653: 491–510.

Voelz, G.J. (2009) 'Contractors and Intelligence: The Private Sector in the Intelligence Community', *International Journal of Intelligence and CounterIntelligence*, 22: 586–613.

Wood, J. and C. Shearing (2006) 'Security and Nodal Governance', paper prepared for seminar at the Temple University Beasley School of Law, Philadelphia, PA, 25 October.

—— (2007) *Imagining Security*, Uffculme: Willan Publishing.

Zimmermann, D. (2006) 'The European Union and Post-9/11 Counterterrorism: A Reappraisal', *Studies in Conflict and Terrorism*, 29: 123–145.

8   European intelligence cooperation

Björn Fägersten

Introduction

The notion of European intelligence cooperation may sound highly improbable. The general difficulties with multilateral intelligence cooperation have been thoroughly covered in the literature (Lefebvre 2003; Clough 2004; Sims 2006; Walsh 2007). Furthermore, why would European governments that have been fighting hard for their fiscal sovereignty be willing to cede it in the security area by coordinating the work of their national security services? On the other hand, the increasing number of transnational risks resulting from our ever more inter-connected societies demand effective international collaboration. Only by sharing information and resources – or producing them collectively – can complex security threats be successfully forecast, analysed and managed. From this perspective, European intelligence cooperation becomes a natural extension of the already high levels of interconnectedness that characterize European states following decades of regional integration. As the former head of the European Union's Center for Intelligence Analysis argues:

> It is perhaps no surprise that the EU, with its relatively small membership and the breadth and depth of its competencies and interrelationships, has made more progress in building an assessment and warning structure than NATO and the UN.
>
> (Shapcott 2011: 126)

This chapter maps current European intelligence cooperation in various fields and analyses its background and challenges. The first section provides an empirical overview of current European arrangements for intelligence cooperation, taking into account the changes brought about within the EU by the Lisbon Treaty.[1] Section two analyses the development of cooperation and how it functions. Finally, section three discusses some of the broader implications arising from European intelligence cooperation, such as what intelligence scholars can learn from it and how it is likely to develop in the future.

Intelligence cooperation in Europe: an overview

This section outlines some of the key arrangements for intelligence cooperation and their role in the European 'intelligence system'. The overview is organized according to the main functions these arrangements are intended to fulfil: supporting law enforcement, informing foreign and security policy, and 'societal protection'.[2]

Intelligence cooperation in support of law enforcement

Police and judicial cooperation has a long pedigree in the affairs of the European Union. Nonetheless, law enforcement is a prerogative of the member states, so that increases in competences at the EU level are only meant to assist member states in their work. Prior to the Maastricht Treaty of 1991, cooperation on these matters was loosely coordinated within the Trevi network (Terrorisme, Radicalisme, Extrémisme et Violence Internationale) (Peek 1994; Occhipinti 2003), in which officials from (mainly) the Ministries of Justice or the Interior of all member states met on a regular basis to further cooperation and information sharing. Under the Maastricht Treaty, Justice and Home Affairs became a policy area of the European Union and the various Trevi working groups where formalized within the EU system.

Without doubt the most prominent arrangement for intelligence cooperation in the law enforcement area is the European Police Office (Europol), tasked with fighting all forms of serious international crime and terrorism. Europol is an official EU agency with three main tasks: acting as a clearing house where member states can exchange information; providing member states with operational and strategic intelligence analysis on criminal activities and trends; and assisting member states in their operational law enforcement work. Information exchange takes place within the Secure Information Exchange Network Application (SIENA), a tool that enables the secure transfer of information between member states, Europol and third parties. The analytical work that takes place at Europol is largely based on its working files, where intelligence on a given topic is assembled from different sources. In order to carry out its tasks, Europol has over 700 personnel and more than 130 liaison officers seconded to its headquarters in The Hague. Liaison officers come from the EU member states as well as partner countries which participate in some of Europol's work. Europol has steadily improved its reputation as a valuable partner for the EU member states. Success has probably been most obvious in areas that do not critically impinge upon member states' authority (cyber crime, money laundering, trafficking in drugs and humans) while the agency has had more of a struggle to establish itself in sensitive areas such as counter-terrorism. In the case of the latter, Europol has also been obstructed by national intelligence services which prefer their own channels of communication and so have been reluctant to supply the necessary intelligence, despite strong political pressure for them to do so (Europol 2002; European Commission 2004a; RAND Europe 2012).

Other forums within the law enforcement field with some relevance to intelligence exchange and collection include the European Union's Judicial Cooperation Unit (Eurojust) and the border management agency Frontex. Eurojust works closely with Europol, and coordinates and assists the work of national magistrates and prosecutors. As such, it is mainly an information end-user, but also to some extent a facilitator of information exchange in the area of criminal intelligence. Frontex is the common European response to the EU's almost total abolition of internal borders, which calls for a more coordinated approach to the common European border. In its work to coordinate member states' operational cooperation along the EU's external borders, Frontex functions as both a consumer and a producer of intelligence and its analysis. Frontex collates data from border authorities inside and outside the EU, other EU agencies and institutions, international organizations and open sources. Based on the analysis of this information, the agency produces annual and biannual risk assessments as well as tailored reports, for example, on joint border operations carried out by member states (Laitinen 2008).

In addition to the cooperative forums discussed above, the EU has technical and legal mechanisms in place for the more or less automatic transfer of information among different users. Although not forums for intelligence cooperation per se, these arrangements greatly facilitate the transfer of what David Omand calls PROTINT (protected personal information held by commercial entities and governments) between European agencies and beyond.[3] One example is the Schengen Information System (SIS), a common database where national agencies can file alerts for wanted or missing persons, as well as details of entry bans or stolen property. This information is then instantly available to law enforcement and customs personnel in all the participating countries. Although the information that can be stored on any individual is quite restricted, additional information may be exchanged using the Supplementary Information Request at the National Entry (SIRENE) system, which has bureaux in each member state. SIS/SIRENE is for public authorities only, but other information systems connect commercial actors with national and EU agencies. Examples include the EU data retention directive, which requires the providers of public communication systems to store data on traffic, locations and subscribers for at least six months, and the EU–US Society for Worldwide Interbank Financial Transfers (SWIFT) and Passenger Name Record (PNR) agreements, which regulate how data on financial transactions and air passengers can be transmitted to authorities in the United States (European Commission 2010).

Intelligence cooperation in support of foreign and security policy

One of the main ambitions behind the Lisbon Treaty is to streamline and strengthen the EU's foreign and security policy. Although territorial defence is still the responsibility of the member states, the EU has launched more than twenty civil and military missions under the auspices of the Common Foreign and Security Policy (CFSP) in the past ten years. These missions range from peace enforcement in the Democratic Republic of the Congo to police training in Afghanistan and state-building in the Balkans. Intelligence support for CFSP missions is provided by the European External Action Service (EEAS), the EU's diplomatic corps headed by the High Representative for Foreign Affairs and Security Policy.

The principal node of intelligence relating to foreign affairs is the EU Intelligence Analysis Centre (IntCen, formerly known as SitCen). A staff of around seventy analyse open and secret information received from the following: member states' security and intelligence services; other EU sources, including delegations in third countries; a variety of open sources; and the agency's own 'information officers', who may be overtly deployed to potential crisis areas. Based on this material, IntCen produces annually around 200 situation assessments of a strategic nature as well as around fifty reports tailored to more specific ends. IntCen works closely with the intelligence directorate of the European Union's military staff (IntDir) through the Single Intelligence Analysis Capacity (SIAC). In practice, this means that the two entities coordinate the requests for information (RFI) they send to member state intelligence suppliers and then produce reports by way of joint task forces, most often with IntCen as the lead agency. The internal work of IntCen is divided up between the Analysis Division, which receives intelligence from member states and produces reports, and the General and External Relations Division, which runs administration, communications and open source collection. In addition to its mission to supply the EU foreign policy machinery with early warning and strategic assessments concerning foreign hot spots, IntCen is also charged with analysing the threat of terrorism, both inside and outside Europe (Shapcott 2009; Ashton 2012a, 2012b). The deployment of EU military missions has also increased the demand for intelligence support of a more operational character, a clear deviation from IntCen's main focus on strategic level analysis.

IntDir manages intelligence analysis on military issues. It is run by officers seconded from the EU member states, and feeds defence intelligence to the EEAS. As with IntCen, its analytical work has expanded over time from early warning and situation assessment at the strategic level to include providing more operational-level support to EU missions. The EU's ambition to take a 'comprehensive approach' to managing crises – essentially merging the civilian and military elements of its missions – means that the work of IntDir is conducted in close proximity to that of the civilian analysts at IntCen. At the moment they work closely within the SIAC framework, but discussions are ongoing about how to further synthesize and streamline intelligence support within the EEAS.

Finally, important intelligence support for foreign and security policy is delivered by the EU Satellite Centre (SatCen). As the EU's only agency devoted to intelligence collection, SatCen produces geospatial and imagery intelligence products on behalf of the High Representative and the EEAS. The primary sources of satellite data are commercial providers, but agreements with specific member states allow SatCen some access to national resources as well. Like the agencies described above, SatCen is increasingly being requested to provide intelligence support for EU missions. To that end, the Centre now has a standing operational support function at its headquarters in Torrejon, Spain. In addition to feeding its intelligence products to the EEAS, SatCen is able to support member states, the European Commission, third states and other international organizations.

Intelligence cooperation in support of societal protection

Intelligence cooperation in support of societal protection aims to inform decision-makers about pending security threats and, if necessary, to thwart these threats.[4] At the operational level, the provision of national security is a treaty-based prerogative of the EU member states and societal protection remains solely in their hands (Treaty of European Union 1992). This has not prevented the EU from adopting policies and strategies in order to promote common work in these areas. As a result, national intelligence and security services cooperate within several multilateral venues, to assist individual member states in their operational work and the EU at the policy and strategy levels.

The most developed multilateral cooperation forums in this vein are the Club de Berne and its later offspring, the Counter Terrorist Group (CTG). Established in the early 1970s during the heyday of terrorist organizations of the extreme Left, the Club de Berne brings together European security services for discussion and joint analysis. The agenda is broad and a variety of working groups convene regularly to cover topics such as counter-espionage, the Russian mafia, domestic terrorism and cyber security. While the Club de Berne has been successful in fostering the exchange of information and experience between European security services, it has no official connection to the European Union. Several EU officials have discussed the idea of bringing 'Berne into Brussels', but the member states – and their security services in particular – have so far fiercely and successfully resisted. However, following the terrorist attacks on the United States on 11 September 2001, politicians and practitioners identified a need for increased security service cooperation on counter-terrorism issues that should also feed into the EU system. The result was the CTG, a multilateral arrangement between roughly the same members that make up the Club de Berne but with an exclusive focus on international radical Islamist-inspired terrorism. Although the CTG is officially independent of the EU, it has a presence in Brussels in the form of a team working within IntCen. The CTG's chair is a rotating position where the country that chairs the EU also chairs the CTG. Representatives of the Group regularly brief various EU bodies and agencies. The CTG has proved a valuable venue not only for multilateral work, but also for identifying commonalities of interest among certain member states, thereby boosting bilateral and 'mini-lateral' cooperation.

Also external to the EU are the various mini-lateral groupings of relevance to intelligence cooperation in the internal security sphere. Most notably, the G6 brings together France, Italy, Germany, Poland, Spain and the UK for discussions and information exchange on a variety of internal security topics. The G6 aims to influence internal security policy in the wider EU but also works to boost cooperation and information exchange among its members. There are other regional mini-lateral groups with similar aims, such as the Salzburg group in Central Europe and groups in the Baltic and Balkan regions.

Cooperation on societal protection also takes place within the EU but, as is noted above, such work mainly aims to support the development of policies and strategies rather than operational work. For example, the EU has a Counter-Terrorism Coordinator (CTC) tasked with overseeing the implementation of a counter-terrorism strategy and monitoring the use and development of the EU's counter-terrorism instruments. Initial high expectations that the CTC would be able to coordinate and drive intelligence cooperation, however, have not been met. In the absence of legislative backing, operational responsibility or strong political support, the CTC has not been able to carve out a strong role in EU counter-terrorism activity and the intelligence work that supports it (Argomaniz and Rees 2012). Finally, the EU has several working groups with some relevance to counter-terrorism policy but less so for intelligence cooperation.[5]

The elephants in the room? Bilateral and transatlantic intelligence cooperation

So far, this overview of intelligence cooperation has covered more or less formalized multilateral cooperation inside and outside the European Union. Obviously, such arrangements and the activities they foster cover only part of the cooperative efforts among Europe's security and intelligence services. The bulk of cooperation, at least from an operational perspective, takes place at the bilateral level. In Europe, bilateral intelligence cooperation is most highly developed between those countries with extensive intelligence capacities. Smaller countries with niche capacities can also be active participants in the high-level bartering that characterizes bilateral intelligence exchange, Sweden's role during the Cold War as a collector and provider of intelligence on the Soviet Union being a case in point (Agrell 2006). Intelligence cooperation is also well developed among states that for historical and geographical reasons enjoy high levels of shared security interests, such as those in the Nordic region.

Bilateral cooperation between European states and non-European partners is mainly geared in two directions, neither of which is particularly symmetric. First, many European countries cooperate extensively with various US intelligence agencies. While the exact nature and depth of such cooperation are difficult to gauge, headlines from recent years offer some pointers. The abduction of Hassan Mustafa Osama Nasr (also known as Abu Omar) from the streets of Milan in 2003 illustrates the practice of CIA-orchestrated renditions, where terrorist suspects are flown to third countries for interrogation. Twenty-three US citizens – most either current or former CIA employees – were subsequently convicted in Italy after being tried in absentia, but the extent of the enabling role played by Italian military intelligence remains unclear.[6] Even more controversial from the perspective of host countries are the secret detention centres that the

CIA supposedly maintained in Europe. Lithuania, Romania and Poland are named in a recent report by the European Parliament, but as many as twelve European states are believed to have been involved in secret CIA programmes (European Parliament 2012). In a more recent example of close bilateral intelligence ties, extensive US surveillance programmes – with varying degrees of host country participation – have been revealed in the Nordic countries.[7] In addition to the cooperation arrangements that have come to light due to controversy over their questionable legality, others have been revealed because of the results they produced. Most attention has been given to the close intelligence cooperation in the field of counter-terrorism, where intra-European and transatlantic cooperation has led to notable successes in recent years.

In general, the dense mesh of bilateral relations that was strengthened following the 9/11 terrorist attacks illustrates the asymmetry of transatlantic intelligence cooperation. Pressed by the US, individual European countries had little chance of resisting calls for intensified cooperation in the 'War on Terror'. Indeed, the development of the CTG, as discussed above, was partly motivated by the urge to gain an autonomous European capacity to perform terrorism risk assessments in the light of tough US pressure to engage in the fight against international terrorism.[8] The decade following the 9/11 attacks also saw many European intelligence and security services establish cooperation with agencies in the Middle East and North Africa (MENA) region. Usually, the relationship is between a Western intelligence agency and a partner agency focused on internal security in one of the countries in those regions.[9] The main objective, at least in the post-9/11 era, has been to help Western governments keep track of potentially dangerous foreign extremists, and/or of citizens from European countries travelling to the region to receive training and guidance. Such cooperation obviously poses great challenges due to different viewpoints on matters such as the rule of law and human rights. At the same time, it is important not to forget that the sometimes lax regulations on interrogation methods have in some instances been the very reason for the cooperation on the part of Western intelligence services. It became clear following the Arab Spring that intelligence cooperation with authoritarian regimes in the MENA region often has its downside, especially when it becomes public. Not only can it provoke criticism from Western advocates of human rights, but it can also nurture popular disdain from within the region should the authoritarian regimes fall. British–Libyan intelligence cooperation, which was exposed following the ousting of Muammar Gaddafi, is a case in point.[10]

Finally, European intelligence cooperation on a variety of issues takes place within the North Atlantic Treaty Organization (NATO). NATO promotes and hosts arrangements for intelligence cooperation in various fields. The Civilian Intelligence Committee (CIC) – formerly known as the Special Committee – brings together NATO member states' heads of security services and civilian intelligence agencies for discussions on threats to the security of the Organization and its member states, such as terrorism and foreign espionage. As NATO has broadened its scope from territorial defence to global crisis management, the

CIC has adapted its work accordingly. However, leaked reports suggest that its member states differ over whether the CIC should or is competent to cover threats relating to out-of-area operations, such as those in Afghanistan.[11] The Committee has a rotating presidency, a formula which provoked some controversy when in 2008 Hungary appointed a KGB-trained officer to chair the meetings.[12] Another important NATO body is the Intelligence Unit (IU), which brings together mostly civilian staff from the member states to perform strategic intelligence analysis on behalf of the Atlantic Council. The IU, which focuses on a variety of transnational threats such as proliferation, state instability and terrorism, works in close cooperation with the military intelligence branch of NATO – the Intelligence Division of the International Military Staff. Other arrangements, such as the Intelligence Liaison Unit at NATO headquarters in Brussels and the Intelligence Liaison Cell at NATO's military headquarters in Mons, are geared towards cooperation and liaison with external partners and organizations. In order to coordinate this diverse intelligence landscape, an Intelligence Steering Board is tasked with overseeing and developing NATO strategic intelligence requirements.[13]

In general, NATO, at least at the strategic level, has had similar intelligence issues to resolve as the EU: how to increase cooperation and information sharing in a multilateral environment that is considered prone to leaks, how to align member state preferences on which topics need consideration and analysis, and, perhaps most importantly, how to integrate the work of different organizational entities such as the security services, the civilian intelligence agencies and the defence intelligence organizations. Unlike the EU, however, NATO has a member state – the US – that in theory can, and to some extent does, supply most of the intelligence within the organization. There is also a well-established hierarchy in which NATO members of the 'Five Eyes' (UK, US, Canada, New Zealand and Australia) share intelligence far more readily among themselves than with other NATO member states (Richelson and Ball 1985; Sloan 2012).

Explaining cooperation

The above section provides an overview of current multilateral intelligence cooperation in Europe. It also discusses parallel and to some extent competing arrangements – for example, bilateral and transatlantic cooperation – that are relevant for gaining an overall understanding of the frameworks involved. While much cooperation evidently takes place on a bilateral basis, the rapid development of multilateral arrangements for cooperation has been striking. This section addresses this puzzle. How can we explain the development of multilateral cooperation in an area that is at the heart of national sovereignty?

As a basis for analysing intelligence cooperation, the vast majority of state interests at play may be summarized as involving a simple trade-off: achieving intelligence and policy gains while minimizing the costs in terms of loss of autonomy and increased vulnerability (Fägersten 2010a). Intelligence gains are the intelligence-related benefits of cooperation. They include access to currently unavailable sources, methods, technologies and information. Policy gains relate to the political motives for cooperation, such as the granting of legitimacy to an actor or organization, the strengthening of political relationships or – in cases where cooperation is publicized – the need to display commitment in the eyes of the public. In their aim to maximize any combination of these gains through intelligence cooperation, however, states are held back by issues of cost as well as risk. The main cost arises when states accept any development that curtails their authority, either in their internal or external affairs. This includes, for example, being dependent on external sources of information in order to be able to make decisions, or being drawn into intelligence operations by alliance commitments. The main risk of intelligence cooperation is linked to the possible disclosure of a country's methods and sources, or the defection of a cooperation partner. This risk, which may be termed a vulnerability, can be the product of incompetence, legal incompatibility or malign motives on the part of others.

Cost-benefit analyses can explain the preference for cooperation in a specific instance or at a specific point in time. If, however, we want to explain a change in cooperation – as in the case of European cooperation – we must look at how and why the balance between costs and benefits has shifted over time. The remainder of this section discusses a set of independent variables that have shifted the balance between the contending state interests described above, thus affecting the prospects for intelligence cooperation in Europe.

Drivers of cooperation

What has made European states more willing to pursue intelligence and policy gains over time? Two factors appear to be determinants in generating demand for cooperation in the European case. The first is the growing perception of a common threat in the form of radical Islamist terrorism. This has increased the demand for both intelligence and policy gains relating to a greater awareness of terrorist movements (in the case of the former) and new institutional arrangements to show commitment (in the case of the latter). Europe has a long history of terrorist activity, but the threat posed by Islamist extremism greatly accentuated the need for international cooperation, in particular in support of societal protection and law enforcement, but also in support of foreign and security policy. It is important to note that an increase in the level of threat will only generate a need for cooperation if it challenges the capacity of individual states. If states can handle a threat unilaterally, they will prefer to do so. In addition, cooperation will only develop on a multilateral basis in cases where many states have similar perceptions of the nature of a threat. In the case of preference asymmetries on the preferred means to counter terrorism, states are more likely to seek bilateral cooperation with like-minded actors. The increased level of threat from Islamist extremists qualified on both counts. Compared to earlier forms of politically motivated terrorism, which had a fairly high degree of local specificity, this phenomenon was perceived as a threat with clearly international dimensions which many states had inadequate resources to counter. One intelligence director, speaking in 2010, summed up the picture:

> The main driver was that all of us, from our respective horizons, saw that the threat [from terrorism] came closer to Europe, and simultaneously increased in volume. Furthermore, terrorists cross borders, which forced us to cooperate. This was not something any state could handle on its own.[14]

The second factor driving cooperation was the internal demand created by the process of European integration. Scholars of integration talk of spillover when cooperative measures in one area create the need for cooperation in adjacent areas (Haas 1968; Schmitter and Niemann 2009). This was clearly the main driver of intelligence cooperation in the field of foreign and security policy, where growing ambitions for a common European foreign and security policy increased the demand for supporting intelligence analysis. IntCen is a case in point. The initial decision to set up the agency, the choice to increase cooperation by seconding national intelligence analysts, the development of a close working relationship with the military intelligence branch of the EU, and the increasing role in operational support were all developments that were motivated by endogenous demands. Not only was intelligence demand created by spillover from other areas of integration, but in line with this concept it was also articulated and championed by actors within the common institutions. IntCen innovatively managed to formulate solutions to problems they themselves had articulated (Shapcott 2005). This highly proactive entrepreneurial approach gained additional leverage due to external shocks, most notably the terrorist attacks in Madrid in 2004 and London in 2005.

Bureaucratic interests as a barrier to cooperation

The drivers discussed above do not tell the full story of European intelligence cooperation. After all, cooperation has developed unevenly in different fields. Part of the explanation for this lies in the obstacles which stand between governmental ambitions and actual outcomes and which obstruct cooperation even in cases where governments favour it. Examples range from counter-terrorism cells that are closed down due to a lack of practitioner support for intelligence-sharing mechanisms that are made ineffective by poor implementation. In the case of Europe, the most potent barrier has been national intelligence staffers whose interests were challenged by suggested schemes for increasing international cooperation. These could include, for example, national-minded analysts who balk at the idea of cooperation in general, but more important was the fact that analysts seemed unwilling to cooperate and share information in a way that challenged pre-existing personal relations and informal networks. The most striking example is Europol and its role in counter-terrorism. European governments called repeatedly for increased intelligence support for Europol from national security services (which in most states are the major holders of such information)

but these calls went largely unheeded (Fägersten 2010b). Even legal instruments
to boost information sharing were largely ineffective in this area. Intelligence
officials who preferred to use their own intelligence channels clearly frustrated
government ambitions on this point. Similar 'bureaucratic resistance' was
evident in the case of the CTG, but with rather different effects. Here, the
political calls (from Brussels as well as from several EU member states) were
for cooperation to be more closely tied to the EU institutions (European Commission 2004). While these suggestions may not have been followed due to a
lack of support from some of the most powerful member states, it was nonetheless striking how effective the national intelligence bureaucrats were in spelling
out the consequences of the formalization and centralization of their already-
existing well-functioning networks such as the CTG. As one intelligence analyst
framed it, 'sure, we can open up a Brussels office but that would not be the place
where we would be sharing intelligence'.[15] Despite repeated calls for coordination and formalization, the security services' counter-terrorism cooperation
remained informal, decentralized and beyond the reach of policy-makers in
Brussels.

Trust and institutional design as enablers of cooperation

Finally, it is relevant to discuss factors that, unlike the drivers, do not increase
the benefits of cooperation per se but rather help governments to manage and
mitigate some of the costs and risks associated with cooperation. First, the
growing trust among actors is an important enabler of cooperation, since it
allows actors to take higher risks on behalf of each other, such as sharing sensitive information or developing joint capabilities. Trust therefore makes intelligence actors willing to accept higher levels of vulnerability, which in turn allows
for increased levels of cooperation. The development of IntCen illustrates how
cooperation is enabled by trust. Initially, only seven EU member states were
invited to participate in the work of the (then) SitCen.[16] Although this was contrary to EU principles, the limited number of participants meant that the new
agency started off with considerable capital in the form of trust, since those
involved were already close intelligence partners. The small and initially
informal agency was expanded, but only by invitation and when trust had been
established beforehand. This was in stark contrast to Europol which as a new,
formal entity – also suffering from some initial problems with security breaches
– faced a long uphill struggle to establish a level of trust that would enable more
effective cooperation (Occhipinti 2003; House of Lords 2009).

   The second enabling factor that made a clear difference to European intelligence cooperation was that of institutional design. How arrangements for cooperation are organized clearly affects the level of cooperation they will generate.
Two design principles are worth closer scrutiny, partly due to their controversial
nature. Some level of hierarchy among cooperating partners can actually pave
the way for increased cooperation in multilateral forums. Where states with
strong intelligence capabilities are offered some level of informal leadership, or

at least a position that matches their power, they tend to support cooperation for the benefit of all. The exclusive starting line-up of IntCen is one example of this. The informal agenda-setting by the big countries in the CTG and the general sensitivity towards big countries' interests in many EU bodies are others.

The remaining relevant design principle is autonomy. If intelligence functions are delegated to a central body, such as an assessment unit, a clearing house or a joint Sigint capacity, then cooperation seems to be enhanced by the autonomy of that body. For example, the discretion given to managers of IntCen (the vagueness of their mandate, their semi-official status and the non-interference in their work by member state politicians) allowed them to maintain a level of cooperation that at times exceeded the level that member states had planned. The same may be said about security service cooperation in the CTG and the Club de Berne. While these bodies did not enjoy any organizational autonomy – their arrangements were fully decentralized – they were allowed to function in a non-politicized environment, something which proved beneficial to cooperation. As one analyst explained, 'this is a venue for real cooperation, not for politics'.[17] At the other end of the spectrum, the arrangements for intelligence cooperation among law enforcement agencies were put under strict bureaucratic and political controls – for very good reasons – and thus cooperation to a large extent followed the lowest common denominator. Interestingly, these somewhat controversial design principles – hierarchy and organizational autonomy – seem to be interrelated. When powerful states sense that their interests are being taken into account (by formal or informal means) they tend to be more willing to delegate authority to third parties or supranational institutions to manage cooperation.

European intelligence cooperation: lessons learned and prospects for the future

Thus far, this chapter has reviewed the current state of European intelligence cooperation and analysed its development over time: the main drivers of cooperation, the major obstacles on the road and the factors that seem to have enabled a level of cooperation that otherwise would have stood little chance of success. While the development of multilateral intelligence cooperation is interesting in its own right, it also gives rise to some general questions. First, what does the development of European intelligence cooperation tell us about this field in general? What lessons may be drawn from it and how might they apply to other regions and settings? In addition, what are the prospects for European intelligence cooperation in the future?

Lessons for intelligence scholars

A comprehensive European intelligence system has been established in under two decades. Intelligence officials from various fields today support EU and NATO member states at the operational as well as the strategic level: assisting in law enforcement, mapping and countering the threat of terrorism, informing foreign and security policy, and upgrading new member states' national intelligence systems in relation to accountability and democratic governance. What can intelligence scholars learn from the development of multilateral intelligence cooperation in Europe?

First, it has been widely argued that multilateral intelligence cooperation is fruitless, since these are not the forums in which states exchange their most secret or 'A-grade' intelligence. Stéphane Lefebvre (2003), for example, argues that 'What is shared and done multilaterally is usually not of a sensitive nature', so that the impact of these arrangements 'has been minimal'. Sims (2006) also points out that multilateral liaison tends to become hollow because it does not allow for high-quality exchange. However, as is illustrated in this chapter, multilateral venues for cooperation can lead to considerable intelligence gains even in the absence of 'A-grade' intelligence. Pooling analytical resources on a multilateral basis can be one way to manage the 'information overload' that could otherwise overwhelm national services.[18] In addition, multilateral pooling has an edge over decentralized bilateral exchanges in situations where states are unable to determine the value of a specific piece of information for other actors. A piece of information that is of little relevance to one actor may actually be 'A-grade' intelligence for another.

Second, multilateral cooperation can play an important role in fostering trust and diffusing norms of democratic governance of intelligence. By way of joint analysis, it also creates a common perception of threats and challenges. A coordinated response to transnational challenges requires a common understanding that is difficult to reach by way of unilateral or bilateral intelligence analysis. By producing common information, multilateral intelligence cooperation paves the way for collective action.

Finally, multilateral cooperation can generate intelligence gains by paving the way for enhanced bilateral or 'mini-lateral' cooperation. A precondition for realizing cooperative gains is to identify a common interest. In many cases such interests are fairly obvious; for example, between neighbouring states with more or less porous borders. Increasingly, however, forces that are generally considered consequences of globalization will create common interests between actors that otherwise might not see themselves as 'natural' partners. Although separated by distance, states may face similar challenges related to cyber security or, for example, they may find that both have minorities of the same origin which support separatist movements in a third country. Multilateral cooperation can be an effective way to identify possible gains from cooperation which may then be captured in a bilateral arrangement. Even between countries that already cooperate, multilateral intelligence gatherings, in a setup that resembles an academic conference, provide a fertile ground for the establishment of broader personal and inter-agency contacts. Hence, by enabling networking and identifying interest commonalities, multilateral intelligence arrangements can generate intelligence gains. Some of these gains may be pursued within the multilateral forum, while others will be captured in parallel bilateral partnerships. This also means that bilateral and multilateral cooperation is not as clearly separated as established theory suggests. The two formats can be intimately intertwined. For example, states can assess threats in a multilateral setting, then manage or counter these threats by way of bilateral cooperation, and finally report back and share best practices in the multilateral forum.

The future of European intelligence

Analysis of European intelligence cooperation in the early 1990s brought to light a hitherto unprecedented development. As a former EU official put it: 'You can't get closer to the heart of national sovereignty than national security and intelligence services. Yet in Brussels we have these analysts working together for the first time' (de Vries 2005). This chapter has discussed the factors that explain how this development has reached its current level. How are these factors likely to play out in the future? What will be the effects on the development of cooperation? The main conclusion is that the scope and depth of European intelligence cooperation are likely to increase in the years to come. However, the pace and character of this increase will be determined by two interrelated variables. First, how far the European Union will be transformed by the financial crisis. Second, the extent to which EU member states want to use the EU to pursue their interests on the international political stage.

What kind of European Union will emerge from the financial crisis? The crisis has proved the complexities involved in operating a common currency alongside a national economic policy. Differences in current account balances, competitiveness and access to financial markets among member states have resulted in a highly unbalanced currency union. In managing the crisis, politicians and institutions have tried to address mounting debt levels by prescribing financial austerity while simultaneously taking steps towards a tighter political union in order to address underlying structural problems. At the same time, both the austerity measures and the steps towards deeper European integration are being met with increasing levels of scepticism in many EU member states. All these aspects – austerity, integration and the legitimacy of both in the eyes of the public – will affect the future of European intelligence cooperation.

First of all, austerity could lead to either less or more cooperation, depending on whether European cooperation is seen as a luxury add-on which cannot be afforded in times of crisis, or as a cost-saving measure that can relieve national budgets through specialization and economies of scale (in the latter case, member states would have to accept that the common European level of cooperation would not only complement, but in some instances replace national competences). This is a calculation that will look different to different member states, so the most likely effect will be one of fragmentation.

Further to this is the point that more integration on a general level is most likely to result in more intelligence cooperation. The analysis of current cooperation suggests strong spillover effects between measures to cooperate in related fields and the need to develop increased joint intelligence capacities. For example, if the Eurozone members move forward with deeper economic and financial integration, it is likely that tighter cooperation on immigration, judicial matters and defence industrial production will follow (Piris 2012). These are all areas that benefit from joint intelligence work. However, it is clear that not all the EU member states will take part in this journey. Britain in particular, but also other countries outside the Eurozone, are reluctant to move towards increasing cooperation. Hence, increased integration (like austerity) may lead to increased fragmentation, where some countries deepen intelligence cooperation while others choose to opt out.

Another question relates to the EU as an instrument for managing European states' security and international interests. Collective action in the foreign, security and defence fields clearly calls for common information and situational awareness, something which the development of IntCen has illustrated. EU strategy documents on both internal and external security indicate the EU's willingness to make progress in areas dependent on intelligence support (Council of the European Union 2008, 2010; European Council 2012). At the same time, EU member states have had difficulties realizing their ambitions in this area. Partly as a result of the financial crisis, the European foreign and security policy has shown signs of 're-nationalization' where member states are more keen to look after their own short-term interests than to pursue common long-term interests (ECFR 2012). If this trend is accentuated, intelligence support at the European level will wane and national resources will be directed elsewhere, such as to strengthen bilateral ties or cooperation within NATO (depending on the issue area).

In sum, several interrelated trends exist which could have possible implications for European intelligence cooperation. Austerity measures could force states to cut down on direct support to international bodies (liaison officers, seconded analysts) and on national intelligence resources that could potentially be used to pursue international aims. Austerity could also force states to seek intelligence gains through international cooperation. Steps towards tighter integration in other policy fields are likely to imply increased demand for more intelligence cooperation, but could also lead to fragmentation, as not all states will take part. It is most likely, therefore, that Europe will see more intelligence cooperation but probably also more fragmented cooperation where some states choose to focus more on bilateral or 'mini-lateral' arrangements and others choose to invest more fully in common European capabilities. In the case of the latter, what would such an increase in cooperation look like?

Law enforcement intelligence is perhaps an area that is less likely to be cut, since the economic benefits of fighting organized international crime are obvious. In the case of Europol the most likely development – assuming increased practitioner support – is that more intelligence will be shared multilaterally rather than sent bilaterally through Europol's network. Statistics from Europol suggest that up to 80 per cent of the information that passes through Europol's information exchange tool is of a bilateral character, hence bypassing Europol headquarters as well as other member states (House of Lords 2009). It is also likely that as European policy-makers are harder pressed to make full use of EU resources and to further integrate civil and military capabilities, Europol will become more deeply involved in, and benefit from, intelligence gathered during the EU's military operations. This could, for example, imply information on organized crime networks relevant for internal EU security.

When it comes to intelligence support for foreign and security policy, increased cooperation is likely to be realized in an increase in member states' supply of national intelligence – assuming that vulnerability can be kept under control – and eventually some form of autonomous collection capacity. Considering the strong incentives to economize on resources, it would be surprising if IntCen did not in time gain the right to ask the global network of EU delegations for political intelligence. Some form of direct access to technical collection platforms is conceivable as well, considering the decline in the cost of such technology and the perceived benefits of 'autonomous' EU resources. In the case of societal protection, a natural development would be to widen the mandate of the CTG beyond the current focus on Islamist terrorism to include international terrorism in general.

In conclusion, there is reason to believe that the scope and depth of European intelligence cooperation will increase in the years to come. Given that some of the possible developments suggested above relate to increased collection capacities at the international level, this calls into question the adequacy of current control and oversight mechanisms. There is a non-negligible risk that future arrangements for European intelligence cooperation will give rise to an accountability gap between national oversight mechanisms and international governance structures. This is particularly relevant at a time when the legitimacy of the broader project of European integration is constantly being called into question. This, too, is an area where we are likely to see increased activity in the future European intelligence system.

Notes

1 For the purpose of this text, intelligence cooperation is defined as cooperation between national agencies with an explicit intelligence mandate and/or the establishment of international bodies with such mandates.
2 'Societal protection' refers to measures to protect a society, including its institutions and values.
3 See Chapter 2 by Sir David Omand (this volume).
4 Although this task at times overlaps with law enforcement intelligence, the main objective is rather different. Law enforcement is focused on bringing criminals to justice by way of securing evidence, while societal protection aims to avoid harm to a society, its values and its institutions. The latter is usually carried out by national security services, and typical work includes countering terrorism, monitoring groups with subversive agendas, and thwarting the actions of foreign intelligence organizations.
5 Other actors with a modest impact on European intelligence cooperation include the Terrorism Working Group (TWG), which brings together staff from interior ministries and security services for discussions on internal aspects of terrorism; the Working Party on Terrorism – International Aspects (COTER), which deals with external aspects such as policies towards third countries and international organizations; and finally, the Standing Committee on Operational Cooperation on Internal

Security (COSI) which is supposed to facilitate and coordinate security cooperation at the operational level. However, during its first years COSI has been occupied with discussions about its own role and to some extent with the implementation of the EU's internal security strategy, and it is not involved in legislation or in any operational work.

6 'Italy's high court upholds convictions of 23 Americans in Abu Omar rendition', *Washington Post*, 20 September 2012.

7 Following the exposure of a US Surveillance Detection Unit (SDU) in Oslo, and its close cooperation with former employees of Norwegian police and defence agencies, investigations concerning similar arrangements were opened in Sweden, Denmark, Finland and Iceland. In none of these cases could the extent to which surveillance had been unlawful be confirmed. Investigations did show, however, that local authorities had been informed to varying degrees about ongoing activities. See, for example, 'Scandinavian protests over U.S. embassy security just politics, ex-counterterrorism official says', *Washington Post*, 17 November 2010.

8 Interview with the head of intelligence analysis at an EU member state's security service, 18 June 2010. The interviews referred to in this chapter were conducted by the author as part of a research project funded by Lund University, Sweden between 2006 and 2011. The material contains forty-two personal interviews with staff and directors representing more than twenty intelligence-related organizations in eleven different countries. All interviewees were promised anonymity in resulting publications.

9 Interview with the director of the agency in charge of external intelligence in one of the larger EU member states, 15 March 2008.

10 'MI5 gave Libyan spies details of dissidents in Britain', *Guardian*, 22 April 2012.

11 Unconfirmed US diplomatic report published by Norwegian *Aftenposten*: 'NATO special committee issues: work plan, intelligence reform, and the Chinese intelligence threat', *Aftenposten*, 13 February 2011.

12 'New NATO intelligence chief was trained by KGB', *New York Times*, 3 February 2008.

13 Apart from these strategic-level arrangements, NATO has arrangements for cooperation on a more operational level, one example being the Intelligence Fusion Centre in Molesworth, UK.

14 Interview with the head of a counterterrorism unit of a medium-sized EU member state, 22 April 2010.

15 Interview with a Brussels-based intelligence analyst, 13 June 2006.

16 During 2002, intelligence analysts were seconded from the external intelligence agencies of the UK, France, Germany, Spain and the Netherlands. In January 2003 these analysts were joined by colleagues from Sweden and Italy.

17 Interview with an intelligence officer responsible for CTG coordination in a medium-sized EU member state, 18 June 2010.

18 A current example is the use of drones in war zones that generate a wealth of information which strains the resources of the agencies in charge. According to the *New York Times*, the footage collected by US drones in Afghanistan and Iraq during 2009 would take twenty-four years to view. See 'Military is awash in data from drones', *New York Times*, 10 January 2010.

Bibliography

Agrell, W. (2006) 'Sweden and the Dilemmas of Neutral Intelligence Liaison', *Journal of Strategic Studies*, 29: 633–651.

Argomaniz, J. and Rees, W. (2012) 'The EU and Counter-terrorism', in S. Biscop and R.G. Whitman (eds), *The Routledge Handbook of European Security*, London: Routledge, pp. 225–234.

Ashton, C. (2012a) 'EU Intelligence Analysis Centre (IntCen). Reply to Question in European Parliament nr E-006017/2012'.

—— (2012b) 'EU Intelligence Analysis Centre (IntCen): Products and Information. Reply to Question in European Parliament nr E-006018/2012'.

Clough, C. (2004) 'Quid Pro Quo: The Challenges of International Strategic Intelligence Cooperation', *International Journal of Intelligence and Counterintelligence*, 17: 601–613.

Council of the European Union (2008) 'Report on the Implementation of the European Security Strategy: Providing Security in a Changing World', S407/08. Online. Available: www.consilium.europa.eu/ueDocs/cms_Data/docs/pressdata/EN/reports/104630. pdf (accessed 28 December 2012).

—— (2010) 'Draft Internal Security Strategy for the European Union: "Towards a European Security Model" ', 5842/2/10. Online. Available: http://register.consilium.europa. eu/pdf/en/10/st05/st05842-re02.en10.pdf (accessed 27 December 2012).

European Commission (2004a) 'Enhancing Police and Customs Co-operation in the European Union'. Online. Available: http://eur-lex.europa.eu/LexUriServ/LexUriServ.do? uriCELEX:52004DC0376:EN:NOT (accessed 28 December 2012).

—— (2004b) 'Proposal for a Council Decision on the Transmission of Information Resulting from the Activities of Security and Intelligence Services with Respect to Terrorist Offences'. Online. Available: http://eur-lex.europa.eu/LexUriServ/LexUriServ. do?uri=CELEX:52005PC0695:EN:NOT (accessed 28 December 2012).

—— (2010) 'EU Information Management Instruments', MEMO/10/349, Brussels.

European Council (2012) 'Conclusions', EUCI 205/12. Online. Available: www.consilium. europa.eu/uedocs/cms_data/docs/pressdata/en/ec/134353.pdf (accessed 28 December 2012).

European Council of Foreign Relations (ECFR) (2012) 'European Foreign Policy Scorecard 2012'. Online. Available: www.ecfr.eu/scorecard/2012 (accessed 28 December 2012).

European Parliament (2012) 'Working Document on Alleged Transportation and Illegal Detention of Prisoners in European Countries by the CIA: Follow-up of the European Parliament TDIP Committee Report', 2012/2033(INI), Brussels.

Europol (2002) 'Annual Report. Document nr 9431/03.'

Fägersten, B. (2010a) *Sharing Secrets: Explaining International Intelligence Cooperation*, Lund: Lund Political Studies.

—— (2010b) 'Bureaucratic Resistance to International Intelligence Cooperation – The Case of Europol', *Intelligence and National Security*, 25: 500–520.

Haas, E.B. (1968) *The Uniting of Europe: Political, Social, and Economic Forces, 1950–1957*, Stanford, CA: Stanford University Press.

House of Lords (2009) European Union Committee, 29th Report of Session 2008–2009, 'Europol: Coordinating the Fight against Serious and Organised Crime, Report with Evidence', 200–208. Online. Available: http://ec.europa.eu/dgs/home-affairs/what-is-new/ public-consultation/2008/pdf/contributions/uk_2_en.pdf (accessed 28 December 2012).

Laitinen, I. (2008) 'Frontex: An Inside View', *Eipascope*. Online. Available: www.eipa. eu/files/repository/eipascope/20090203161640_SCOPE2008–3_5_IllkaLaitinen.pdf (accessed 24 January 2013).

Lefebvre, S. (2003) 'The Difficulties and Dilemmas of International Intelligence Cooperation', *International Journal of Intelligence and Counterintelligence*, 16: 527–542.

Occhipinti, J.D. (2003) *The Politics of EU Police Cooperation: Toward a European FBI?*, Boulder, CO: Lynne Rienner.

Peek, J. (1994) 'International Police Co-operation within Justified Political and Judicial Frameworks: Five Theses on Trevi', in J. Monar and R. Morgan (eds), *The Third Pillar of the European Union: Co-operation in the Fields of Justice and Home Affairs*, Brussels: European Interuniversity Press, pp. 201–208.

Piris, J.C. (2012) 'The Issue: Could Rescuing the €-17 Fatally Weaken the EU? My Verdict: No, There Are Several Models for a "Two-speed Europe"', *Europe's World*, 22. Online. Available: www.europesworld.org/NewEnglish/Home_old/Article/tabid/191/ArticleType/articleview/ArticleID/22044/language/en-US/Default.aspx (accessed 27 December 2012).

RAND Europe (2012) *Evaluation of Implementation of the Europol Council Decision and of Europol's Activities*, Rand Technical Report.

Richelson, J.T. and Ball, D. (1985) *The Ties That Bind: Intelligence Cooperation between the UKUSA Countries – the United Kingdom, the United States of America, Canada, Australia, and New Zealand*, Boston, MA: Allen & Unwin.

Schmitter, P.C. and Niemann, A. (2009) 'Neo-functionalism', in A. Wiener and T. Diez (eds), *European Integration Theory*, 2nd edn, Oxford: Oxford University Press, pp. 45–66.

Shapcott, W. (2005) 'Oral Evidence', in House of Lords, European Union Committee, 'After Madrid: The EU's Response to Terrorism, Report with Evidence', pp. 53–62.

—— (2009) 'Situation Report – Interview with William Shapcott', *Jane's Intelligence Review*, 21: 58.

—— (2011) 'Do They Listen? Communicating Warnings: An Intelligence Practitioner's Perspective', in C. de Franco and C.O. Meyer (eds), *Forecasting, Warning, and Responding to Transnational Risks*, Basingstoke: Palgrave Macmillan, pp. 117–126.

Sims, J.(2006) 'Foreign Intelligence Liaison: Devils, Deals, and Details', *International Journal of Intelligence and Counterintelligence*, 19: 195–217.

Sloan, E. (2012) 'Canada and NATO: A Military Assessment', Strategic Studies Working Group Papers, Canadian International Council, Canadian Defence and Foreign Affairs Institute.

Treaty of European Union (1992) Article 4:2. Online. Available: http://eur-lex.europa.eu/LexUriServ/LexUriServ.do?uri=OJ:C:2010:083:0013:0046:en:PDF (accessed 27 December 2012).

Vries, G. de (2005) 'Gijs de Vries on Terrorism, Islam and Democracy'. Interview in *Euractiv*, published 4 March. Online. Available: www.euractiv.com/security/gijs-vries-terrorism-islam-democracy/article-136245 (accessed 20 March 2013).

Walsh, J.I. (2007) 'Defection and Hierarchy in International Intelligence Sharing', *Journal of Public Policy*, 27: 151–181.

9 Intelligence-led policing in Europe

Lingering between idea and implementation

Monica den Boer

Introduction

Intelligence-led policing (ILP) has been a recent hype in national and international discourse on law enforcement.[1] Within the international context it is widely suggested that this model of policing, which intends to embed the rational and managerial use of information in processes of policing with the intention to reduce crime in a preventive manner, is more effective than purely responsive styles of policing. This chapter takes an in-depth look at the concept of ILP as it is practised in the member states of the European Union (EU). The ambiguity of the concept may have consequences for the way in which ILP is welcomed and used in police agencies throughout Europe. These ambiguities are caused by unresolved strategic choices concerning the level and direction of intelligence sharing (hierarchical and layered versus horizontal and networked); the organizational context and the actors involved in ILP (general versus specialist); the extent to which intelligence may be used to manage a police organization or to 'manage and predict risks in the outside world' (managerialism versus risk assessment); and the way in which ILP will develop in the near future.

There is a fundamental normative debate in the domestic security field about the mandate and professional capacity of police organizations with regard to intelligence gathering and analysis. Intelligence agencies are of the view that this is a highly demanding, complex and secretive task which cannot be delegated to the public police forces (see e.g. Gregory 2008: 47–61). However, with the blurring of the line between ordinary police practices such as surveillance and the (proactive) high policing practices of gathering information on activists and terrorists, intelligence has definitely gained an undeniable position in the discourse of mainstream policing. Several European countries have introduced intelligence-led policing as an important if not the leading model of policing into their work practices. Hence, this chapter takes the law enforcement discourses about ILP as a point of departure.

Traditionally, ILP is associated with running informants under proactive policing methods with the purpose of collecting sensitive information on the basis of which an analysis can be made. However, as time has passed, ILP has gradually transformed into an overall practice in which information is brought together in the form of analytical products. This knowledge, which is supposed to be acquired in a systematic, rational and professional fashion, provides input for decisions by police managers and state prosecutors about priority setting, employment of capacity, instruments, and longer term strategies such as educational development within the police forces and cooperation with public and private agents (Johnston 1999; Stenning 2000). Moreover, the introduction of ILP has been facilitated by an increased focus on transnational criminal networks and the apparent need for new police management models (Gill 1998).

According to Ratcliffe (2008), some universal drivers explain the push for the ILP model. These drivers include trends such as new governance challenges, technological innovation, proactive information gathering and multi-agency policing. The popularity of ILP hinges upon several factors. First, ILP allows police organizations to keep their former responsive style of policing intact while at the same time seeking to innovate along proactive lines of performance. Reactive policing was increasingly regarded as an insufficient response to rising crime levels, both at the local and global levels (transnational organized crime and terrorism). In other words, the lack of an effective response culminated in a demand gap: high volumes of crime persisted despite numerous law enforcement interventions. Second, ILP is a managerial model which allows for the control of information-based processes from the top to the bottom of the organization. In other words, analytical intelligence products like risk assessments can assist police leadership to make informed strategic choices about the employment of police personnel and the definition of strategic focus points. Third, ILP allows police organizations to create interconnections, both internally between police processes and externally with other (security) actors. For instance, intelligence plays a crucial role in predicting public order problems, and this can assist in the preparation of police operations. Fourth, the ILP philosophy encourages police organizations to take recourse to alternative means, such as early detection, interference, disturbance and the improvement of criminogenic environments. These alternative means of intervention may weigh less heavily on the already overburdened criminal justice system, because an interception of illegal goods, for instance, may not always culminate in legal proceedings against a suspect. The flipside of proactive intervention is however that it may be a challenge for law enforcement organizations to demonstrate the effectiveness of their intervention, for instance, in terms of choking off a profitable market for a criminal organization. Statistics on the cost-effectiveness of proactive, intelligence-led operations are generally hard to get, but those interventions may lead to a greater sense of safety among citizens. Fifth, because of its rationality-based approach, ILP supports priority setting, which is seen as important from a managerial and budgetary perspective, given the scarce capacities. Last but not least, intelligence-led policing is facilitated by the vast possibilities offered by information and communications technology. In sum, these arguments fold into a rather convincing rhetoric which explains the attractiveness of the ILP model.

However, as we will see in more detail below, despite the popularity of ILP in several European countries, there is also cultural and legal resistance to the introduction of intelligence gathering for ordinary law enforcement purposes. While ILP was originally introduced for the purposes of counter-terrorism, it has already been stretched towards the control of organized crime, serious crime, public order management, immigration and border control. This may imply a whole series of practical and ethical consequences which often tend to be over-looked. These consequences may range from privacy issues to the potential pro-fessional misuse of intelligence, or the exploitation of intelligence for ordinary criminal justice procedures. On a deeper level, ubiquitous intelligence to which law enforcement organizations may have unlimited access causes fears related to Bentham's Panopticon: a surveillance society where citizens remain under the constant gaze of law enforcement organizations (see e.g. Hoogenboom 1994; Whitaker 1999). In some Western European societies such as Great Britain, this is already a concern. Although widely used surveillance methods like CCTV and automatic number plate recognition (ANPR) do not by themselves produce intel-ligence products, the information may be used to compose intelligence pictures on the transactions, movements, and numerous other activities of all citizens all of the time.

Towards an understanding of intelligence-led policing

Intelligence-led policing is one of several policing concepts which have gained ground in police forces around the world. In recent decades police forces have implemented models such as community policing (COP), problem-oriented policing (POP), hot spot policing and, more recently, reassurance policing (Pon-saers 2001). The implementation of these conceptual models is rarely mono-disciplinary. In practice there is a strong overlap between POP and ILP, but even COP is blending with ILP as the need for generating community intelligence has become more emphasized. Carter and Carter (2009: 311) even regard ILP as a 'complementary expansion of the community policing concept'. MacVean (2008: 70) refers to the community as being the 'ears and eyes' of the police, which involves a social contract on the one hand, and an explicit intelligence relationship on the other. Maguire and John (2006) argue that ILP is not neces-sarily incompatible with community and neighbourhood policing and that it can incorporate perspectives of partner agencies and local communities (see also Innes *et al.* 2009; Lowe and Innes 2012). The International Association of Chiefs of Police (IACP) even advocates a model that integrates intelligence-led policing with community policing (IL3CP).[2]

In contrast, it may be conceivable that in the ILP model the police (and not the citizens or their elected representatives) determine crime-fighting priorities, which contrasts strongly with the spirit of the community policing model (see e.g. Kleiven 2005; Keane and Kleiven 2009). Despite these inherent conceptual tensions between different models of policing, in practice these concepts have blurred significantly as police organizations generally apply a selection of tactics, logics and instruments deemed appropriate for particular contexts and threats. Sometimes ILP is regarded as old wine in new bottles, as preventive policing was regarded as one of the prime processes of policing since the start of the nineteenth century. The attraction of ILP seems to be mainly that it is a much 'smarter' model of policing than the other models, as it is supposed to be more effective in view of endemic patterns of crime. Intelligence creates the basis for knowledge and the codification of best practices, which facilitate knowledge-based decision-making (instead of arbitrary, ill-founded, ad hoc or reactive policing). However, the 'smart' character of ILP places high demands on the police profession and its culture, since police officers are supposed to 'think out of the box', to change their culture from 'need-to-know' to 'need-to-share', and to reach beyond the traditional information silos. But the problem is that ILP tends to be defined and implemented in different ways. Hence, as a conceptual model, intelligence-led policing lacks a homogeneous definition and its implementation tends to be rather differentiated (Van den Hengst and Staffeleu 2012: 188).

The House of Lords European Union Select Committee uses a simple definition of ILP: 'using today's knowledge to shape tomorrow's policing' (House of Lords 2007–2008), referring primarily to its forecasting abilities. In this context, ILP is generally associated with scenario building, risk assessment and threat analysis (Maguire 2000). Several national and international law enforcement agencies have embraced this methodology and have incorporated it into their information products. By analysing information, law enforcement organizations seek to be 'one step ahead' of crime and the criminal. In recent years ILP has been built around risk assessments and risk management (De Lint 2006). Although claimed as a policing framework that builds on previous paradigms, including community policing, problem-oriented policing and the continuous improvement or partnership model of policing (McGarrell *et al.* 2007), it was essentially a response to the reactive, crime-based focus of community policing with calls for police to employ informants and surveillance to combat recidivist offenders. Moreover, it is technologically and financially feasible for governments to record nearly everything that is said or done within their borders (every phone conversation, electronic message, social media interaction, the movements of nearly every person and vehicle). Governments with a history of using all the tools at their disposal to track and monitor their citizens may make full use of this capability (Villasenor 2011). Technology trends facilitate ILP-based capabilities. Vast databases of captured information create what amounts to a surveillance time machine, enabling intelligence and security services and police agencies to intercept communications prior to someone's designation as a surveillance target. The data needs to be acquired, managed, aggregated, and made accessible and searchable with appropriate analysis tools. This throws up the urgent need to clarify and specify the application of data protection principles to ILP in connection with the application of new technologies (for issues concerning oversight, see Den Boer 2013).

Intelligence-led policing is thus seen as an approach which seeks to reduce crime and to transfer resources from a retrospective or reactive response to crime to a proactive or pre-emptive approach on the basis of the strategic analysis of crime data, what is known about offenders and offender groups, and contextual information. The knowledge that has already been acquired is used in a more rational way to determine where crimes are likely to occur and to discern patterns of crime: 'intelligence tells officials everything they need to know before they knowledgeably choose a course of action. For example, intelligence provides law enforcement executives with facts and alternatives that can inform critical decisions' (Peterson 2005: 15). This can support police organizations in targeting particular individuals, activities and locations. Intelligence-led policing is said to have originated in the United Kingdom (Tilley 2003: 311). Tilley argues that:

> [T]he main impetus for intelligence-led policing comprises the supposed failure of the police to address the systemic sources of crime and crime patterns.... Intelligence-led policing draws on the notion that the police can and do know a great deal about offending patterns. Intelligence-led policing involves effectively sourcing, assembling and analyzing 'intelligence' about criminals and their activities to better disrupt their offending, by targeting enforcement and patrol where it can be expected to yield highest dividends.
>
> (Tilley 2003: 313)

Another reason for the introduction of ILP may well have been a failure of information processing (Deukmedjian and De Lint 2007). At the international level, Interpol regards the strategic analysis of information and intelligence as a means to inform higher level decision-makers, provide early warning of threats, and support senior decision-makers 'in setting priorities to prepare their organizations to deal with emerging issues' which may imply the reallocation of resources to different areas of crime.[3]

Within the United Kingdom, it was particularly the Kent County Constabulary that was influential in spreading the concept of ILP. This came after the use of intelligence-led policing in Northern Ireland, where the Royal Ulster Constabulary (RUC) had been involved in a long-term anti-terrorism campaign against the Irish Republican Army (IRA). Tilley (2003: 321) claims that there does not seem to be a real philosophy behind the development of ILP, but one could argue that it reflects an awareness within law enforcement circles that the policing of criminal activities on the basis of intelligence seems more apt to modern times as the world develops into a global society with a high frequency of transnational transfers and transactions, as well as hyper-mobility, anonymity and fragmented governance (Bekkers *et al.* 2006; Den Boer 2012). In addition, the concept of ILP – even though there is confusion on the definition – has the potential to be transplanted from one region to the other, as well as from one country or organization to the other.

For a theoretical grounding of ILP we must consult a variety of authors, including Brodeur, Ratcliffe, Gill and Harfield. Ratcliffe (2008) advocates a definition of ILP which emphasizes the business and managerial aspects of data analysis and criminal intelligence. In this view ILP provides a decisional framework which facilitates the reduction of problems and crime, and which is based on strategic management and effective enforcement strategies. The leading idea behind this definition is the need to focus on the most prolific and serious offenders and the ways in which information and intelligence can be used more rationally, seeking to reduce human error, arbitrary decision-making, tunnel vision, prejudice and lack of professionalism. In Ratcliffe's view, the elementary components of ILP are interpretation, influence and impact, which are interrelated processes in the intelligence cycle, which tends to involve the collection of data on the basis of certain objectives and specified issues, followed by validation and assessment, interpretation, dissemination, and an impact assessment, leading to a potential reformulation of objectives (Phillips 2008: 27).

Contrary to this instrumental vision of intelligence, Gill and Phythian (2006) argue that intelligence is 'ubiquitous'. Confidential and classified information gathering seems omni-present in post-9/11 global societies that express high anxiety levels about terrorism. Moreover, intelligence is an ambiguous product which can be misused. Gill examines the erroneous use of intelligence in cases like the intelligence failure before the onset of the Iraq war in 2003 (Gill 2005, 2006), thereby proclaiming the need for better oversight and parliamentary control (Gill 2007). Gill's argument is closely related to Brodeur's, who developed the 'high policing' paradigm that focuses on the protection of the state by means of political surveillance. High policing can be performed by means of undercover policing methods, an approach that has been expanded since 9/11 (Brodeur 2007). Characteristics of the high policing paradigm are its encompassing character, the conflation of powers, the protection of state interests and the abundant use of informants which pervades all levels of society. This comes with wide and highly uncontrollable powers for the agencies that carry the relevant mandate. Currently, political surveillance by the state is facilitated by technology-enhanced surveillance of transactions, behavioural patterns and movements of citizens, all feeding into total information awareness (TIA) on the part of government bodies. High policing is claimed to be totally dependent on the collation, analysis and dissemination of intelligence, which leads to the observation that it should be described as 'intelligence-leading' instead of 'intelligence-led policing' (Brodeur and Leman-Langlois 2003: 15). State surveillance has been transformed into surveillance by a variety of public and private agents (Lippert and O'Connor 2006), and the incremental growth of intelligence powers has often not been subjected to legal boundaries. In sum, high policing has become an accepted and normalized paradigm of policing in the 'security control society' (Sheptycki 2007).

In a networked model, law enforcement actors can interact in a direct capacity on the basis of professional discretion, while in a bureaucratic model they require authorization to pass on intelligence between different hierarchical layers. The attraction of transnational police networks is that they handle intelligence in a flexible manner, and that they can 'adapt, adjust, and act quickly to address issues that require immediate action' (Bayer 2010: 98). Although transnational law enforcement networks are often able to 'connect the dots' with a capacity to act powerfully and successfully (Bayer 2010: 98), the major challenge for sovereign states is that networked intelligence is a liquid commodity which cannot necessarily be trusted if it is not made subject to professionalization, standardization and verification procedures. In any case, the 'horizontal' or networked model of intelligence-led policing advocates intelligence as a collaborative exercise, in which ordinary police officers also play an essential role as a resource for gathering information: 'intelligence is everyone's job' (Peterson 2005: 11).

The risk of intelligence cocooning is still high because of a lack of trust and reciprocity among intelligence owners. This may give further rise to a competition between intelligence channels (such as bilateral vs. multilateral), and between networks (high trust environments, low institutionalized environments) and bureaucracies (trust through the cultivation of intelligence professionalism and the establishment of sectoral intelligence agencies) (Den Boer 2002a). If the governance of intelligence is apparently still a challenge, how are we doing on the practical-operational side of things?

Police intelligence processes and products

The intelligence process may be defined as a logical chain of actions: preparation, collection, processing, analysis, dissemination and monitoring. Cope (2004: 190) distinguishes the following stages in the intelligence cycle: (1) acquisition of information; (2) analysis of intelligence; (3) review and prioritizing; (4) actioning intelligence through tasking meetings; (5) evaluation and analysis of impact of action. Van den Hengst and Regterschot (2012: 24) distinguish three elementary processes, namely analysis, dissemination and decision-making. The analysis often includes a historical reconstruction of a number of criminal cases and arrives at a descriptive analysis of hotspots, hotshots and 'hot times' but ideally an analysis includes an estimation (what may happen when a reoffender is released from prison or what effect results from preventive measures) and advice as to what should be done with the analytical knowledge. Hence, when it concerns the analysis of intelligence, there seems to be a wide gap between theory and practice (Cope 2004), in the sense that the theory prescribes a detailed and phased process of intelligence gathering and validation, while in reality the practice is more mundane.

A variety of actors may be involved in this process, for instance, 'analysts' and 'decision-makers'. While analysts are theoretically crucial for intelligence-led policing, Cope provides a rather sobering image of their position in a Canadian context:

> Frequently analysts' work was sidelined, 'a lot of products are window-dressing', an analyst commented. Products were also described as 'wallpaper' by both analysts and police officers and were ignored when planning operations. Rather than being used proactively, analytical products were demanded at the end of an operation to summarize the outcomes or used to justify an operation that was already planned. Although analysis was

distributed in reports for tasking meetings and made accessible through officers' briefings, on computers and posted on notice boards, feedback or queries about analytical products were rarely received.

(Cope 2004: 192)

Complex intelligence products are often not acted upon in terms of operational policing. Meanwhile, police officers tend to rely mostly on their traditional frames of understanding and thereby ignore the potential value of analytical products (Cope 2004: 201).

Further down the intelligence-processing chain, decision-makers either reject or accept intelligence for further use. Van den Hengst and Regterschot (2012: 23) add that decision-making on the basis of information and intelligence is not merely conducted in specialist or managerial venues within the police organization, but also by operational field officers. The decision-making process is subdivided into presentation (transfer of the knowledge on the basis of analysis); interaction (between analyst and 'decision-maker'); and the exploitation or use of the analyses in decision-making (Van den Hengst and Regterschot 2012: 23). Applied to intelligence gathering on criminal cooperation structures, this requires several categories of information being brought together in an analytical file; for instance, details on whether internal or external violence has been or may be used. Furthermore, this process may generate an analysis of illicit profit by the criminal organization and of the way this is invested and/or laundered; of the contacts with facilitators in the 'legal upper world' such as lawyers, police officers or estate agents; of the methods by which the criminal organization seeks to conceal its practices from the outside world; and of the diversification and fluidity of criminal flows of goods and money (Den Boer 2010a; Van Mantgem *et al.* 2012: 25). Although the prime focus of ILP has always been on crime, there has been a gradual expansion to adjacent fields, such as public order offences, radicalization and corruption. Hence, the ILP model may be rather expansionist, not only in terms of its potential transfer to other (presumed) safety deficits, but also to other sectors. In this context, one could think of the growing popularity of intelligence-based risk assessments in sectors like finance, health, energy, food and transport.

The 4×4 intelligence model is known as a grading system for the reliability of intelligence (reliability, validity, restriction and distribution). In the United Kingdom, the 5×5 intelligence model is used in the National Intelligence Model (Keane and Kleiven 2009: 330), which includes handling/distribution as a third variable. The EU police agency Europol applies the 5×5 intelligence model, which is not very different from the standards of confidentiality and handling codes that are used in the member states. Within the domain of foreign and military affairs (such as within NATO), a 6×6 intelligence ranking model is used.[4]

The 5×5 intelligence model

Different concepts may be used for the intelligence process within security organizations. The concept used most frequently is that of the 'intelligence

Table 9.1 Confidential National Intelligence Report (Form A)

ORGANIZATION and OFFICER	XYZ Police DC 3271N Joe Bloggs			DATE/TIME OF REPORT	0600 hours on 05/01/2007
INTEL SOURCE or INTEL REF No.	0017			REPORT U.R.N.	
	A Always reliable	**B** Mostly reliable	**C** Sometimes reliable	**D** Unreliable	**E** Untested source
SOURCE EVALUATION	**1** Known to be true without reservation	**2** Mostly reliable	**3** Sometimes reliable	**4** Unreliable	**5** Untested source
INTELLIGENCE EVALUATION	**1** Known to be true without reservation	**2** Known personally to the source but not to the officer	**3** Not known personally to the source but corroborated	**4** Cannot be judged	**5** Suspected to be false
	PERMISSIONS			RESTRICTIONS	
	1	**2**	**3**	**4**	**5**
HANDLING CODE To be completed at time of entry into an intelligence system and reviewed on dissemination	May be disseminated to other law enforcement and prosecuting agencies, including law enforcement within the EEA and EU compatible (No Code or Conditions)	May be disseminated to UK non-prosecuting parties (Code 3.7 conditions apply)	May be disseminated to non-EEA law enforcement agencies (Code 4.7 and/or conditions apply, specify below)	Only disseminate within originating agency/ force Specify internal recipients)	Disseminate intelligence receiving agency to observe conditions as specified below

REPORT SUBJECT	CRAIG RAMAGE – COMMUNITY INTELL – FEUD

Intelligence dated 05/01/2007 provides that
Approximately 0020 hours on Friday, 5 January 2007, Craig Mitchell RAMAGE, born 05/07/1982 of 24/3 Oxland Avenue, attended at the A&E of the Royal Infirmary and was treated for injuries, which he freely stated were the result of a fight with a Jimmy DONALDSON. During treatment, RAMAGE was heard to say to an unknown male who had accompanied him to the hospital, that Jimmy DONALDSON would have his house 'torched' next week in revenge.

		EVALUATION		
	S	1		H
	A	4		5

Source: image taken from www.scotland.gov.uk/Resource/Img/169855/0050938.gif (accessed 14 September 2012).

cycle'. Intelligence products that emerge frequently in the lexicon of police intelligence exchange are 'threat analysis' and 'risk assessment' (Sheptycki 2004), which theoretically facilitate the rational management of human and material resources as they provide longer term pictures of future trends. 'Scenario building' has gained ample ground in national as well as international intelligence cultures. Risk assessments can hold a series of predictive values on a wide range of safety issues, such as warning signs on potential reoffenders. Several police agencies are in the process of establishing so-called real-time intelligence rooms, where technology is used to support a multi-agency interface to facilitate rapid emergency response and ambient intelligence (electronic sensors built into environments which identify and may respond to the presence of people). The introduction of the real-time intelligence concept has also occurred at the international level of policing. Interpol has established a Major Events Support Service to facilitate the real-time exchange of messages and police data with member states through its Command and Coordination Centre and Real-Time Analytical Intelligence Database (RAID).[5]

Implementation of ILP in EU member states

Several member states of the EU already possess a (pre-)existing infrastructure for intelligence-led policing. Almost all countries have faced the challenge of transnational organized crime and terrorism in different forms, sizes and degrees. Italy has been struggling with the mafia and with domestic terrorism for many years, resulting in the creation of an administrative superstructure against the mafia, drugs and terrorism above the relevant law enforcement organizations. In Germany, every province (Land) has its own Landeskriminalamt with its own intelligence functions, while the Federal Bundeskriminalamt holds primary responsibility for the investigation of the most serious forms of transnational organized crime. The Netherlands and the United Kingdom have gradually centralized the managerial responsibilities and intelligence functions for transnational organized crime in the form of national criminal investigation agencies. Most intelligence units which have a central coordinating role among EU member states act simultaneously as national contact points (such as Europol National Units) for matters concerning Europol, Interpol and the Schengen Agreement. The trend to establish national contact points and intelligence units has also developed out of EU strategies such as the 1997 Action Plan on Organized Crime and the 1999 Tampere Action Plan on Justice and Home Affairs Cooperation. The EU has furthermore given strong impetus to the creation of national football intelligence units and financial intelligence units (FIUs).

More recently one may observe trends towards the general application of intelligence collection inside the EU member states. While it was previously focused on specific forms of transnational organized crime (people smuggling, human trafficking, drugs trafficking), intelligence is increasingly regarded as a general police commodity and has become more strongly embedded in police processes overall, building on the established fact that field officers who are on duty have always been expected to relay information on what they observe in streets and neighbourhoods. Hence, on the one hand we may witness a process of centralization and specialization of intelligence, in particular when it concerns transnational criminal networks, while on the other intelligence is woven into the main police processes and procedures. The implementation of intelligence-led policing models can be in the hands of a steering group or specific portfolio holder among chief constables. Within law enforcement circles the support of the police leadership is seen as a pivotal condition for the successful implementation of new police concepts and strategies, including that of intelligence-led policing.

United Kingdom

Following the integration of the European Crime Intelligence Model (ECIM), every EU member state should now have a National Intelligence Model in place. The UK pioneered this development. The National Intelligence Model (NIM) was implemented by the forty-three police forces in England and Wales by 1 April 2004. The Code of Practice of the Association of Chief Police Officers (ACPO) on the NIM, issued in 2005 by the Home Secretary under the Police Reform Act 2002, provided a statutory basis for the introduction of a set of principles. Hence, in the United Kingdom, the NIM became 'the major vehicle for conducting intelligence-led policing' (Tilley 2003: 321), and was then further developed by the National Criminal Intelligence Service (NCIS). In theory, the NIM works by interconnecting different levels in the information and intelligence hierarchy, ranging from local to national to international. Some critics have argued that 'NIM' is a misnomer because it 'does not, in and of itself, facilitate the acquisition, collation and management of intelligence' (Harfield 2008: 2). Moreover, as Carter and Carter (2009: 312) have argued, the implementation of NIM in the UK was held up because 'many did not understand the concept' and it could be interpreted in different ways (Ratcliffe (2010) refers to a similar misunderstanding in the Australian context). Moreover, it required a reallocation of resources – which always gives rise to tensions within organizations – as every police force now needed an analytical capability (Carter and Carter 2009: 313). However, in comparison to the US, it was easier for the British police service to adopt NIM, 'having had a solid history of sophisticated law enforcement intelligence' (Carter and Carter 2009: 213) in relation to the Irish Republican Army.

The Netherlands

In the Netherlands, national drivers for change were ongoing discussions about the restructuring of the police organization and its information exchange processes, the adoption of a new strategy which advocated the interconnection of the global and local levels, and the arrival of new complex threats such as cybercrime. In line with the British police forces, the Board of Chief Police

Commissioners in the Netherlands adopted a Dutch National Intelligence Model (NIM) in 2008 (Van den Hengst and Staffeleu 2012: 188). The implementation of the NIM had to be fulfilled by the twenty-five regional police forces and the national police agency, on the basis of a National Intelligence Agenda (NIA) containing the priority subjects (Van den Hengst and Regterschot 2012: 24). The main challenge was therefore to implement a form of standardization which – at the same time – would correspond to the needs and practices of the individual police forces. The Board of Chief Police Commissioners established a national intelligence programme committee (Van den Hengst and Staffeleu 2012: 189) to guide and support the police forces with the implementation of ILP. The procedure required that the national committee apply an incremental model, gradually including a wider number of elements in the information organization with the aim to eventually reach the same implementation level nationwide. The employment by the forces of highly educated analysts was also encouraged by the committee. Van den Hengst and Staffeleu (2012: 190) found that the relative number of employees working in the information organization within the police forces was on average 5.7 per cent, with little regional differentiation. An intelligence planning calendar was also introduced as binding for all forces.

In parallel with the implementation of NIM, there was also an endorsement in 2005 of the concept of nodal policing, which advocates the use of intelligence to discern flows of criminal activities and the concentration of criminal activities at certain infrastructural hotspots: international harbours, airports or motorways. An issue in ILP in the Netherlands is the overly technocratic application of intelligence, such as through digital surveillance and the surveillance of motorways through ANPR. The concept of nodal intelligence gathering tends to depart from the vertical layering of intelligence-gathering processes as it presupposes the exchange of intelligence between police forces and other stakeholders, such as the border control authority (Koninklijke Marechaussee) and the public and private sector (Den Boer 2010a).

As ILP is now the leading organizational concept in the Dutch police organization, every police process is in principle subject to an intelligence flow, and all police officers are supposed to make a contribution. The recent law on police information demands an exchange of information with other national and international law enforcement organizations.[6] This norm applies in all situations, with only a few exceptions allowing for non-compliance (otherwise regarded as a breach of professional duty) (Kop *et al.* 2011: 25). As of 1 January 2013, a single national police force is directly accountable to the Minister of Security and Justice.[7] The intelligence process will have to be restructured across different levels and various national expert units (such as the National Criminal Investigation Service), with the support of a police-based Real Time Intelligence Centre (RTIC).[8]

General observations on the national implementation of ILP

On a formal level, several member states have special legislation covering special police investigation methods (the use of informants, infiltrators) which are building blocks in the ILP model. The weaknesses of ILP in the Netherlands and the United Kingdom have however been defined as follows:

> [P]olice officers continue to be involved in response-led policing and no time remains for proactive work.
>
> > (Tilley 2003: 333)

> ILP produces an information and intelligence overload; too much information of little practical value.
>
> > (Van den Hengst and Staffeleu 2012: 188)

> [I]t is difficult to create and maintain a continuous flow of intelligence, analysis, and preparation of target packages, and difficult to conduct operations on the basis of intelligence.
>
> > (Tilley 2003: 333)

> [P]olice officers perceive several obstacles, such as complex data protection rules and high security demands, particularly with regard to proactive intelligence-gathering.
>
> > (Van den Hengst and Staffeleu 2012: 188)

> [T]here is a lack of training and senior officer commitment. Specialist units have difficulty communicating with one another, despite new legislative changes which should enhance the free flow of information between the agencies.
>
> > (Tilley 2003: 333; Vis 2012)

> ILP has met with unsympathetic attitudes, cultural resistance and low morale among police officers who perform administrative tasks, because they feel excluded from this policing task.
>
> > (Tilley 2003: 333)

> ILP throws up a range of potential ethical and operational problems, such as concerning the employment of covert means of investigation and a disproportionate use of privacy-invasive intelligence-gathering.
>
> > (Tilley 2003: 334)

> [I]t is difficult to show evidence that the application of ILP leads to the reduction of crime and criminal opportunities.[9]

In sum, a successful implementation of ILP requires that several conditions be met. Carter and Carter argue that 'the concept of ILP must be created through an inclusive development process that ensures that it is integrated with an agency's goals and functions, its capabilities, and the characteristics of both the agency and the jurisdiction it serves'. There are 'no shortcuts' in this process and the implementation of ILP should not be seen as 'an add-on responsibility' of each agency (Carter and Carter 2009: 317).

The interface between national and international intelligence-led policing

National police agencies are actively involved in intelligence exchange with relevant agencies in other nation-states. This intelligence exchange is generally managed in a bilateral and direct fashion, for instance, through liaison officers. A new approach is gaining ground: multilateral and mediated intelligence exchange through professional agencies that have an explicit intelligence mandate, such as Europol, the EU Border Management Agency (Frontex) and the EU Intelligence Analysis Centre (INTCEN). Intelligence exchange between EU member states has been encouraged since the 1970s when the fight against terrorism became a security priority in Europe, and it has become a common dimension in the discourse of European police cooperation, particularly around issues such as transnational organized crime. EU-wide strategies which promoted an intelligence-based approach to transnational organized crime were the 1997 Action Plan on Organized Crime and the 1999 Tampere Programme on the EU Area of Freedom, Security and Justice. Large-scale terrorist attacks in the US (2001) and Europe (2004, 2005) provided a further boost to intelligence-led law enforcement strategies.

This approach was further refined in the Hague Programme of 2004, which included the objective of establishing and implementing a methodology for intelligence-led law enforcement at the EU level. It introduced the Organized Crime Threat Assessment (OCTA) as part of the European Crime Intelligence Model (ECIM). From then on intelligence-led policing was officially regarded as an approach to be established throughout Europe in order to raise the quality of intelligence and threat assessments. In October 2005 the EU Justice and Home Affairs Council adopted the objective to establish a common methodology for intelligence-led law enforcement, which was to be further enhanced through concerted and coordinated long-term action by all EU bodies and agencies involved in these efforts, together with the member states. The Council noted and welcomed the intention of the European Commission to bring forward proposals, prepared in cooperation with the relevant bodies and agencies, as well as from the member states, for further action in this area. This conclusion clearly endorsed and deepened the establishment of intelligence exchange within a multi-agency framework.

The 2010 Stockholm Programme reiterates the call for a 'proactive and intelligence-led approach'.[10] The word 'intelligence' was however used only four times in this document, twice in relation to financial intelligence units with a view on the fight against money laundering. The ensuing Stockholm Action Programme also only employs 'intelligence' twice in its sixty-nine pages; in relation to financial intelligence the objective of the European Commission is to lay down – in 2014 – new regulations on the improvement of customs and police cooperation in the EU. This would include reflections on the use of under-cover police officers, on Police Cooperation and Customs Centres, as part of an EU approach to intelligence-led policing, and on common actions to improve operational police practices. Interestingly, the EU Internal Security Strategy of 2010 does not mention the term 'intelligence', although the words 'information' and 'information sharing' are used several times.[11] This indicates that the concept of intelligence is primarily used in certain quarters within the area of freedom, security and justice. The question is therefore whether this strategic ambition of improving information sharing is really alive in the member states and whether active preparations are being made for its implementation and operationalization.

According to the House of Lords Report, Europol is believed to be:

> uniquely well placed to establish among the police forces of the Member States a common understanding of intelligence-led policing. Europol should work with the Heads of National Units and the European Police College to organize training which will encourage the adoption and use of Intelligence-Led Policing as the common working method.
>
> (House of Lords 2007–2008: point 76)

Hence, while Europol is positioned as the intelligence coordinator, a remaining issue is whether – despite Europol's right to request cooperation from the member states – the agency generates sufficient levels of trust and commitment in the member states to overcome institutional reluctance in domestic intelligence circles.[12] Europol is aware of this challenge and has built communication links and shared databases to facilitate interaction between law enforcement officials. There is now a Europol Information System (EIS) and a Europol Analysis System; the latter comprises software which is used by all police forces in the EU member states and beyond. Yet levels of cooperation with the role of Europol in the exchange of law enforcement data vary considerably among EU member states, and expressions of commitment do not mean shared strategic perspectives on the necessity and added value of Europol's role in European intelligence exchange.

So far there is still no European Intelligence Agency in existence, and despite the push for more multi-agency security cooperation, the bulk of intelligence cooperation still does not take place at the European level (Müller-Wille 2008). Frontex also relies on partnerships with national bodies in the member states that hold responsibility for border control and related intelligence processes. INTCEN, which was established under the umbrella of the EU Common Foreign and Security Policy, is supposed to undertake a common assessment of particularly critical issues in relation to the foreign policy of the EU. The House of Lords Select Committee is of the opinion that INTCEN (formerly 'SitCen') is better adapted than Europol to the exchange of intelligence among security services rather than among law enforcement agencies).[13]

Conclusions and future outlook

Intelligence-led policing is regarded by some as the miracle recipe for meeting several law enforcement challenges. In essence, the concept is far from being new and innovative, as intelligence has always been intricately linked with security. From a historical perspective it may be argued that ILP was already introduced by the British police in the 1830s. Hence, ILP may well be defined as old wine in new bottles. What is relatively new is that ILP is now used for several different purposes and processes beyond the horizon of criminal investigation. Intelligence as a process and product can be provided by a variety of private, public, collective and commercial agents. ILP may complement the traditional police emphasis on locality, where intelligence makes it possible to establish information patterns about the flow of illicit goods and criminal suspects (Phillips 2008: 27; MacVean 2008: 66).

Popular as the pro-ILP rhetoric may have become, ILP's proactive intervention sits uneasily with legitimacy and output monitoring. Moreover, the chronic lack of trust among law enforcement organizations may lead to the emergence of archipelagos of intelligence in the transnational policing domain, causing diverse and 'fluidly evolving forms of policing and internal security' that are resistant to 'adequate individual and democratic accountability' (as is often the case with transnational arrangements) (Walker 2003: 132; see also Den Boer 2002b; Sheptycki 2004). ILP is built on the assumption that law enforcement organizations share intelligence in order to maximize their effectiveness. Within international security environments, ILP is strongly promoted by a number of internal security agencies in the EU. The House of Lords Select Committee even encouraged its own government to persevere in its attempts to embed these concepts in the policing culture of all member states.[14]

More comparative empirical research is required to analyse information and intelligence flows in the police forces of different countries (see Van den Hengst and Staffeleu 2012: 1930). A question which still lingers is to what extent there is any (proven) added value from ILP when compared to other models of policing. It is supposed to be more proactive, rational and effective, but what about sustainable results? Finally, ILP applications challenge the ordinary accountability arrangements of public police forces, certainly when they exchange and act upon intelligence in a multilateral international context (MacVean 2008: 65, 68). This leads to transnational intelligence 'clouds' in which ownership of intelligence can no longer easily be identified. Police organizations are not the only actors that deal with intelligence. In the national context, intelligence about people, their mobility and transactions is collected by several agencies and institutions, each for its own purpose. Governmental authorities extend their knowledge about citizens by gathering and interconnecting information and intelligence. Several countries have developed strategies for a digital future, seeking to achieve more effectiveness in policing by smart data exchange. In a rapidly internationalizing and borderless environment, intelligence no longer merely belongs to the realm of government, but also to citizens themselves.

A question for the future is whether police organizations will be able to make sensible use of collective intelligence, for instance, to solve a crime or to prepare themselves for a riot. Is intelligence to be regarded as a new technique of 'governmentality' through which the masses are subjected to constant monitoring and mental disciplining? Intelligence and intelligence policing have surmounted the already complex debate on data collection and data protection.

Notes

1 The author would like to thank the editors of this volume, and Paul Minnebo (Europol) and Willy Bruggeman (Federal Police Council Belgium) for their thorough and useful comments. Any omissions are the sole responsibility of the author.
2 See www.theiacp.org/PublicationsGuides/Projects/IntelligenceLedCommunityPolicing/tabid/1006/Default.aspx (accessed 14 September 2012).
3 See www.interpol.int/INTERPOL-expertise/Intelligence-analysis (accessed 7 September 2012).
4 Europol Information Management: Products and Services. Online. Available: www.mvr.gov.mk/Uploads/Europol%20Products%20and%20Services-Booklet.pdf (accessed 14 September 2012).
5 See www.interpol.int/INTERPOL-expertise/Command-Coordination-Centre (accessed 14 September 2012).
6 'Wet van 21 juli 2007, houdende regels inzake de verwerking van politiegegevens (Wet politiegegevens)' [Law of 21 July 2007 Pertaining to the Rules on the Processing of Police Data]. Online. Available: http://wetten.overheid.nl/BWBR0022463/geldigheidsdatum_28–11–2012 (accessed 17 January 2013).
7 'Invoering van de politiewet, en aanpassing van overige wetten aan die wet (Invoerings- en aanpassingswet Politiewet 201X)' [Introduction of the Police Law and Adaptation of Additional Laws to this Law (Introduction and Adaptation Legislation Police Law 201X)], 30 August 2012. Online. Available: http://wetten.overheid.nl/BWBR0031794/geldigheidsdatum_17–01–2013 (accessed 17 January 2013).
8 *Concept Inrichtingsplan Nationale Politie* [Draft Plan for the National Police], 25 June 2012. Online. Available: www.rijksoverheid.nl/documenten-en-publicaties/rapporten/2012/06/25/inrichtingsplan-natinale-politie.html (accessed 17 September 2012).
9 However, see e.g. Bureau of Justice Assistance (2008) 'Reducing Crime Through Intelligence-led Policing'. Online. Available: www.bja.gov/Publications/ReducingCrimeThroughILP.pdf (accessed 8 November 2012).
10 European Council (2010) 'The Stockholm Programme – An Open and Secure Europe Serving and Protecting Citizens', 2010/C 115/01Par 4.1.
11 European Commission (2010) 'The Internal Security Strategy in Action: Five Steps Towards a More Secure Europe', Communication from the Commission to the European Parliament and the Council, Brussels, 22.11.2010 COM (2010) 673 final. Online. Available: http://ec.europa.eu/commission_2010–2014/malmstrom/archive/internal_security_strategy_in_action_en.pdf (accessed 11 July 2012).
12 House of Lords Select Committee on European Union, 29th Report, 2007–2008. Online. Available: www.publications.parliament.uk/pa/ld200708/ldselect/ldeucom/183/18307.htm (accessed 11 July 2012).
13 Ibid., point 29.
14 Ibid., point 82.

Bibliography

Bayer, M. (2010) *The Blue Planet. Informal International Police Networks and National Intelligence*, Washington, DC: National Defense Intelligence College.

Bekkers, V., Van Sluis, A. and Siep, P. (2006) *De Nodale Oriëntatie van de Nederlandse Politie: Over Criminaliteitsbestrijding in de Nederlandse netwerksamenleving. Bouwstenen voor een beleidstheorie*, Rotterdam: Public Innovation/Erasmus Universiteit. Online. Available: www.politieenwetenschap.nl/pdf/nodale_orientatie.pdf (accessed 20 December 2012).

Brodeur, J-P. (2007) 'High and Low Policing in Post 9/11 Times', *Policing: A Journal of Policy and Practice*, 1: 25–37.

Brodeur, J-P. and Leman-Langlois, S. (2003) 'Surveillance-fiction or Higher Policing?', in K. Haggerty and R. Ericson, *The New Politics of Surveillance and Visibility*, Toronto: University of Toronto Press.

Carter, D.L. and Carter, J.G. (2009) 'Intelligence-led Policing. Conceptual and Functional Considerations for Public Policy', *Criminal Justice Policy Review*, 20: 310–325.

Cope, N. (2004) 'Intelligence Led Policing or Policing Led Intelligence? Integrating Volume Crime Analysis into Policing', *British Journal of Criminology*, 44: 188–203.

De Lint, W. (2006) 'Intelligence in Policing and Security: Reflections on Scholarship', *Policing and Society*, 16: 1–6.

Den Boer, M. (2002a) 'Intelligence Exchange and the Control of Organised Crime: From Europeanisation via Centralisation to Dehydration?', in J. Apap and M. Anderson (eds), *Police and Justice Co-operation and the New European borders*, The Hague: Kluwer Law International.

—— (2002b) 'Towards an Accountability Regime for an Emerging European Police Governance', *Policing and Society*, 12: 275–290.

—— (2010a) 'New Mobile Crime', in P. Burgess (ed.), *Handbook of New Security Studies*, London: Routledge.

—— (2010b) 'Towards a Governance Model of Police Cooperation in Europe: The Twist Between Networks and Bureaucracies', in F. Lemieux (ed.), *International Police Cooperation. Emerging Issues, Theory and Practice*, Collompton, Devon: Willan Publishing.

—— (2012) 'Go With the Flow and Undo the Knots: Policing Strategies in an Interconnected World', in F. Allum and S. Gilmour (eds), *Handbook on Transnational Organized Crime*, London: Routledge.

—— (forthcoming 2013) 'Counter-terrorism, Security and Intelligence in the EU: Governance Challenges for Collection, Exchange and Analysis', *Intelligence and National Security*.

Deukmedjian, J.E. and De Lint, W. (2007) 'Community into Intelligence: Resolving Information Uptake in the RCMP', *Policing and Society*, 17: 239–256.

Gill, P. (1998) 'Making Sense of Police Intelligence? The Use of a Cybernetic Model in Analysing Information and Power in Police Intelligence Processes', *Policing and Society*, 8: 289–314.

—— (2005) 'The Politicization of Intelligence: Lessons from the Invasion of Iraq', in H. Born, J. Johnson and I. Leigh (eds), *Who's Watching the Spies? Establishing Intelligence Service Accountability*, Washington, DC: Potomac.

—— (2006) 'Not Just Joining the Dots but Crossing the Borders and Bridging the Voids: Constructing Security Networks after 11 September 2001', *Policing and Society*, 16: 26–48.

—— (2007) 'Evaluating Intelligence Oversight Committees: The Case of the UK Intelligence Security Committee and the "War on Terror"', *Intelligence and National Security*, 22: 14–37.

Gill, P. and Phythian, M. (2006) *Intelligence in an Insecure World*, Cambridge: Polity Press.

Gregory, F. (2008) 'The Police and the Intelligence Services – with Special Reference to the Relationship with MI5', in C. Harfield, A. MacVean, J. Grieve and D. Phillips (eds), *The Handbook of Intelligent Policing*, Oxford: Oxford University Press.

Harfield, C. (2008) 'Introduction: Intelligent Policing', in C. Harfield, A. MacVean, J. Grieve and D. Phillips (eds), *The Handbook of Intelligent Policing. Consilience, Crime Control and Community Safety*, Oxford: Oxford University Press.

Hoogenboom, B. (1994) *Het politiecomplex: Over de samenwerking tussen politie, bijzondere opsporingsdiensten en particuliere recherche*, Arnhem: Gouda Quint.

House of Lords Select Committee on European Union (2007–2008) 29th Report, point 66.

Innes, M., Abbott, L., Lowe, T. and Roberts, C. (2009), 'Seeing Like a Citizen: Field Experiments in "Community Intelligence-led Policing"', *Police Practice and Research: An International Journal*, 10: 99–114.

Johnston, L. (1999) 'Private Policing in Context', *European Journal in Criminal Policy and Research*, 7: 175–196.

Keane, N. and Kleiven, M.E. (2009) 'Risky Intelligence', *International Journal of Police Science and Management*, 11: 324–333.

Kleiven, M.E. (2005) 'Where's the "Intelligence" in the National Intelligence Model?', unpublished thesis, University of Portsmouth. Online. Available: http://brage.bibsys.no/politihs/bitstream/URN:NBN:no-bibsys_brage_9206/1/where's_%20the_%20intelligence.pdf (accessed 14 September 2012).

Kop, N., Wal, R. van der and Snel, G. (eds) (2011) *Opsporing belicht. Over strategieën in de opsporingspraktijk*, Apeldoorn: Politieacademie.

Lippert, R. and O'Connor, D. (2006) 'Security Intelligence Networks and the Transformation of Contract Private Security', *Policing and Society*, 16: 50–66.

Lowe, T. and Innes, M. (2012) 'Can We Speak in Confidence? Community Intelligence and Neighbourhood Policing v2.0', *Policing and Society*, 22: 295–316.

MacVean, A. (2008) 'The Governance of Intelligence', in C. Harfield, A. MacVean, J. Grieve and D. Phillips (eds), *The Handbook of Intelligent Policing. Consilience, Crime Control and Community Safety*, Oxford: Oxford University Press.

Maguire, M. (2000) 'Policing by Risks and Targets: Some Dimensions and Implications for Intelligence-led Crime Control', *Policing and Society*, 9: 315–336.

Maguire, M. and John, T. (2006) 'Intelligence-led Policing, Managerialism and Community Engagement: Competing Priorities and the Role of the National Intelligence Model in the UK', *Policing and Society* (Special Issue: *Intelligence in Policing and Security: Reflections on Scholarship*), 16: 67–85.

McGarrell, E., Freilich, J. and Chermak, S. (2007) 'Intelligence-led Policing as a Framework for Responding to Terrorism', *Journal for Contemporary Criminal Justice*, 23: 142–158.

Müller-Wille, B. (2008) 'The Effect of International Terrorism on EU Intelligence Cooperation', *Journal of Common Market Studies*, 46: 49–73.

Peterson, M. (2005) *Intelligence-led Policing: The New Intelligence Architecture*, Washington, DC: U.S. Department of Justice. Online. Available: www.it.ojp.gov/documents/Revised_Laser_Intell-Led_Polcing.pdf (accessed 17 August 2012).

Phillips, Sir D. (2008) 'Police Intelligence Systems as a Strategic Response', in C. Harfield, A. MacVean, J. Grieve and D. Phillips (eds), *The Handbook of Intelligent Policing*, Oxford: Oxford University Press.

Ponsaers, P. (2001) 'Reading About "Community (oriented) Policing" and Police Models', *Policing: An International Journal of Police Strategies and Management*, 24: 470–497.

Ratcliffe, J. (2008) *Intelligence-led Policing*, Cullompton, Devon: Willan Publishing.

—— (2010) 'Intelligence-led Policing and the Problems of Turning Rhetoric into Practice', *Policing and Society*, 12: 53–66.

Sheptycki, J. (2004) 'Organizational Pathologies in Police Intelligence Systems. Some Contributions to the Lexicon of Intelligence-led Policing', *European Journal of Criminology*, 1: 307–332.

—— (2007) 'High Policing in the Security Control Society', *Policing. A Journal of Policy and Practice*, 1: 70–79.

Stenning, P. (2000) 'Powers and Accountability of Private Police', *European Journal on Criminal Policy and Research*, 8: 325–352.

Tilley, N. (2003; reprinted 2005) 'Community Policing, Problem-oriented Policing and Intelligence-led Policing', in T. Newburn (ed.), *The Handbook of Policing*, Cullompton, Devon: Willan Publishing.

Van den Hengst, M. and Regterschot, H. (2012) 'Intelligence gestuurd politiewerk: een maturity model', *Het Tijdschrift voor de Politie*, 74: 23–27.

Van den Hengst, M. and Staffeleu, E. (2012) 'Different Information Organizations to Produce the Same High Quality Intelligence: An Overview of the Police Forces in the Netherlands', *Policing: A Journal of Policy and Practice*, 6: 187–193.

Van Mantgem, J. van, Grapendaal, M. and Van der Wel, M.A. (2012) 'De CSV-manager 4.2: waar strategisch en tactisch elkaar ontmoeten', *Het Tijdschrift voor de Politie*, 74: 23–26.

Villasenor, J. (2011) 'Recording Everything: Digital Storage as an Enabler of Authoritarian Governments', *Governance Studies*, Center for Technology Innovation, The Brookings Institution. Online. Available: www.brookings.edu/~/media/research/files/papers/2011/12/14%20digital%20storage%20villasenor/1214_digital_storage_villasenor.pdf (accessed 20 December 2012).

Vis, T. (2012), *Intelligence, politie en veiligheidsdienst: verenigbare grootheden?*, Tilburg: Universiteit van Tilburg.

Walker, N. (2003; reprinted 2005) 'The Pattern of Transnational Policing', in T. Newburn (ed.), *The Handbook of Policing*, Collompton, Devon: Willan Publishing.

Whitaker, R. (1999) *The End of Privacy. How Total Surveillance is Becoming a Reality*, New York: The New Press.

10   The next 100 years?

Reflections on the future of intelligence

Wilhelm Agrell

An unlikely prediction and some guesswork

At the beginning of the twenty-first century, there has been a growing interest in the history of intelligence in general, and the history of intelligence institutions in particular (Andrew 2009; Aid 2009; Weiner 2007). This interest is not limited to the Anglo-Saxon world (Rentola 2009; Davidsen-Nielsen 2008). Behind this is probably the historical fact that the 'short twentieth century' was a formative period for intelligence and security services as we know them today, but there is also an awareness that things will not remain as they are forever, that societies and their interrelations are bound to change, and as a consequence so will the need for and the conduct of intelligence. Intelligence is an evolving social activity, so looking back may not only be a way to understand and to a considerable extent discover the past, but also to get some insights, however limited and uncertain, about the dynamics shaping the future of intelligence. But will future intelligence represent a new era, completely detached from the past, where history would be irrelevant or even misleading? Christopher Andrew, in the concluding chapter of his account of MI5, argues forcefully against this notion: 'For the first time in recorded history, there has been a widespread assumption that the experience of all previous generations is irrelevant to present policy. Institutions, like individuals, however, diminish their effectiveness if they fail to reflect on past successes and failures' (Andrew 2009: 849).

The future, or rather the perception of the future, always tends to reflect the present, and our inability to take into account fundamental changes, even though history is made up of them, is sometimes stunning, as is our limited ability to see the complex indirect consequences of technological, social and cultural change. We could call this phenomenon the unavoidable cognitive prison of the present. It tends to distort and restrict perceptions of the future, especially concerning activities like intelligence, which are dependent on and shaped by developments on a number of more or less interrelated fields. Intelligence, by definition, is a mirror of the complexity of historical change. Therefore, the discussion of the future of intelligence has in past decades tended to reflect the dominating perceptions of the nature of security and threats, from the late Cold War paradigm of the 1980s, to the broadened definition of security and intelligence users in the

1990s to the post-9/11 hegemony of counter-terrorism as the future main dominating task of intelligence (Goodman 1996; Charters *et al.* 1995). Much of the recent literature on the future of intelligence is thus rapidly ageing, already transforming into a source for the history of thinking about intelligence, or what some future writer may define as the history of the philosophy of intelligence.

But in the case of intelligence the cognitive prison of the present has a further dimension; it is also a part of the subject itself. One of the fundamental recurring problems experienced in the conduct of intelligence over the past century is the limited ability of intelligence to discover and comprehend changes incompatible with expectations, perceptions or simply with what has been stated in dozens or hundreds of previous assessments. Therefore, the limited ability to assess the future of intelligence is also an important limitation in the conduct of intelligence, perhaps even the most important one, as reflected in some of the vast literature on surprises (Wohlstetter 1962; Betts 1982, 2007; Kam 1988). However, one thing stands out as reasonably certain. The least likely of all unlikely predictions about the future of intelligence must be that it will remain as we know it today, that intelligence will develop along familiar lines and that we simply have to prolong the trends of the past years and decades or of the past century.

But why should we worry at all about the future of intelligence if we cannot foresee it? One simple answer is that we will do it anyway. There is always a perception of the future, well founded or not, that guides policy, public debate and the internal development of the field. If we would make no effort to reflect along these lines, assuming that the future is unknowable – as it is in a strict logical sense – we will most likely remain stuck in the cognitive prison and unintentionally and perhaps unknowingly make precisely the worst of all guesses, the mirror image of the present and its more or less distorted perception of the past.

Yet these perceptions of the past, the history of intelligence and the societies in which intelligence has developed and functioned (or malfunctioned), is basically all we can rely on to get some kind of structure on thinking about intelligence on a more general level. John Keegan in one of his famous books on warfare, *The Face of Battle*, writes about what he calls the usefulness and deficiencies of military history, of history as the only way, aside from personal experience, to grasp what battle is all about, but at the same time it is producing myths, distortion and over-simplification (Keegan 1998). In a similar way the history of intelligence, even when well researched and well written, may be of limited immediate relevance for thinking about the future. The past is not a scheme; cases or 'lessons' are seldom as unambiguous as they are presented and taught.[1] Thus what is the usefulness of intelligence history from this specific perspective?

In all social development there are long lines. History never stops, and the ruptures perceived to end one era and begin another often appear less abrupt and dramatic in retrospect. Therefore, the long lines, to the extent that they can be identified, would be of considerable help, not perhaps to predict the future but to provide some elements likely to prevail into the future. In intelligence these long lines consist of fundamental and timeless methods and recurring failures, the 'permanent operating factors' that the literature of surprises deals with and that Christopher Andrew encourages institutions and individuals to reflect about. To take one example, the means to stage deception will inevitably change continuously, since the success of deception depends on adaptation to current conditions, technical possibilities and information flows. But the basic principle of the deception scheme as an induced cognitive trap is not likely to change, since it is based on group dynamics and the functions of the human mind (Whaley 1973). These elements of intelligence methodology are essential for reflections about the future of intelligence in organizational, social and intellectual terms – of course with the caveat that some factors assumed to be timeless and unchanging may not be as permanent as we may perceive them at present.

Another central element in macro-historical discussions are the attempts to identify not the permanent or slowly changing factors but the mechanisms of change, the prime movers or 'triggers' in a historical process, as they were discussed in Chalmer Johnson's work on revolutionary change (Johnson 1966). While these prime movers are not always obvious and often appear in complicated interactions, they can provide some elements of foresight as to the interplay of factors in future developments. The mechanisms will not make it possible to predict or model the future, but should help people to think and reason about it.

To say something about the future of intelligence we have to guess, but to guess in a structured way. If twentieth-century intelligence had some 'great moments' along with a number of well-known as well as hidden or undiscovered failures, so will most likely twenty-first-century intelligence have all those as well, although it would take a novel writer and not a historian or social scientist to fathom them. And likewise, twenty-first-century intelligence will experience further ruptures and surprises, apart from those already belonging to the short history of the century. Perhaps, but only perhaps, these coming failures and their consequences are rather more predictable than the possible great moments.

The first or last century of intelligence?

Looking back on a century of intelligence, in the words of Jeffrey T. Richelson (1995), a fundamental question is whether or not this represents a foundational period, where intelligence rose to become a core element in national and eventually international security, and in the course of this also transformed from amateurism to a profession, or rather a field of professions. An alternative interpretation would be that the century of intelligence instead represents a unique period in first of all European and North American history, in much the same way as we now perceive the role of armed conflicts in politics and the transformation of the means of warfare, where the twentieth century stands out as a brief, devastating period in human history, fuelled by the combination of ideology, industrial technology and a fatal interpretation and employment of the Clausewitzian concept of war. From such a perspective, intelligence may be seen as the product of a period with specific circumstances, as mirrored in the subdivision of the intelligence field in intelligence/counter-intelligence and subversion/counter-subversion. The rise of twentieth-century institutional structures cannot be separated from these specific circumstances and it would hardly have taken place without them. Most of the institutions still dominating the intelligence field were literally born under fire. But then again, intelligence in the way we know and define it today may be not only the product but rather a reflection of these specific historical circumstances. Intelligence as a social phenomenon and instrument was not invented in 1909, or not even in 1587 when Francis Walsingham drafted his *Plot for Intelligence out of Spain* (Dedijer 1983; Hutchinson 2007: 216). In one sense intelligence is constantly restarted throughout history. Late nineteenth-century intelligence was in many European countries focused on the national and international threat from anarchistic terrorism, just as early twenty-first-century intelligence has focused on the threat from international terrorism.

So, if the perception of twenty-first-century intelligence as simply a continuing gradual process of adaptation and modernization would end up as a rather poor one, so would probably the corresponding concept of 'the end of intelligence', as mirrored in the brief debate in the 1990s over institutions without a mission and the need for survival strategies in terms of redefinition and reorientation. Intelligence will inevitably transform; the question is which factors will determine this transformation. But at the same time, the factors of change also change over time. If we look at technology, this transformation of the dynamics of change may be observed. In the nineteenth century new technology was the product of invention, engineering and industrial entrepreneurship. In the course of the twentieth century, new technology became the output of massive commercial, national and eventually multinational research and development efforts. So while the dynamics and social impact of new technology continue, the institutions and procedures behind the innovations have changed completely.

A number of fundamental driving factors may be identified behind the establishment and transformation of intelligence in the twentieth century, which does not necessary imply that no other factors or circumstances have been relevant. However, there are at least five factors that run through the whole period and cut across the various national experiences:

1 The evolution in demand for intelligence on threats, whether actual or perceived. Imaginary threats can affect intelligence just as much as real threats.
2 The double impact of technological change, both affecting the intelligence targets and the potential to collect, communicate and process intelligence material.
3 The evolution of the societies in which intelligence operates or of which it is a part.
4 The remarkable stability and survivability of intelligence institutions and networks.
5 The prevailing nature of certain methods and problems in the conduct of intelligence.

The need to know

In the beginning there had to be a customer. Not only did British intelligence in its modern form start with the beginning of the twentieth century, but so did military and security intelligence in a number of European countries. The invention was the establishment of permanent or at least semi-permanent intelligence organizations, with an assigned task within a military staff structure and a state bureaucracy, the introduction of the concept of the *deuxième bureau*, an entity with the task of monitoring the others. When a few years ago the Swedish military intelligence organization wanted to celebrate its hundredth anniversary, a thorough search in the intelligence archives of the old General Staff managed to turn up a document from early 1905, where funding was provided for the establishment of a network for secret intelligence collection led by two junior officers (Frick and Rossander 2004). The reason for this invention was obvious, and so was the target: Norway. The unequal union between the two Scandinavian countries was coming apart through a process of mutual nationalism, and the former brothers were transforming into enemies in a destructive and all too well-known process of polarization.

As it turned out, war on the Scandinavian peninsula was averted at the brink and secession was accomplished without bloodshed. But Swedish military intelligence continued to exist, though no longer directed at a secessionist threat. This pattern seems to be common, and illustrates one of the basic dynamics of intelligence organizations, whether as independent institutions, as a department or merely as a function carried out within a bureaucracy or organization. Once intelligence has been 'invented' in fiscal or organizational terms it seems that it is seldom 'uninvented', as new needs always tend to appear on the horizon. Swedish military intelligence turned from Norway to the rising threat from the Russian Baltic Fleet, replaced in the 1920s by the perceived threat of Bolshevik subversion, followed by Stalin's rearmament and expansion towards Finland and the Baltic States, German expansion in Scandinavia during the Second World War, the post-war re-establishment of the Baltic Fleet, the gradual Cold War expansion of the Soviet capability for amphibious warfare, the post-Cold War Russian transfer of offensive resources from the Central Front towards the flanks following the withdrawal from united Germany, the continued strategic instability posed by the Kaliningrad enclave and the security implications of the underwater pipeline being built by Russian Gazprom through the Baltic. There is nearly always a need to know, although the exact focus of that need may change, and then change back again.

The evolution of the means of warfare was perhaps the most powerful dynamic factor affecting the conduct of intelligence until the end of the Cold War. Intelligence grew into large structures with thousands or tens of thousands of employees and innumerable agents, subcontractors or assets, not primarily due to bureaucratic momentum, which set in later, but originally to meet the demand for intelligence from new means of warfare that certainly resorted to, or was preparing to resort to, the employment of destructive force. Intelligence was in itself not decisive, but in combination with a military potential it was, as underlined by Keegan in one of his later works (Keegan 2003).[2] But intelligence itself also became dependent on an ever-increasing flow of raw information, data banks and continuously updated assessments. We can certainly discuss the actual impact of intelligence on the subsequent events or non-events, from Magic (US), Ultra (UK) and G-Schreiber (Sweden), to the massive efforts of Cold War intelligence and counter-intelligence. 'Did intelligence matter?' (Herman *et al.* 2006) is a highly relevant question, but it is perhaps less relevant for the development of the structures and patterns, the very idea of intelligence as something vital to national and international security. Here the perception of intelligence seems to have been more important than the actual direct or indirect impact.

However, without this massive demand-pull from the process of militarization and focus on national security, it is hard to see how the establishment of twentieth-century intelligence within the realm of national security would have come about. And just as in the field of research and development of new technologies and systems, the pattern set by the military applications was transferred to other fields, and thus created other intelligence needs (Treverton 2009).

Technology and the intelligence revolutions

Technology stands out as a crucial element in this process of transformation in a number of interlinked ways. Any effort to comprehend the evolution of twentieth-century intelligence and further developments must take into consideration this multiple impact of technology. First of all, technological change has been an important aspect of the transforming security environment, creating the need for intelligence. What made the Russian Baltic Fleet a growing concern for Swedish intelligence prior to the First World War was not so much political considerations as the replacement of the losses in the Tsushima battle with a new generation of capital ships. This interaction is perhaps the most studied aspect of military intelligence, especially during the Second World War and the Cold War, when technological intelligence and military R&D became increasingly interlinked (Jones 1979). This technological driver is not limited to the traditional military domain, as illustrated both by irregular warfare and the wider significance of intelligence on scientific research and industrial R&D.

The second impact of technological change concerns the intelligence objects. The development of information technology and patterns of information exchange has been the single technological and social factor with the most direct impact on the conduct and potential of intelligence, a process that started well before the twentieth century but which gathered momentum with the exponential expansion of telecommunications. If we could foresee the developments in communications technologies, this would most likely give a general idea of the transformation of future intelligence collection, and the potential to monitor a vast number of human activities – to the extent that this would be considered politically, legally and ethically acceptable or at least tolerable.

The monitoring of telecommunications also illustrates the third aspect of technological change: the employment of technology for passive or active intelligence collection. Some of these systems were simply mirroring or adapting information technology, such as the first generation decoding machines at Bletchley Park or at the Swedish Defence Radio Agency, or varieties of antennas and receivers. Other technologies could be employed for active intelligence collection with sensors outside the sphere of telecommunications. Employment of technology for intelligence purposes was however not limited to collection, but also encompassed processing, storage, analysis and dissemination of information, in short the technological basis for the intelligence cycle.

The development of twentieth-century intelligence was conceptual and organizational to be sure; but first and foremost it was technological. The massive impact of collection and later processing technologies was what transformed intelligence from a slow, incomplete and delayed gathering of information on specific spots to broad, near real-time coverage of a wide spectrum of objects and activities. It seems unlikely that the powerful momentum of multiple technological impacts on the conduct of intelligence would cease or even wind down, unless we are to speculate over a possible future with decreased efforts in R&D, growing and widespread scepticism towards new technologies, or social or political developments severely hampering international scientific and R&D cooperation.

Institutional survivability and professional heritage

The 100-year anniversaries are themselves an indication of a considerable institutional continuity in the intelligence field. There are remarkably few cases from the twentieth century of intelligence organizations being permanently dissolved, even when their original mission has disappeared, or after major political controversies, scandals or performance failures. Intelligence directors come and go, but the organizations generally remain. Major reorganizations are in many cases cosmetic, as the staff remain intact or simply get recycled in a new organizational chart. Even after major regime changes, as in the former Warsaw Pact states of Eastern Europe, the intelligence services are generally not disbanded for good. In some cases they were thoroughly reorganized, in others the personnel were dismissed, only to be re-employed after some time as their competence was needed by the new regimes (Born *et al.* 2005). Only in a state that itself also ceased to exist, the German Democratic Republic (GDR), were the intelligence and security services totally and permanently disbanded, even though their heritage continues to cast long shadows.

In Western countries, institutional stability has been remarkable. Behind this is the closed nature, special role and relative inaccessibility of these organizations, also for policy-makers. This reflects both a well-established intelligence culture, and a corresponding reluctance among policy-makers to become too deeply involved in intelligence matters, sometimes for good reasons. If the way intelligence services operate remains a black box for most policy-makers, this is even more the case when it comes to signals intelligence. A potentially important development, however, is the opening up of this black box, or rather black chamber, through the pressure of legislation and systems for approval of access to electronic communications affecting citizens. These kinds of judicial and institutional processes tend to be incremental and never-ending. Furthermore, the changes that they constitute are often more permanent than developments on the organizational level, and the major consequences are often indirect and – at least originally – unintentional.[3]

It is necessary, however, to underline that a substantial part of twentieth-century intelligence were the structures and techniques developed and employed by totalitarian systems and authoritarian regimes, especially in the field of domestic surveillance and political control. These aspects of the development of intelligence as an institutional, constitutional and legal phenomenon cannot simply be regarded as temporary exceptions. The totalitarian and authoritarian experience had, and continues to have, a profound impact on intelligence, both in terms of the institutional sustainability discussed above, and in a more indirect way through the diffusion of methods, organizational principles and perceptions of professionalism, perhaps best illustrated by the massive recycling of the German intelligence heritage after the Second World War (Aldrich 2001; Naimark 1995; Pryser 1999).

Will the major intelligence institutions, as we know them from the twentieth and early twenty-first century still be around towards the end of the twenty-first century? And if so, in what form will they still appear? Or will there be new forms of intelligence organizations and structures? If it is a correct observation that intelligence organizations, for a number of reasons, have a higher degree of survivability than other sectors of public administration, it is possible that the traces of early twenty-first-century organizations may still be visible by the end of the century. Tasks will certainly change, along with names and internal structures, a process that is likely to reflect how the performance and roles of the organizations are perceived by users, financers and voters, and how these categories in their turn will change over time.

The future of intelligence as activity and social phenomenon

If twentieth-century intelligence was shaped by the demands and diffusion from the security domain and the perceptions of external and internal threats against states, the future of intelligence may be expected to reflect the evolving nature of security and the dynamics of threats and, above all, threat perceptions. A future stable European peace would certainly, as in previous long interwar periods, affect the attitudes to and transformation of intelligence as a security instrument in this part of the world. The 'soft power' of diplomacy, negotiations, economic interdependence and social integration is not necessarily something that will be conducted with the same forms of intelligence support as traditional twentieth-century national security, though it is hard to imagine any international order where intelligence becomes redundant. There are many organizations or networks operating without a defined intelligence support, but this is often provided in an informal and sometimes unconscious way. It may also be argued that a security system not primarily based on quantifiable and well-defined military means will be even more dependent on intelligence support, although focused on other issues and objects and supporting decision-making in a different and more integral way than traditional security intelligence (Sheptycki 2009).

International organizations have, for a number of obvious reasons, remained weak in terms of intelligence. It is not likely that the divide between these organizations and the traditional intelligence institutions could be permanently overcome in the sense that the national institutions would be subordinate to a new international order. Certainly, these international organizations can build their own intelligence functions, as some of them are already in the process of doing, but these new intelligence actors are bound to encompass all the problems and limitations of international organizations as such, along with the inherent problems of every intelligence structure. A possible alternative course of action would be for international organizations to build different forms of intelligence structures. However, the main problem with intelligence is often not the conduct of intelligence itself, but the limited ability of the receiver to use intelligence output in forwarding the goals of the organization.

Apart from this there is the phenomenon of new or emerging intelligence actors. While the established intelligence triad – national/transnational security, law enforcement, business/competitive intelligence – is transforming and adapting to new threats and opportunities and new demands from users, new intelligence fields with new actors are taking shape in several traditionally non-intelligence or even anti-intelligence environments. This organic and often unstructured process could be just as important or even more important than the eternal issue of intelligence institutions and reforms.

During the twentieth century it was generally taken for granted that new intelligence actors could learn from the old ones. The future may contain an opposite pattern, at least in some respects. The emerging intelligence fields could provide examples of alternative modes of intelligence, perhaps even methods that reduce some of the – seemingly – eternal shortcomings of traditional intelligence like groupthink, segmentation of information and production for the sake of production. New intelligence actors may, for reason of their specific demands and premises, build intelligence systems along different lines and based on other principles than those inherited from the last century.

Intelligence has throughout history been a problematic activity when it comes to a wider social acceptance, often for very good reasons. The spy is an occasional hero, especially in his or her virtual role in popular culture, but he is also a loathed traitor. And while most citizens might accept that their own country resorts to spying or other forms of intelligence activities abroad, the acceptance of domestic surveillance and especially systematic intelligence gathering is far more conditional and fluctuating. Spying, under whatever euphemism, is never generally liked or accepted. In this sense intelligence, at least as soon as individuals are directly or indirectly affected, remains in a grey zone of ethically dubious social activities, always dependent on transparent goals, secure procedures and effective oversight to ensure legitimacy. On this fundamental social and cultural level, it is hard to see whether intelligence would ever come in from the grey zone to become just another social field, another part of business and government administration, unless of course intelligence transforms and becomes just that. But then again, who in that brave new world would perform the intelligence task out there?

The future of intelligence as a field of knowledge production

The most obvious limitation in the twentieth-century concept of intelligence has been the tendency to focus on the production of masses of information, presented and perceived as knowledge, but in many cases being quite the opposite, the production or rather creation of institutional and social ignorance,[4] defined here not as the conscious lack of knowledge but the flawed perception of knowing, while in fact not knowing, or comprehending. If intelligence, in the words of Francis Bacon, could be regarded as the 'light of the state', then the main hazard is perhaps not darkness but the misconception that the illuminated spot around the lamppost constitutes the world.[5]

The conduct of intelligence in terms of the technological basis, collection ability and focus changed dramatically during the twentieth century. What did *not* change in a corresponding way was the underlying theory of cognition, the idea that in the end intelligence is about facts, about the 'real' world, and that this will be revealed more or less by itself through a linear and to an increasing extent industrialized knowledge production system (Herman 1996: 305–338). Perhaps because of this conviction, and the immense expansion of intelligence collection and use (and misuse) of technology as the universal solution to almost every upcoming intelligence task or problem, analysis has remained a small and sometimes insignificant bypass link in the huge intelligence machinery. Analysis has not only been diminutive in terms of staff and financial resources, it has also, due to the design of the intelligence cycle and its assumed rationality, been assigned a reactive role, often far down the intelligence assembly line (George and Bruce 2008; Marrin 2009; Agrell 2009; Charters *et al.* 1996).

As a consequence, analysis has not developed in a way similar to collection. In certain fields it could be argued that analysis has not developed at all or even moved backwards under the pressure from mass collection and mass dissemination. There has been only limited and scattered development of the field since the publication of Sherman Kent's classical book on strategic intelligence in 1949 (Kent 1949). Kent argued for the introduction of scientific methods in intelligence, not only to comprehend specific problems and fields but to make verifiable assessments. The non-development of a scientific approach to an array of analytic problems is a striking feature of twentieth-century intelligence; there is not only an 'under-theorization' in the study of intelligence and the impact of intelligence on international relations, as Christopher Andrew observes (Andrew 2004), but also a crucial under-theorization in intelligence itself (Johnston 2005).

Looking ahead, it is hard to see how this unsatisfactory state of the art can continue for any prolonged period of time. This underdevelopment or under-theorization thus constitutes an area with the most obvious growing potential for change. Sooner or later a process is bound to start, similar to the one familiar in most research fields, with an explicit and visible interest in methodological development, the establishment of a methodologically relevant literature and a theoretical discourse.

An intellectual process of this kind may in itself become a factor changing not only the concepts and intellectual perspective of intelligence analysis, but also affecting the wider intelligence culture and thus in the end the way intelligence is organized, employed and regarded. It is hard to see how a serious focus on methodological issues could be accomplished within the framework of the traditional closed twentieth-century intelligence organizations. Thus, structures may change and the walls of secrecy slowly crumble, not necessarily because of an open source revolution or the growth of public demand for transparency, but because of the need for future intelligence systems to be able to supply reliable and above all verifiable assessments.

Like scientific research, intelligence analysis is about uncertainty. The similarities are sometimes striking and it may be argued that there is a process of convergence where intelligence analysis increasingly relies not only on scientific output and competence but also on borrowed or transformed methods, applied to specific intelligence problems. This also illustrates the other side of the convergence; with an increasing role for science in early warning, prediction and prescription over a wide range of political issues, science and research organizations are, with all the well-known problems from the intelligence field, becoming intelligence oriented, a process constituting a vital element in what may be called a social intelligence revolution, the emergence of intelligence-based societies or, if not that, then at least intelligence-demanding ones.

A century of intelligence proliferation and transformation?

Intelligence will not disappear. Not even the current intelligence institutions are likely to go away, at least not rapidly, and certainly not without preceding major upheavals. However, most of them will probably be found under different names, some not even referring to the traditional twentieth-century concept of the intelligence field. Others may have merged and transformed into a shape still unknown (and perhaps unthinkable) today. And intelligence as a social activity and phenomenon may appear in different contexts and be perceived through other norms, values and expectations than twentieth-century national intelligence.

Given the main elements in the transformation of intelligence discussed here, how will the globalized, transformed field of intelligence look in the coming century? Leaving aside the reservations concerning the cognitive prison of the present, as well as the impact of the unforeseeable dimensions of historical change – the 'secrets' and 'mysteries' of future history – there are at least six fundamental processes of change that could be identified, and as time passes either become the object of closer study or be discarded:

1 *A decreasing relevance and subsequent breakup of the prevailing national intelligence paradigm.* Intelligence reform within an existing framework is, at least in the long run, not a viable strategy. It is hard to imagine *any* major new intelligence challenge as a task for primarily national institutions or systems. From this also follows that the institutionally, professionally and constitutionally important divide between foreign and domestic intelligence will inevitably lose relevance and become increasingly diffuse, perhaps not so much due to political pull but to various push factors caused by the indirect consequences of structural changes.

2 *The rise of new fields of knowledge with intelligence relevance.* With more and diversified intelligence demands the principle of in-house expertise is becoming infeasible and counterproductive. This is likely to be the most powerful factor affecting the analytic and assessment function of intelligence. It is however not certain that expertise and knowledge will be brought into intelligence structures; a reverse process is thinkable where it is the intelligence expertise and knowledge that are brought into strategic fields of knowledge production in research, public administration or business.

3 *Diminishing relative importance of exclusive sources and methods.* With the powerful technological and social momentum behind the open source revolution, the relative share of exclusive intelligence collection is bound to shrink (Treverton 2001; Steele 2000). Future intelligence demands may furthermore revaluate open sources from being a traditional second-rate asset to the main source category, for instance, if the open source arena in itself becomes the intelligence target. It should in this context be observed that the exclusive sources and methods are by no means constant but similarly transforming, perhaps best illustrated by the adaptation of Comint to new information technologies.

4 *The rise of new actors using, producing and providing intelligence.* This is not a future scenario but a rapid ongoing process, not only driven by intelligence demands – especially not in the traditional sense – but by the economic potential of the control and exploitation of the information content on the Internet. The major change will come once the intelligence potential of the ongoing digital information revolution is being exploited in a systematic way.

5 *The loss of intellectual monopoly in a competitive knowledge environment.* Traditional intelligence institutions will not only be affected by decreasing relevance of the national intelligence paradigm and the competition from open sources and new actors. Like many other providers of expertise, intelligence will be challenged and eventually lose a monopoly hitherto based on the access to exclusive sources, the use of special methods and the possession of unique 'deep' knowledge.

6 *Increasing emphasis on reliability in a fragmented world of information.* With new fields of knowledge becoming relevant, the impact of the open source revolution and claims from competing providers of expertise, the

crucial element in the intelligence process will tend to shift from information collection to knowledge validation. This, and not traditional intelligence output, may become the primary task of intelligence.

The common denominator for these processes is a transformation not only of institutions and methods, but in the very concept of intelligence as a separate, bureaucratized entity. Using a twentieth-century term, this may be described as intelligence proliferation, a process where intelligence will become more widely employed and integrated, but at the same time increasingly diverse, diffuse and hard to define. Thus, those in the future eventually attempting to write the history of twenty-first-century intelligence may not only be faced with the task of reconstructing such a process of proliferation, but also with a profoundly transformed subject matter. Is it even certain that they will find it relevant to define their studies as the history of *intelligence*?

However, I have a feeling that whatever we manage to come up with about the future of intelligence, it will most likely amuse someone who may rediscover these long-forgotten efforts at the end of the century and perhaps use them in a lecture on early twenty-first-century perceptions and mindsets. Most efforts to look into the future of intelligence have a far shorter time-span, where the imminent intelligence problems and their possible solution are the focus and prediction or prescription seldom goes beyond the next anticipated intelligence reform. This is perhaps in one way safer ground, but also an area where the future can quickly become the past, or rather bypassed by developments.

Facing the future we are all mentally trapped, intelligence systems and those who study them alike. We are stuck in our mindsets, frames of reference and the current dominating discourse. But of course the future itself is a powerful trap of genuine unpredictability and immense complexity, where every theory we could formulate is bound to fail. The scholar trying to figure out the future of intelligence is sharing some of the fundamental methodological problems of the intelligence analyst, also trapped in a prison of the present facing the interaction of prime movers and circumstantial factors in the process of historical change. If intelligence ever comes closer in the future to dealing with this paramount challenge in analysis and assessment, we will possibly as a byproduct be able to identify the lines of the future of intelligence rather more accurately than seems possible today.

Notes

1 One prominent example of the over-simplification of cases is the Israeli intelligence failure prior to the Yom Kippur or October War 1973, often referred to as the paramount example of cognitive traps and groupthink in intelligence analysis. This interpretation rested on the account of the Agranat Commission published in 1974, which for security reasons withheld the role of possibly the most important Israeli intelligence asset at the time, the Egyptian official Ashraf Marwan. Yom Kippur remains an important historical case, but perhaps in a slightly different way than originally perceived. See Bar-Joseph (2005).

2 Keegan quotes David Kahn's assessment that all the code-breaking efforts of Poland prior to the outbreak of the Second World War in 1939 came to nothing, as intelligence can only work through strength (Kahn 1991: 91).

3 A recent example of this is the effort of the Swedish government to give the signals intelligence service access to communications to and from the country through the fibre-optic cables (they had tapped a considerable amount of cables and satellite links before with secret approval or silent consent from the government). First presented in 2005, the proposed bill stated that the existing intelligence oversight body could handle the approval. When the bill was finally put before Parliament in 2008, a new independent approval body was suggested and a few months later the government agreed to this in the face of fierce public and parliamentary pressure as well as pressure from within the ruling alliance. It proposed a new independent intelligence court to decide if permission was to be granted for specific Comint operations.

4 Ignorance as a factor in understanding intelligence has been surprisingly overlooked, outside the specific field of intentional disinformation of other actors or the public. Besides a few works in economy dealing with the phenomenon of random choices, ignorance as a social phenomenon has been sparsely studied, with the important exception of Proctor and Schiebinger (2008).

5 The 'light of the state' analogy originally appeared in a script by Bacon for a festival at Gray's Inn in 1594. Essex used it in a letter to a Doctor Hawkins two years later. See Dedijer (1983).

Bibliography

Agrell, W. (2009) 'Intelligence analysis after the Cold War: New paradigms or old anomalies?', in G. Treverton and W. Agrell (eds), *National Intelligence Systems: Current Research and Future Prospects*, Cambridge: Cambridge University Press.

Aid, M. (2009) *The Secret Sentry: The Untold History of the National Security Agency*, New York: Bloomsbury Press.

Aldrich, R.J. (2001) *The Hidden Hand: Britain, America and Cold War Secret Intelligence*, London: John Murray.

Andrew, C. (2004) 'Intelligence, international relations and "under-theorisation"', in L.V. Scott and P. Jackson, *Understanding Intelligence in the Twenty-first Century*, London: Routledge.

—— (2009) *The Defence of the Realm. The Authorized History of MI5*, London: Allen Lane.

Bar-Joseph, U. (2005) *The Watchman Fell Asleep: The Surprise of Yom Kippur and its Sources*, New York: State University of New York Press.

Betts, R.K. (1982) *Surprise Attack: Lessons for Defense Planning*, Washington, DC: Brookings Institution.

—— (2007) *Enemies of Intelligence. Knowledge & Power in American National Security*, New York: Columbia University Press.

Born, H., Johnson L.K. and Leigh, D. (eds) (2005) *Who's Watching the Spies? Establishing Intelligence Accountability*, Washington, DC: Potomac Books.

Charters, D.A., Farson, S.A. and Hastedt, G.P. (eds) (1995) 'Special Issue on Intelligence Analysis and Assessment', *Intelligence and National Security*, 10.

—— (eds) (1996) *Intelligence Analysis and Assessment*, London: Frank Cass.

Davidsen-Nielsen, H. (2008) *Spionernes krig. Historien om Forsvarets Efterretningstjeneste* [The War of the Spies. The History of the Defence Intelligence Service], Copenhagen: Politikens Forlag.

Dedijer, S. (1983) 'The Rainbow Scheme: British Secret Service and Pax Britannica', in Wilhelm Agrell and Bo Huldt (eds), *Clio goes Spying: Eight Essays on the History of Intelligence*, Lund: Lund Studies in International History.

Frick, L.W. and Rossander, L. (2004) *Bakom hemligstämpeln* [Behind Classified Secret], Lund: Historiska Media.

George, R.Z. and Bruce, J.B. (eds) (2008) *Analyzing Intelligence: Origins, Obstacles and Innovations*, Washington, DC: Georgetown University Press.

Goodman, A.E. (1996) 'The future of US intelligence', *Intelligence and National Security*, 11: 645–656.

Herman, M. (1996) *Intelligence Power in Peace and War*, Cambridge: Cambridge University Press.

Herman, M., McDonald, J.K. and Mastny, V. (2006) *Did Intelligence Matter in the Cold War?*, Oslo: Instutt for Forsvarsstudier.

Hutchinson, R. (2007) *Elisabeth's Spy Master: Francis Walsingham and the Secret War that Saved England*, London: Phoenix.

Johnson, C. (1966) *Revolutionary Change*, Boston, MA: Little, Brown and Company.

Johnston, R. (2005) *The Analytic Culture of the U.S. Intelligence Community*, Washington, DC: Central Intelligence Agency.

Jones, R.V. (1979) *Most Secret War: British Scientific Intelligence 1939–1945*, London: Coronet Books.

Kahn, D. (1991) *Seizing the Enigma*, Boston, MA: Houghton Mifflin.

Kam, E. (1988) *Surprise Attack: The Victims' Perspective*, Cambridge, MA: Harvard University Press.

Keegan, J. (1998) *The Face of Battle: A Study of Agincourt, Waterloo and the Somme*, London: Pimlico.

—— (2003) *Intelligence in War: Knowledge of the Enemy from Napoleon to Al-Qaeda*, London: Hutchinson.

Kent, S. (1949) *Strategic Intelligence for American World Policy*, Princeton, NJ: Princeton University Press.

Marrin, S. (2009) 'Intelligence analysis and decision-making: Methodological challenges', in P. Gill, S. Marrin and M. Phythian, *Intelligence Theory: Key Questions and Debates*, New York: Routledge.

Naimark, N.M. (1995) *The Russians in Germany: A History of the Soviet Zone of Occupation, 1945–1949*, Cambridge, MA: Harvard University Press.

Proctor, R. and Schiebinger, L. (eds) (2008) *Agnotology: The Making and Unmaking of Ignorance*, Stanford, CA: Stanford University Press.

Pryser, T. (1999) 'From Petsamo to Venona', *Scandinavian Journal of History*, 24: 75–89.

Rentola, K. (2009) 'Suojelupoliisi kylmässä sodassa' [The Security Police in the Cold War], in M. Simola (ed.), *Ratakatu 12, Suojelupoliisi 1949–2009* [Ratakatu 12, The Security Police 1949–2009], Helsinki: WSOY.

Richelson, J.T. (1995) *A Century of Spies. Intelligence in the Twentieth Century*, Cambridge: Cambridge University Press.

Sheptycki, J. (2009) 'Policing, intelligence theory and the new human security paradigm: Some lessons from the field', in P. Gill, S. Marrin and M. Phythian (eds), *Intelligence Theory: Key Questions and Debates*, London: Routledge.

Steele, R.D. (2000) *On Intelligence: Spies and Secrecy in an Open World*, Fairfax: AFCEA International Press.

Treverton, G.F. (2001) *Reshaping National Intelligence for an Age of Information*, Cambridge: Cambridge University Press.

—— (2009) *Intelligence for an Age of Terror*, Cambridge: Cambridge University Press.

Weiner, T. (2007) *Legacy of Ashes: The History of the CIA*, New York: Doubleday.

Whaley, B. (1973) *Codeword Barbarossa*, Cambridge, MA: The MIT Press.

Wohlstetter, R. (1962) *Pearl Harbor: Warning and Decision*, Stanford, CA: Stanford University Press.

11 Conclusions

It may be 10 September 2001 today

George Dimitriu and Isabelle Duyvesteyn

Introduction

True intelligence is about the future and what is likely to happen in the time ahead (Clark 2007: 172). The security situation in Western societies has changed significantly since the collapse of the Soviet Union. There is no longer a single and clearly visible enemy threatening Western security. Nowadays intelligence communities are confronted with the combined threat of terrorists, insurgents, organized criminals, proliferators, hacktivists, as well as state actors or their proxies. Furthermore, as David Omand has pointed out in Chapter 2, globalization, the revolution in the communications domain and other technological developments have impacted upon the work of intelligence agencies as any other sector of society, and will continue to do so in the foreseeable future.

In 1985 Walter Laqueur, looking ahead at the future of intelligence services, noted that the public had mixed feelings. During crises and war the public would call for the strengthening of these agencies, while in relatively peaceful times an aversion against intelligence grew. During the 1970s and 1980s, public debates in the US took place on subjects such as intelligence leaks, the ethics of certain collection methods, the role of intelligence in the Vietnam War and covert action in foreign policy. In the end, Laqueur concluded, congressional investigations, adverse publicity, and extracted or volunteered revelations led to a decline in the level of effectiveness of intelligence activity.

With regard to the future, Laqueur emphasized the need for more training and education, not only for the intelligence professionals but – more importantly – also for intelligence consumers (Laqueur 1985). US intelligence historian David Kahn would echo these words in 2001 in his assessments of the future of intelligence. A fundamental challenge would remain in the future: How to get statesmen and generals to accept information that they do not like (Kahn 2001, 2009). Kahn therefore reasoned that in order to fully realize their potential, future intelligence agencies needed to improve their assessments and become more convincing for leaders to accept their reports.

The contributors to this volume have followed in Laqueur's and Kahn's footsteps and attempted a comprehensive overview of the future of intelligence. While choices in the past have bound intelligence agencies to a certain path dependency, the situation now, as Wilhelm Agrell recognizes in Chapter 10 (this volume), demands that intelligence agencies can no longer extend and extrapolate from previous trends and will have to engage in more out-of-the-box reasoning.

Conceptualizing intelligence

To discuss intelligence, we need to have a common understanding of what intelligence is. Many have wondered why a business so old and important in state affairs as intelligence still lacks an accepted definition or a solid theoretical basis. Motivated by the need to develop theories about how intelligence works, attempts have been made to define the term (Warner 2011), but what complicates this is that it may be understood as an activity, a process and a product (Lowenthal 2002: 8). Critics may question the need for a common definition, as in practice we seem to know what intelligence is about. States have been able to build intelligence organizations, to develop doctrines and procedures, and to implement intelligence in national decision-making without agreeing upon a common definition. It would be a mistake, however, to underestimate the value of commonly agreed-upon definitions, especially in fields in which ambiguous terms can easily be exploited for political purposes. The many different interpretations of the phenomenon 'terrorism' illustrate this problem. While there are innumerable definitions of terrorism, what someone considers an act of terror may be explained by others as a legitimate use of force. Different explanations can lead to different responses, varying from robust counter-terrorism measures to overt support for a freedom struggle. The same applies to intelligence. Without a proper definition, activities such as influence operations may be explained as either intelligence activities or acts of diplomacy. Covert actions may be explained as either military intervention or counter-intelligence activity. Without a clear demarcation, future debates will continue on whether the conclusion of the absence of weapons of mass destruction in Iraq was actually an intelligence failure or a policy failure.

When seeking a proper definition of intelligence, most scholarly attempts are narrow and entangled in sub-processes and minor characteristics. For example, many definitions encapsulate elements of the intelligence cycle, the necessity of secrecy and the relation to national security (Kent 1949: vii; 76; Kirkpatrick 1997: 365; Joint Chiefs of Staff 2001: 208). While most definitions seem to be logical, the concepts on which these definitions are based are open to different interpretations as well, making consensus even more difficult to achieve. Broader and more abstract definitions are therefore useful. Intelligence may be described as 'knowledge', or 'processed information' to serve 'decision-makers', to 'optimize resources', or to 'reduce uncertainty and ignorance' (Central Intelligence Agency 1999: vii; Kahn 2001). One shortcoming, however, is that most theoretical and definitional enterprises are largely focused on intelligence itself, ignoring its consumers.

Furthermore, critics have noted that there is an omission in intelligence literature: it is predominantly conceptualized by intelligence scholars using a bottom-up approach that largely overlooks the perspective of the policy-makers (Marrin 2009: 147–148; Sims 1995: 7). As Stephen Marrin (2009) notes, descriptions of unidirectional information flows have placed conceptual blinders on scholars and failed to integrate intelligence and decision-making literature. He therefore argues for a more consumer-centric approach to conceptualizing intelligence, which makes sense since intelligence services are controlled by policy-makers, budgeted by policy-makers and receive their directions from policy-makers. Ultimately, those who hold power will decide what is to be done by intelligence services and what intelligence needs to be about.

While coming up with valuable suggestions, Marrin's approach offers an incomplete framework to conceptualize intelligence and to discuss its future. Intelligence needs to be regarded from a policy-making perspective, but intelligence and policy-makers are part of a complex constellation of systems which consists of (among others) people, organizations, networks, states, institutions, influence and relationships; thus the necessity to understand the environment in which an intelligence system operates. Furthermore, we need to ask to what extent the context has changed. In the early 1980s the security paradigm was predominantly focused on states and collective security instead of groups and individuals (Sheptycki 2004). Different technological developments, such as the transmission and storage of data, have since had a dramatic impact.

Finally, most theories of intelligence regard it as it would be in a perfect world: services present intelligence to serve decision-makers who in turn can make informed decisions. In the real world, however, intelligence services are confronted with an increasing number of competitors, budget cuts, 'blaming and shaming', media attention, and a growing interest and scrutiny from society. We live in a world in which policy-makers rapidly come and go, striving not only for the good of the state, but also serving their own individual interests such as remaining in power or winning the next political battle. As a consequence, intelligence services continuously face difficult dilemmas, as those whom they serve and who control them not only value accuracy, completeness and objectivity but also good timing and the confirmation of their policy preferences. In sum, intelligence cannot be regarded without considering the circumstances and the complex environment in which it is situated. Intelligence is a product of its time and environment.

Technological developments

Technological developments have an impact on society at large, on the state, and on conceptions of power. As we will show below, technology enhances certain aspects of intelligence while on the other hand restricting it, and it has a similar impact on the intelligence services' opponents, whether they be state or non-state actors.

As several authors in this volume argue, the communication revolution is one of the most important factors that shape the future role of intelligence. New media and the internet have created a new virtual battlefield for insurgents and terrorists to engage adversaries and reach audiences. With the empowerment of the individual, everyone can now write news reports and instantly disseminate them worldwide. Whereas in the past states and media corporations controlled the distribution of reports, citizens now make their own news. Terrorists, insurgents and ordinary civilians are no longer passive consumers of information; they are news-makers as well. All have the potential to find supporters, to inform, manipulate and mobilize (Kurth Cronin 2006; Weimann 2006: 64–91, 110).

The revolution in the communication domain enables not only active citizenship but also leads to a shifting security threat. The internet offers a means for terrorists from different parts of the world to gather and plan terrorist attacks online, in a virtual world which is not easily penetrated by intelligence services. Moreover, so-called lone wolves can radicalize in the virtual domain without any noticeable indicators in the physical world. Technological developments also extend the reach of intelligence services, opening up new possibilities through data mining, unmanned aerial vehicles (UAVs or drones), surveillance systems, detection devices, forensic and biometric capabilities, automated analysis tools and geo-mapping. As several authors in this volume (among them David Omand) have noted, in the near future it will be increasingly difficult to avoid leaving digital traces. It should be recognized, however, that technological superiority is not decisive if the opponent decides to play a totally different game. For example, the primitive use of Improvised Explosive Devices (IEDs), avoiding the use of mobile phones and computers and the reliance on very primitive means of communication by terrorists and insurgents, has severely hampered the work of Western intelligence services in Iraq and Afghanistan.

What do the technological developments mean for the intelligence services in the future? The contributors in this volume have made several suggestions. To begin with, it means an exponential growth of non-state actors that can 'provide and procure' intelligence, leaving aside whether this is a disadvantage to intelligence services or can be complementary, as is noted by Gregory Treverton (Chapter 3). As Jennifer Sims (Chapter 6) points out, civilians with mobile phones, cameras and the internet have become intelligence collectors and disseminators. The first news of the US operation against Osama Bin Laden was a tweet from a Pakistani who lived in Abbottabad and noticed helicopters above his house. The technological developments have put enormous pressure on intelligence services as it becomes more difficult to be the first with the news. According to Wilhelm Agrell (Chapter 10), this may lead to the shift of intelligence agencies from information collection agencies to knowledge validation organizations and knowledge management organizations. Similarly, according to Sims, the new communication developments lead increasingly to the mass production of information and data overload. While automatic processing of intelligence and analysis is flourishing, eventual intelligence analysis needs a human component. As both Arthur Hulnick (Chapter 5) and Mark Lowenthal (Chapter 4) note, intelligence analysis still has an intellectual feature that largely takes place in the minds of analysts. They have a message of caution that intelligence services should invest more in the training and education of young analysts in the profession.

Finally, on a warning note, new technical possibilities emerge at such a speed that governments are hardly able to oversee their consequences or implement judicial guidelines for their use by law enforcement. Furthermore, ethical discussions about sensitive issues such as data mining and the use of drones do not take place prior to their introduction but occur simultaneously. Since there is hardly any time for thorough research into the use of new technologies, it is questionable whether governments and intelligence services can identify all second and third order effects before their use. The same applies to the creation of proper instruments and institutions for accountability and oversight.

Whatever conclusions may be drawn from technological developments and their implications for intelligence, the state of technology is never fixed or finished; we are just in the midst of a communication revolution and the pace of developments is increasing exponentially. Technological developments not only influence the intelligence services, they also impact upon the environment in which intelligence operates.

The social context

Inevitably, the evolution of intelligence is related to the society in which it is embedded and in which it operates. Technological developments have expanded access to knowledge and increased ways of expression. The communication revolution seems to expand the gap between the public and intelligence services. As Gregory Treverton summarizes in this volume, intelligence is closed and passive, while society and the current media environment has increasingly become more open and active. Walter Laqueur already noted in 1985 the growing aversion of Western society against war, conflicts and the working of intelligence and security services. In Western democracies, citizens increasingly challenge the practices of their governments. It is too simplistic to attribute these challenges only to people's disaffection with domestic security measures and worries about their privacy or (in the worst case) fears of an Orwellian state. There are also other factors at work.

In modern Western societies, war and conflict have become less popular and less legitimate as a tool for foreign policy (Gaddis 1987: 240). The justifications for deploying and using force, whether troops or drones, has become the subject of public scrutiny. According to some scholars, this may be attributed to changes in demographics and strategic culture. A pioneer in this debate is historian and military strategist Edward Luttwak, who argued that modern society is shifting towards a 'post-heroic culture' in which there is no longer room for the 'warrior tradition' or noble ideas such as martial sacrifice and fighting for a greater cause (Luttwak 1995, 1996; Ignatief 2000; Everts 2002). According to others, individuals simply oppose violence against foreign communities based on moral and expedient calculations (Merom 2003). Based on variations of the democratic peace theory, they suggest that the decline in public appetite for war and conflict is a reason why politicians are increasingly reluctant to fall back on sanctioning violence (Doyle 1983; Maoz 1998; Gowa 1999; Merom 2003: 244; Huth and

Allee 2003; Berinsky 2009: 3). While the debates on 'post-heroic culture' and democratic peace theory take place primarily outside the realm of intelligence studies, the concepts do seem to play a role as the distinctions between intelligence operations and the use of military force become increasingly blurred.

David Omand concludes that citizens increasingly tolerate less risk with regard to their personal safety, and that security has shifted from guaranteeing the integrity of national territory to the protection of the citizen (see also Sheptycki 2004). He reminds us that risk management is not only about avoiding objective threats such as foreign invasion but, more importantly, about perception. Statistically, the chances of dying in a car accident may be 100 times more likely than in a terrorist attack, but it is terrorism that generates the most fear. The paradox is, however, that when people feel safe, they tend to be less concerned about the state of intelligence services. In relatively peaceful times, the incentive for further investments fades away and governments can easily carry out budget cuts. When crises occur, citizens will again call for a greater intelligence effort, while at the same time paying less attention to moral values and feeling fewer scruples about the means used by intelligence services (Ruttenberg 2001; Alter 2001; Dershowitz 2002: 131–164). These often changing demands do not make it easier for intelligence services to function to the satisfaction of the general public.

In sum, the Western public expresses a latent aversion for intelligence and conflict, but demands a delicate balance to cope with the dangers of 'risk society' (Beck 1992, 2008). Many of the authors in this volume agree that the influence of the public on intelligence is most likely to increase. Intelligence services will have to deal with mounting public pressure for accountability, transparency and oversight. Intelligence has an increasingly sceptical public, suspicious of developments in surveillance, data mining and monitoring, especially after revelations about torture, drone attacks and renditions. Problems related to these developments cannot be solely ascribed to intelligence services because in the last resort it is politicians and not intelligence agencies who are to blame for these practices. However, this does not change popular perceptions. In the end, the perceived practices of intelligence may bring such negative connotations that policy-makers may feel the need to change its name, as hinted by Agrell. This is what happened, for instance, with the term Psychological Operations (PSYOP), which was changed, due to its negative connotations, to Military Information Support to Operations (MISO) by the US in 2010 (Csrnko 2010; Exum 2010: 219).

As several authors in this volume argue, developments in technology and society have resulted in a stronger and more influential public voice and a partly value-driven, partly interest-driven opinion about intelligence. Furthermore, as den Boer points out (Chapter 9), borders become less relevant, globalization continues, and intelligence no longer merely belongs to the realm of the state but becomes expropriated by its citizens. The services' primary consumers are those who hold power. It is also up to these decision-makers to explain the necessity and importance of intelligence to the public and to stimulate and contribute to the debate on the balance between collective security and individual liberty.

Policy-makers have an important responsibility for shaping public opinion to create resilience and influence people's subjective security perceptions. While intelligence services need to educate the policy-makers and politicians, it is up to those in power to educate society.

The role of the state

Governance, including the governance of security, has been radically transformed since the 1980s. Western states have been transformed into enabling states, resulting in decreased state interference in the economy and a stronger emphasis on the creation and supply of public goods through market mechanisms (van der Meer 2009). Western politics, as Jelle van Buuren observes (Chapter 7), have also developed a system of multi-level, multi-centred security governance. Multi-level governance is characterized by the sharing of power across multiple levels. Power is no longer solely concentrated in state actors, but in different semi-state and non-state actors as well. Furthermore, multi-level governance means a more equal power distribution between different tiers of governance, while at the same time relations are increasingly determined through networks (van den Berg and Toonen 2007). In Manuel Castells' view (2009), a network society can be characterized as an open, highly dynamic and innovative social system without a centre of gravity, but operating as a connection of different nodes of power communicating with each other through common codes and values. Ongoing globalization and the further development of the network society will lead to an increased blurring of the distinction between intelligence and domains such as policing, armed forces, private intelligence companies, international intelligence communities of intergovernmental organizations such as NATO and the EU, and policy-makers. This may raise concerns about accountability, responsibility and power distribution, and lead to questions by intelligence services about their mission, vision and purpose. These issues will be dealt with in turn.

First, the distinction between domestic and external threats has faded. Terrorists, insurgents and cyber activists can wreak havoc on the lives of Western citizens while based abroad, a reason why Omand, van Buuren and Agrell foresee an increasingly artificial separation between domestic and foreign intelligence. Law enforcement, police, domestic security and foreign intelligence will have to work together. As Monica den Boer convincingly argues, intelligence-led policing (ILP), originally introduced for the purpose of counter-terrorism, has already been applied in other fields such as the fight against organized crime, public order management, immigration and border control.

Second, the development of multi-layered governance has led to a further diffusion of power, as well as the growth of horizontal (different disciplines) and vertical (different tiers and levels) intelligence networks. We can think here of intelligence networks of intergovernmental organizations such as the UN, NATO and the EU. Furthermore, van Buuren notes the closer connections between private security companies and intelligence services, which blur the distinction between what is public and what is private in the world of intelligence. Treverton even discusses the idea of involving citizens voluntarily as amateur analysts in the intelligence process.

Third, another increasingly fuzzy distinction is that between intelligence and the use of armed force. Currently, the communication from 'sensor to shooter' occurs within seconds. A striking example is the positive identification and fixing of a target by a UAV with the help of signals and imagery intelligence, and the subsequent release of a Hellfire missile from the same platform. The military is now increasingly involved in counter-terrorism tasks. According to Arthur Hulnick, the cooperation between Special Operations Forces (SOF) and intelligence services has become an essential element in the US counter-terrorism campaign since 9/11. This also shows clearly in recent reports, which indicate that the US Defense Intelligence Agency (DIA) has forged a tight relationship with the SOF community. Admiral William McRaven, Commander of US Special Operations Command, has called for increased cooperation between SOF and intelligence operatives (Miller 2012).

What are the implications of these developments for the future of intelligence? First of all, and most importantly, multi-level networked states and the accompanying blurring of distinctions between activities and responsibilities on different levels will significantly challenge oversight and accountability arrangements. As den Boer argues, this leads to transnational intelligence clouds in which ownership of intelligence can no longer be easily identified. Moreover, it may be unclear for which actors intelligence services are actually working. Who is accountable for unsavoury practices when the collection of intelligence has been outsourced to different private subcontractors? Proxy services are not always easily controlled, but their activities often reflect heavily on those whom they serve (Dimitriu 2013). At the international level similar problems occur. Björn Fägersten (Chapter 8) argues that international cooperation may lead to unintentionally embarrassing situations, of which the exposure of British–Libyan intelligence cooperation following the ousting of Muammar Gaddafi is a typical example.

Second, as most of the authors note, the shift to a network society will have a strong impact on how Western societies will view intelligence organizations, structures and institutions. Intelligence production will no longer be the playing field solely of intelligence services, but will, as den Boer observes, be increasingly provided by a variety of private, public, collective and commercial agents. New intelligence cooperation initiatives at supranational levels will alter long-established institutions such as the 'quid pro quo' adage, while at the same time communities of interest and multilateral working relationships may come and go. While the hybridization of intelligence networks and multi-disciplinary intelligence sharing may have some positive impact on the future of intelligence, such as increased output and effectiveness, Fägersten doubts whether the future will only bring more cooperation. He foresees more fragmented cooperation, such as 'coalitions of the willing'. This makes sense, as equal cooperation requires a balance in investments, a high level of trust, the will to share sensitive intelligence and a somewhat common idea of future threats. What if the economic divide between Northern and Southern Europe widens? As Sims notes, when competition between states increases in intensity and perceptions of threats rise, incentives to withhold information will also grow. In sum, as Bob de Graaff warns in the Introduction, increased international collaboration and the rise of networks may not be a panacea for the improvement of future intelligence. The internationalization and blurring of intelligence will undoubtedly challenge the sovereignty of Western states.

Questions of power

In the realm of International Relations, traditional realist views have focused primarily on the material aspects of 'hard power', such as technical capabilities, resources, manpower, capital, strength and strategy (Morgenthau 1973 [1948]; Gilpin 1981). More recently, scholars have paid attention to the softer elements of power, for example, motivation, persuasion, national cohesion and will (Merom 2003; Nye 2011). An added element in the current era is the increased importance of information, concerning the ability to shape perceptions and influence and persuade designated target audiences. This is the realm of strategic influence, narratives and communication, public diplomacy, negotiations and outreach.

As a result of technological developments, power has been shifting increasingly to non-state actors such as NGOs, international companies, terrorists and insurgents. Consequently, as Sims points out, the traditional focus of intelligence on nation-states and their capabilities, intentions and activities no longer captures the whole picture, and as Agrell adds, the shifting of intelligence targets has obviously profound implications for the practice of intelligence itself. He rightly concludes that soft power needs a different kind of support from intelligence agencies. At the same time, states are not paramount actors in the information domain. It is questionable whether Western states with all their layers of bureaucracy and hierarchy are actually capable of successfully competing with flexible and adaptive non-state actors. Sims concludes that power shifts in the future may not only occur among states but also within them. Large corporations that manage the global information infrastructure are becoming the new power brokers. Furthermore, each citizen with a mobile phone and a connection to the internet is empowered to swiftly inform others or to release manipulated information. This results in disorderly clusters that willingly or unwillingly challenge state power.

The more information becomes associated with power, the more the line between intelligence services and ruling powers blurs. As de Graaff points out, intelligence analysts may become increasingly involved with sense-making and constructing realities. Instead of presenting reality, intelligence professionals may be shaping it. De Graaff rightly wonders whether society will accept such a pronounced role for intelligence services and their entanglement with politics. The increased politicization of intelligence brings additional risks. First of all, it is doubtful whether analysts will get the time, resources and opportunities to build deep knowledge about possible future threats, as Lowenthal advocates. With the increased chances of politicization of intelligence, there will be a tendency for intelligence services to be focused on the topical problems of the day. As politics becomes more and more mediatized (Castells 2009: 507), they will mostly be driven by the perceived short-term threats to the public. Moreover, politicians who are preoccupied with these threat perceptions will not allow much space for intelligence professionals who want to focus on the objective threats that may appear in the future but are still outside the public gaze.

As Peter Gill points out in his description of the relation between knowledge and power, in its ideal form, the relationship is one of independent intelligence services that present intelligence which governments then act upon (Gill 2005: 12–33). But with the 'politicization' of intelligence, the knowledge–power role is reversed. The will to act by policy-makers precedes the delivery of knowledge by intelligence services. The information delivered by intelligence services will be judged according to its ability to support the desired actions. An often quoted example of this is the 'cherry picking' of policy-makers in the US and the UK relating to intelligence on weapons of mass destruction prior to the invasion of Iraq in 2003 (Morrison 2011). This subjective use of intelligence can temporarily empower governments but ultimately misleads the public. Of course, there are various possible relationships between knowledge and power, this being only a negative example.

Changes in the concepts of power will likely have their impact on the future development of intelligence services. The further blurring of borders between power and intelligence may be one of the consequences. It is increasingly unclear which actors actually possess power and how power is distributed. Ultimately, fragmented and diffused power will impact on the ability of policy-makers to formulate preferred policy outcomes and, as a consequence, to optimize strategies, convert resources and direct intelligence.

Conclusions

When Walter Laqueur (1985) wrote about the future of intelligence almost three decades ago, he advocated a reorientation of its focus. In those days, Laqueur opined that there was an overemphasis on military-strategic intelligence, instead of a focus on political-strategic and economic intelligence. In the context of the Cold War this was probably logical. Laqueur's vision of the reorientation of intelligence has not been heeded. Agrell foresees the rise of new fields of knowledge in the future, but at this moment policy-makers mainly demand actionable or military-tactical intelligence. This is, as Omand observes, a preference which seems to show continuity with what Laqueur noted thirty years ago.

One is reminded again of Laqueur's statement of three decades ago on the brittle relationship between society and intelligence. A delicate balance is required between the growing aversion of the public, at least in Western societies, against torture and the use of force and violations of the private sphere on the one hand, and the demand for personal security and protection against terrorism on the other. In the future this popular opinion will probably increase in strength, while at the same time a steady number of almost real-time images of the use of armed force and consequences of sometimes unsavoury intelligence practices will enter everyone's living-room. Therefore, as the authors in this volume argue, intelligence services in Western democracies can expect mounting public pressure for accountability, transparency and democratic oversight in the years to come.

In Western democracies, there is a constant need for those who hold power to explain the role and necessity of intelligence services to the public. This will become increasingly important. Official communication on the role of intelligence services, however, has to compete with media which seek dramatic and newsworthy stories lacking any responsibility for balance (Stimson 2004). Moreover, changing ideas of power and the blurring of borders between intelligence and power could lead to a highly ambiguous role for intelligence. The role of intelligence services to interpret the world for policy-makers could, for instance, lead to a temptation to shape public perceptions about those services.

To conclude: the distribution of power will become increasingly diffuse, as Western states are turning increasingly into network societies and becoming characterized by multi-level governance, which will impact on intelligence. Once an exclusive tradecraft of civil servants and the military, intelligence will increasingly become a playing field of different public and private organizations, international networks as well as ordinary people. This will seriously challenge proper oversight and accountability. Attention should be paid to what intelligence is in essence about. Intelligence does not exist just for its own sake, but always serves another purpose. It enables optimal use of resources and serves policy-makers in their process of deciding which way to go in war and peace. For these same reasons, intelligence will probably continue to play an important role in the foreseeable future. In spite of all far-reaching changes in recent decades, an observation made by Laqueur almost three decades ago still holds true today:

> Intelligence is an essential service, but only a service. It is an important element in the decision-making process, but only one element: its usefulness depends entirely on how it is used and guided.... It can never be a substitute for policy or strategy, for political wisdom or military power. In the absence of an effective foreign policy even the most accurate and reliable intelligence will be of no avail.
>
> (Laqueur 1985: 8, 11)

Bibliography

Alter, Jonathan (2001) 'Time to Think About Torture', *Newsweek*, 5 November.
Beck, Ulrich (1992) *Risk Society, Towards a new Modernity*, London: Sage Publications.
—— (2008) *World at Risk*, Cambridge: Polity Press.

Berg, Caspar F. van den and Toonen, Theo A.J. (2007) 'National Civil Service Systems and the Implications of Multi-level Governance: Weberianism Revisited?', in Jos C.N. Raadschelders, Theo A.J. Toonen and Frits M. van Der Meer (eds), *The Civil Service in the 21st Century, Comparative Perspectives*, New York: Palgrave Macmillan, pp. 103–120.

Berinsky, Adam J. (2009) *In Time of War, Understanding American Public Opinion from World War II to Iraq*, Chicago, IL: University of Chicago Press.

Castells, Manuel (2009) *The Rise of the Network Society: The Information Age: Economy, Society, and Culture*, Malden, MA: Wiley-Blackwell.

Central Intelligence Agency: Office of Public Affairs (1999) *A Consumer's Guide to Intelligence: Gaining Knowledge and Foreknowledge of the World Around Us*, Washington, DC: Central Intelligence Agency.

Clark, Robert M. (2007) *Intelligence Analysis, A Target-centric Approach*, 2nd edn, Washington, DC: CQ Press.

Csrnko, Major General Thomas R. (2010) 'Memorandum for all soldiers and civilians associated with the Psychological Operations Regiment', United States Department of the Army, 23 June.

Dershowitz, Alan M. (2002) *Why Terrorism Works: Understanding the Threat, Responding to the Challenge*, New Haven, CT: Yale University Press.

Dimitriu, George (2013) 'Interrogation, Coercion and Torture: Dutch Debates and Experiences after 9/11', *Intelligence and National Security*, 547–565.

Doyle, Michael W. (1983) 'Kant, Liberal Legacies, and Foreign Affairs', *Philosophy and Public Affairs*, 12: 205–235.

Everts, Philip (2002) *Democracy and Military* Force, Basingstoke: Palgrave.

Exum, Andrew (2010) 'Information Operations', in Thomas Rid and Thomas Keaney (eds), *Understanding Counterinsurgency: Doctrine, Operations, and Challenges*, New York: Routledge, pp. 216–229.

Gaddis, J.L. (1987) *The Long Peace: Inquiries into the History of the Cold War*, New York: Oxford University Press.

Gill, Peter (2005) 'The Politicization of Intelligence: Lessons from the Invasion of Iraq', in Hans Born, Loch K. Johnson and Ian Leigh (eds), *Who's Watching the Spies? Establishing Intelligence Service Accountability*. Dulles, VA: Potomac Books, pp. 12–33.

Gilpin, Robert (1981) *War and Change in World Politics*, Cambridge: Cambridge University Press.

Gowa, Joanne S. (1999) *Ballots and Bullets: The Elusive Democratic Peace*, Princeton, NJ: Princeton University Press.

Huth, Paul K. and Allee, Todd L. (2003) *The Democratic Peace and Territorial Conflict in the Twentieth Century*, Cambridge: Cambridge University Press.

Ignatieff, Michael (2000) *Virtual War, Kosovo and Beyond*, New York: Henry Holt/Metropolitan Books.

Joint Chiefs of Staff (2001) *Department of Defense Dictionary of Military and Associated Terms*, Washington, DC: Government Printing Office.

Kahn, David (2001) 'An Historical Theory of Intelligence', *Intelligence and National Security*, 16: 79–92.

—— (2009) 'An Historical Theory of Intelligence', in Peter Gill, Stephen Marrin and Mark Phythian (eds), *Intelligence Theory: Key Questions and Debates*, New York: Routledge, pp. 4–15.

Kent, Sherman (1949) *Strategic Intelligence for American Foreign Policy*, Princeton, NJ: Princeton University Press.

Kirkpatrick, Lyman B. Jr. (1997) 'Intelligence', in Bruce Jentelson and Thomas G. Paterson (eds), *Encyclopedia of US Foreign Relations*, Vol. 2, New York: Oxford University Press.

Kurth Cronin, Audrey (2006) 'Cyber-mobilization: The New Levée en Masse', *Parameters*, 36: 77–87.

Laqueur, Walter (1985) 'The Future of Intelligence', *Society*, 23: 3–11.

Lowenthal, Mark M. (2002) *Intelligence: From Secrets to Policy*, 2nd edn, Washington, DC: Congressional Quarterly Press.

Luttwak, Edward N. (1995) 'Toward Post-heroic Warfare', *Foreign Affairs*, 74: 109–122.

—— (1996) 'A Post-heroic Military Policy', *Foreign Affairs*, 75: 33–44.

Maoz, Zeev (1998) 'Realist and Cultural Critiques of the Democratic Peace: A Theoretical and Empirical Re-assessment', *International Interactions*, 24: 3–89.

Marrin, Stephen (2009) 'Intelligence Analysis and Decision-making' in Peter Gill, Stephen Marrin and Mark Phythian (eds), *Intelligence Theory: Key Questions and Debates*, New York: Routledge.

Meer, F.M. van der (2009) 'Public Sector Reform in Western Europe and the Rise of the Enabling State: An Approach to Analysis', in R.R. Mathur (ed.), *Glimpses of Civil Service Reform*, Hyderabad: Icfai University Press, pp. 171–195.

Merom, Gil (2003) *How Democracies Lose Small Wars: State, Society, and the Failures of France in Algeria, Israel in Lebanon, and the United States in Vietnam*, Cambridge: Cambridge University Press.

Miller, Greg (2012) 'DIA Sending Hundreds More Spies Overseas', *Washington Post*, 1 December.

Morgenthau, Hans ([1948] 1973) *Politics among Nations: The Struggle for Power and Peace*, Boston, MA: Random House.

Morrison, John (2011) 'British Intelligence Failures in Iraq', *Intelligence and National Security*, 26: 509–520.

Mueller, J. (1989) *Retreat from Doomsday: The Obsolescence of Major War*, New York: Basic Books.

Nye, Joseph (2011) *The Future of Power*, New York: Public Affairs Books.

Ruttenberg, Jim (2001) 'Torture Seeps into Discussion by News Media', *New York Times*, 5 November.

Sheptycki, James W.E. (2004) 'Organizational Pathologies in Police Intelligence Systems: Some Contributions to the Lexion of Intelligence-led Policing', *European Journal of Criminology*, 1: 307–332.

Sims, Jennifer (1995) 'What is Intelligence? Information for Decision-makers', in Roy Godson, Ernest R. May and Gary Schmitt (eds), *Intelligence at the Crossroads, Agendas for Reform*, Washington, DC: National Strategy Information Center.

Stimson, James A. (2004) *Tides of Consent: How Public Opinion shapes American Politics*, Cambridge: Cambridge University Press.

Warner, Michael (2011) 'Wanted: A Definition of "Intelligence"', in Loch K. Johnson (ed.), *Intelligence: Critical Concepts in Military, Strategic and Security Studies*, New York: Routledge, pp. 113–123.

Weimann, Gabriel (2006) *Terror on the Internet: The New Arena, the New Challenges*, Washington, DC: United States Institute of Peace.

Index

CPSIA information can be obtained
at www.ICGtesting.com
Printed in the USA
BVOW06s0030030118
504236BV00008B/47/P

9 781138 951952